KR

Adria

The Official Guide to
Ancestry
Family Tree

Matt S. Grove

Ancestry®

Library of Congress Cataloging-in-Publication Data

Grove, Matt.
  The official guide to Ancestry Family tree / by Matt Grove.
     p. cm.
  ISBN 1-59331-038-2 (alk. paper)
  1. Ancestry Family tree. 2. Genealogy—Computer programs. 3.
Genealogy—Data processing. I. Ancestry Family tree. II. Title.

  CS21.G76 2003
  929'.1'02855369—dc21

                                      2003012180

Published by Ancestry®, an

imprint of MyFamily.com, Inc.

P.O. Box 990

Orem, UT 84059

10 9 8 7 6 5 4 3 2 1

Printed in the United States of America

Table of Contents

Table of Contents

Table of Contents

Getting Started with Ancestry Family Tree

With genealogy fast becoming one of the most popular and exciting hobbies around the world, Ancestry.com, the most trusted source for connecting families, is pleased to present Ancestry Family Tree. Whether you are a novice or an experienced family historian, you will find that Ancestry Family Tree is an extremely user-friendly software program designed to help you keep your genealogy in superb order. Using its many features you will be able to create a lasting legacy to share with family members for years to come.

As you begin using Ancestry Family Tree, you will quickly discover that the basics are easy to master. As you input information, you will be using Pedigree Chart and Family Group Sheet formats with which you are likely already familiar. Using these views you will enter names, dates, and places as well as notes and sources for your information. With each name that is entered, the real magic of Ancestry Family Tree comes to life. The software performs an automated search of Ancestry.com databases* and the number of results is displayed conveniently in a link next to the name.

As you create individual records for each family member—or import them via a GEDCOM file—you will begin to create a connected database of family history information. From there, the guide will teach you how to include data from other sources (such as a family member who may already have done research) that will save you time and help your research grow.

In addition to getting you started with these simple steps, this guide will also show you how to use the additional features of this program to broaden your search using the built-in search connection to Ancestry.com and your other favorite sites. You will also learn how to print out your findings in attractive and readable reports, and to create multimedia slideshows and scrapbooks. And, for those who would like to share their genealogy with others using the World Wide Web, you will also find everything you need to create your own family history webpage.

Genealogy has never been easier than with Ancestry Family Tree. Start now and discover for yourself how much fun family history can be. Chapter 1 provides you with a detailed overview of the Ancestry Family Tree program, how it works, and all the many things you can do with it. It also provides a description of Ancestry Family Tree's workspace so that you will quickly know your way around.

So, let's dive right in. A world of discovery is at your fingertips!

*Internet connection necessary for this feature.

Introduction to Ancestry Family Tree

In this chapter, you will learn all about Ancestry Family Tree: how it works and what you can do with it. You will also find here an overview of the forms you will complete for your different ancestors to create individual, marriage, and family records. These forms make up Ancestry Family Tree's workspace.

In this chapter

• Overview of Ancestry Family Tree
• Ancestry Family Tree workspace

Overview of Ancestry Family Tree

Ancestry Family Tree allows you to create and store family records. A collection of electronic records is referred to as a *database.* Using the software you can create any number of family databases. Several types of records are involved in creating and maintaining family databases, but the two most important are the *individual record* and the *marriage record.* For every person represented in an Ancestry Family Tree family database, there is an individual record. Likewise, for every married couple or mother and father pair represented in the database, there is a marriage record (even for a mother and father who were never married.

Individual records

For each individual you can enter the person's name, of course, and date and place data for specific events such as birth, death, and burial. You can also enter notes, source citations, and additional events for each individual. You can choose to enter information about LDS church ordinances, and there are specific places for you to enter aliases, physical description, and other personal data not related to events.

Marriage records

A marriage record identifies a married couple (or a mother and father if they were not married). Besides date and place of marriage you can enter notes, source citations, and additional events for each marriage, and you can choose to enter LDS sealing data.

Sources and source citations

A *source* is the origin of the information you enter, such as a published family history. Ancestry Family Tree lets you create a record for each source of information included in a database. For an individual's name and for each of various events (birth, marriage, death, burial, and additional events), you can create a *source citation* that refers to a specific source record.

Many sources are located in repositories—libraries, government archives, etc. You can create a record of details about each repository for the sources you cite in the database.

Media collections

For each individual in a family database you can create a *media collection.* A media collection can include three types of electronic media files: photo images, video clips, and sound clips.

You can arrange the photo images in a media collection into "slide shows" and "scrapbooks" for viewing, and you can attach an audio clip to each photo image. You can even attach a media file to a source record or citation and to a repository record.

Searching the database

An Ancestry Family Tree family database is easily searchable. You can search the entire database for an individual, search for a descendant of a selected individual, or search for a marriage.

Ancestry Family tree also lets you use *search filters* that can help you find one or more individuals. You can use two types of filters to narrow your search for individuals. The *relationship filter* allows you to limit the search to a group of individuals based on their relationship to a selected individual (for example, all descendants of the selected individual). A *field filter* allows you to limit the search to a group of individuals based on information that exists in the database for the individuals (for example, year of birth).

Importing and exporting data

You can electronically import and export genealogical data as GEDCOM files. Using this common file format, you can share your data with other researchers and receive data from other researchers—even those who use genealogy software other than Ancestry Family Tree.

Importing data into an existing family database often results in duplicate records within the database. Ancestry Family Tree allows you to eliminate duplicate records by searching for them and merging them into one record.

Ancestry Family Tree also allows you to identify and export the records of individuals who are qualified for LDS temple ordinances. You can create a GEDCOM export file optimized for processing by TempleReady™, a software program that prepares the GEDCOM file for submission to the temple.

Charts and reports

You can present the data stored in a family database by creating and printing any of several types of charts and reports using Ancestry Family Tree. Some reports present information mainly about a specific individual, while others include information about selected groups of people.

Searching the World Wide Web

Ancestry Family Tree makes it easier for you to search the fantastic genealogical resource that is the World Wide Web. A vast amount of genealogical information is available on the Web; Ancestry Family Tree lets you maintain a list of your favorite websites and search them for information quickly and conveniently. In addition, Ancestry Family Tree's Internet menu lets you instantly connect to and search the most popular resources for genealogical information at Ancestry.com.

Publishing your data on the Web

You can use Ancestry Family Tree to publish your family history data on the World Wide Web, where other researchers can see it and use it to enhance their own research. You can publish your own family database as a webpage that anyone can access via the World Wide Web. You can also create an Online Family Tree hosted by Ancestry.com. Using this free service, you can easily place your family history data online, where you and anyone else whom you choose to allow can contribute to it.

Ancestry Family Tree workspace

When you are working in Ancestry Family Tree, you will be using one of three different *views*: the Pedigree view, the Family view, or the Name List view. Each view presents a different "picture" of information about individuals in your family database. To move among the views, you simply click the **Pedigree**, **Family**, and **Name List** tabs at the top of the view.

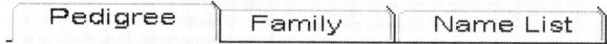

Pedigree	Family	Name List

Pedigree view

The Pedigree view shows a five-generation pedigree for the individual who is in the *primary* position—at the far left of the view.

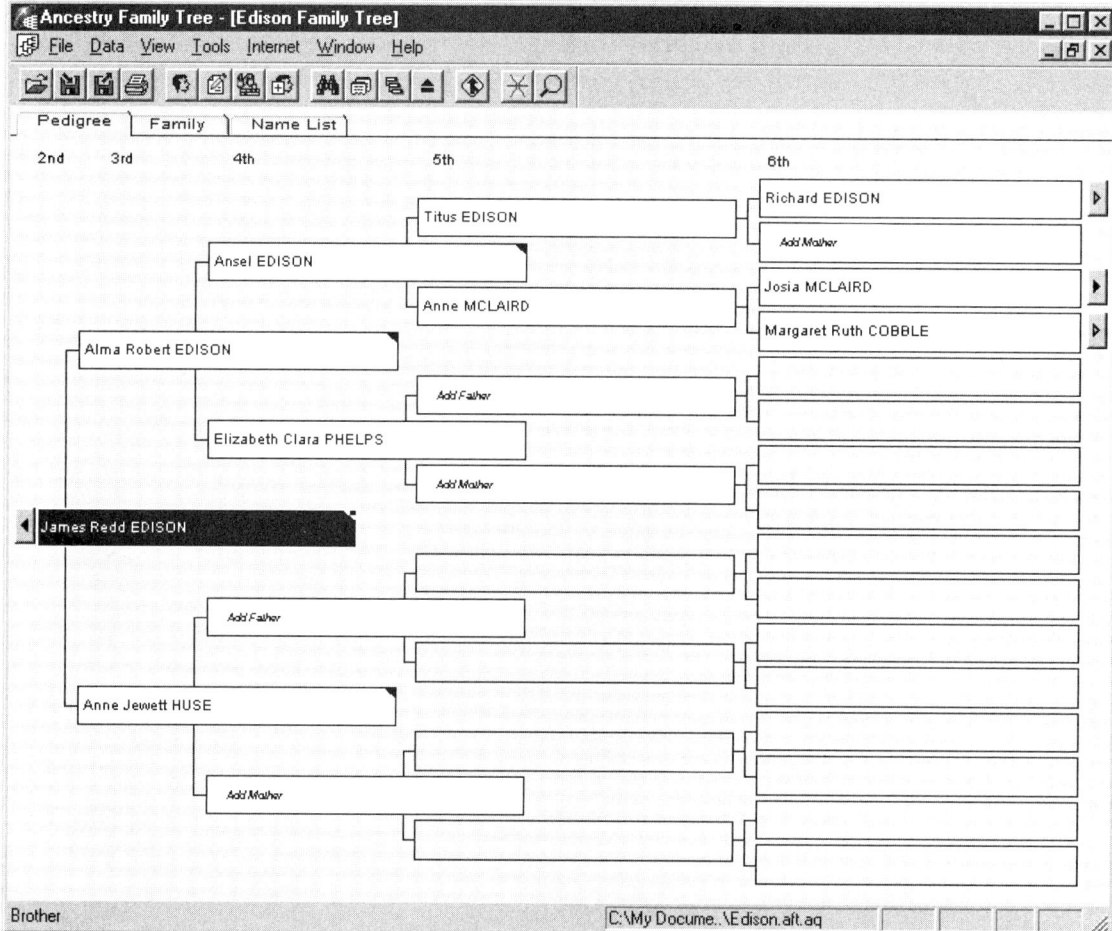

To view descendants of the primary person, click the arrow button to the left of the individual. To view ancestors who extend beyond the fifth generation shown in the view, you can click arrow buttons to the right of those individuals.

Dates and places of birth, marriage, and death appear for individuals in a drop-down information box when you place the cursor over an individual name (depending on the settings selected on the InfoBox page of the Preferences form, which determines overall Ancestry Family Tree user preferences. Refer to chapter 2, Installation and Setup, to learn how to define information box preferences).

Family view

The Family view shows all of the individuals in a *family group*—a mother, father, and their children. The parents of the primary person (who appears in the upper-left in this view) are shown as well. Note that the information box for the primary person appears consistently in the upper-left corner in the Family view.

Again, to view descendants of the primary person, you can click an arrow button to the left of the individual. To view ancestors of the primary person's parents, you can click arrow buttons to the right of those individuals. The Family view can also show how each individual in the view is related to a selected individual—the *root person*. (Note the Father and Mother labels, above; refer to "Identifying relationships among individuals" in chapter 4, Working with Individuals in a Database, to learn how to set relationship indicators.)

The Family view allows you to perform many data-entry tasks for the individuals in a family database. You can access the marriage record of the primary person and his or her spouse, or the marriage record of the primary person's parents (**Marriage** buttons); create a new marriage record for the primary person (**Add Spouse** button); and add children for the primary person (**Add Child** button). (You can also perform these tasks by making selections on the tool bar and menus, as described below.)

Name List view

The Name List view is an alphabetical name index of every individual in a family database, along with RIN, sex, and the date and place of the first event (if any) for which data exists for the individual.

RIN	Name	Sex	Event	Date	Place
15	Berger, Harrison	M			
7	Bradley, Jonathan	M			
23	Cobble, Margaret Ruth	F			
3	Edison, Alma Robert	M	Marriage	3 Aug 1860	Providence, Rhode Island
13	Edison, Ansel	M			
17	Edison, Emma	F			
25	Edison, Emma Dickson	F	Birth	Jul 1891	Raleigh, North Carolina
1	Edison, James Redd	M	Birth	1 Jul 1866	Baltimore, Maryland
5	Edison, Jonathan Anton	M	Birth	1 Dec 1868	
21	Edison, Richard	M			
9	Edison, Richard Albertus	M	Birth	1889	Raleigh, North Carolina
19	Edison, Titus	M			
6	Edwards, Echo	F	Birth	1 Dec 1887	
8	Edwards, Edwina	F			
12	Harris, Thora	F			
4	Huse, Anne Jewett	F	Marriage	3 Aug 1860	Providence, Rhode Island
2	Landers, Emma Valentina	F	Birth	30 Jul 1868	Buffalo, New York
18	Landers, Emma Valentina	F	Marriage	15 Dec 1886	Raleigh, North Carolina
10	Landers, Jeremiah	M			
20	McLaird, Anne	F			
22	McLaird, Josia	M			
24	McLaird, Oliver	M			
11	Morton, Amelia	F			
16	Phelps, Elizabeth Clara	F			
14	Smith, Henrietta	F	Birth	10 Jul 1900	Ogden, Weber County, Utah, USA

If you highlight an individual in the Name List view, that person will become the primary person in the Pedigree and Family views.

The tool bar

The tool bar appears in each of the three views. It lets you instantly access various records and features in Ancestry Family Tree.

The table below describes the function of each button on the tool bar.

Button	Description
	Click the Open Database button to access the Open Family Database form, which allows you to find and open a family database on your computer. Refer to chapter 4, Working with Individuals in a Database, to learn how to open an existing family database.
	Click the Import button to open the Import GEDCOM File form; it lets you find and import a GEDCOM file. Refer to chapter 10, Importing and Exporting Files and Merging Records, to learn how to import data.
	Click the Export button to open the GEDCOM Export form, which allows you to export data from a family database in GEDCOM format. Refer to chapter 10, Importing and Exporting Files and Merging Records, to learn how to export data.
	Click the Print Reports button to open the Reports and Charts form, which allows you to create and print various reports and charts containing information from a family database. Refer to chapter 11, Creating Reports and Charts, to learn how to present your data using reports and charts.
	Click the Edit Individual button to open the Edit Individual form; it allows you to add to or modify information in the record of the selected individual. Refer to chapter 4, Working With Individuals in a Database, to learn how to edit individual records.
	Click the Edit Notes button to open the Notes form, which allows you to add to or modify notes for the selected individual. Refer to chapter 6, Working With Notes, to learn how to edit notes for an individual.
	Click the Multimedia button to open the Media Collection form, which allows you to add to or modify the media collection for the selected individual. Refer to chapter 8, Working With Media Collections, to learn how to edit media collections.
	Click the Add Individual button to add a new individual to the database. Refer to chapter 4, Working With Individuals in a Database, to learn how to add an individual.
	Click the Search button to open the Find Individual form; it allows you to specify an individual whose record you want to view. Refer to chapter 9, Searching the Database, to learn how to search for individual records.
	Click the Browse List button to open the Search for Individual form, which lets you search the database for one or more individuals. Refer to chapter 9, Searching the Database, to learn how to search for individual records.
	Click the Descendancy List button to open the Descendancy List form, which shows all descendants of the selected individual. Refer to chapter 9, Searching the Database, to learn how to use the descendancy list.

Button	Description
⏏	Click the Home Person button to return the focus of the current view to the database's root person—the first individual entered in the database.
⬆	Click the Merge button to open the Merge Individuals form, which lets you search for and merge duplicate records. Refer to chapter 10, Importing and Exporting Files and Merging Records, to learn how to merge duplicate records.
✳	Click the Create World Wide Web Page button to open the Web Page Wizard, which allows you to create a webpage from a family database. Refer to chapter 13, Publishing Your Data on the World Wide Web, to learn how to create a webpage.
🔍	Click the Search Ancestry.com button to search the Ancestry.com Website for records relating to the individual who is currently highlighted in the Ancestry Family Tree view.

The menu bar

The menu bar also appears in each of the three views. The menu items let you instantly access various records and features in Ancestry Family Tree, including some that are not accessible via the tool bar. To use the menus, simply click a menu and then click the menu item you want.

File   Data   View   Tools   Internet   Window   Help

Refer to the tables below for descriptions of the various menu items.

File menu

Menu item	Description
New	Lets you create a new family database file. Refer to chapter 3, Working with Family Databases, to learn how to create a new family database.
Open	Lets you open an existing family database file. Refer to chapter 4, Working with Individuals in a Database, to learn how to open an existing family database.
Close	Closes the family database file that is currently open.
Backup	Use to create a backup copy of a family database file. Refer to chapter 3, Working with Family Databases, to learn how to create a backup copy of a family database.
Restore	Lets you restore a family database file from a backup copy. Refer to chapter 3, Working with Family Databases, to learn how to restore a family database from a backup copy.
Copy	Use to copy the family database file that is currently open and save it with a new name. Refer to chapter 3, Working with Family Databases, to learn how to copy an existing database.

Menu item	Description
Delete	Lets you delete an existing family database. Refer to chapter 3, Working with Family Databases, to learn how to delete an existing database.
Import	Allows you to import data saved in the GEDCOM format. Refer to chapter 10, Importing and Exporting Files and Merging Records, to learn how to import data.
Export	Lets you export data from the family database file that is currently open in GEDCOM format. Refer to chapter 10, Importing and Exporting Files and Merging Records, to learn how to export data.
Import from Web	Connects you to Ancestry.com and allows you to download GEDCOM data from Online Family Trees to which you have access. Refer to chapter 10, Importing and Exporting Files and Merging Records, to learn how to import a GEDCOM file from an Online Family Tree.
Export to Web	Lets you export data from the family database file that is currently open to the Ancestry World Tree at Ancestry.com or as an Online Family Tree. Refer to chapter 13, Publishing Your Data on the World Wide Web, to learn how to create an Online Family Tree.
Print Reports	Use to create reports and charts. Refer to chapter 11, Creating Reports and Charts, to learn how to present your data using any of various reports and charts.
Exit	Closes Ancestry Family Tree (and any family database file that is currently open).

Data menu

Menu item	Description
Edit Individual	Lets you edit the record of the individual who is currently highlighted in the Ancestry Family Tree view. Refer to chapter 4, Working with Individuals in a Database, to learn how to edit individual records.
Edit Notes	Lets you edit the notes for the individual who is currently highlighted in the Ancestry Family Tree view. Refer to chapter 6, Working with Notes, to learn how to edit notes for an individual.
Edit Media Collection	Allows you to edit the media collection for the individual who is currently highlighted in the Ancestry Family Tree view. Refer to chapter 8, Working with Media Collections, to learn how to edit media collections.
Add Individual	Lets you add a new individual record to the family database file that is currently open. Refer to chapter 4, Working with Individuals in a Database, to learn how to add an individual.

Menu item	Description
Add Father	Lets you add a father for the individual who is currently highlighted in the Ancestry Family Tree view. Refer to chapter 4, Working with Individuals in a Database, to learn how to add an individual based on relationship to another.
Add Mother	Lets you add a mother for the individual who is currently highlighted in the Ancestry Family Tree view. Refer to chapter 4, Working with Individuals in a Database, to learn how to add an individual based on relationship to another.
Add Spouse	Lets you add a spouse for the individual who is currently highlighted in the Ancestry Family Tree view. Refer to chapter 4, Working with Individuals in a Database, to learn how to add an individual based on relationship to another.
Add Child	Lets you add a child for the individual who is currently highlighted in the Ancestry Family Tree view. Refer to chapter 4, Working with Individuals in a Database, to learn how to add an individual based on relationship to another.
Add Parents	Lets you add additional parents for the individual who is currently highlighted in the Ancestry Family Tree view. You can use this menu item only with individuals for whom parents (the primary parents) already exist in the database. Refer to chapter 4, Working with Individuals in a Database, to learn how to add additional parents to an individual.
Unlink Individual	Lets you remove relationship links from the individual who is currently highlighted in the Ancestry Family Tree view. Refer to chapter 4, Working with Individuals in a Database, to learn how to unlink individuals.
Delete Individual	Lets you delete the individual who is currently highlighted in the Ancestry Family Tree view from the family database file. Refer to chapter 4, Working with Individuals in a Database, to learn how to delete an individual record from a family database.
Order	Use to rearrange the order of multiple parents, spouses, and children for the individual who is currently highlighted in the Ancestry Family Tree view. Refer to chapter 4, Working with Individuals in a Database, to learn how to rearrange the order of multiple parents, spouses, or children.
Edit Primary Marriage	Allows you to edit the primary marriage for the individual who is currently highlighted in the Ancestry Family Tree view. This menu item is only available for individuals who are married. Refer to chapter 5, Working with Marriages, to learn how to edit a marriage record.

Menu item	Description
Edit Parent's Marriage	Lets you edit the marriage record of the primary parents of the individual who is currently highlighted in the Ancestry Family Tree view. This menu item is only available for individuals for whom there are parents in the database.
Edit Parent Links	Use to edit relationship links between the individual who is currently highlighted in the Ancestry Family Tree view and his or her parents. This menu item is only available for individuals for whom there are parents in the database. Refer to chapter 4, Working with Individuals in a Database, to learn how to edit parent links.

View menu

Menu item	Description
Pedigree	Opens the Pedigree view for the current family database file.
Family	Opens the Family view for the current family database file.
Name List	Opens the Name List view for the current family database file.
Toolbar	Click to show or hide the Ancestry Family Tree tool bar.
Status Bar	Click to show or hide the status bar at the bottom of the Ancestry Family Tree view.

Tools menu

Menu item	Description
Search	Lets you search for individuals in the family database file that is currently open. Refer to chapter 9, Searching the Database, to learn how to search for individual records.
Browse List	Use to view a list of individuals in the family database file. Refer to chapter 9, Searching the Database, to learn how to search for individual records.
Descendancy List	Lets you view a list of descendants of the individual who is currently highlighted in the Ancestry Family Tree view. Refer to chapter 9, Searching the Database, to learn how to use the descendancy list.
Relationship Indicators	Use to set indicators that specify the relationship of every individual to a specific individual. Refer to chapter 4, Working With Individuals in a Database, to learn how to set relationship indicators.
Home	Use to place the database's root person in the current view.

Menu item	Description
Merge	Allows you to find and merge duplicate individual records. Refer to chapter 10, Importing and Exporting Files and Merging Records, to learn how to merge duplicate records.
Relationship Examiner	Lets you determine the relationship between any two individuals in the database. Refer to chapter 4, Working with Individuals in a Database, to learn how to use the relationship examiner.
Calculators	Use to open the Date Calculator and the Soundex calculator. Refer to chapter 4, Working with Individuals in a Database, to learn how to use the Date Calculator and the Soundex calculator.
Edit Source List	Lets you view a list of sources for the family database file that is currently open, and create, edit, or delete source records. Refer to chapter 7, Working with Sources and Source Citations, to learn how to work with source records.
Edit Repository List	Lets you view a list of source repositories for the family database file that is currently open, and create, edit, or delete repository records. Refer to chapter 7, Working with Sources and Source Citations, to learn how to work with repository records.
Preferences	Lets you define overall Ancestry Family Tree user preferences. Refer to chapter 2, Installation and Setup, to learn how to define user preferences.
Database Check/Repair	Use to have Ancestry Family Tree search for and repair database problems. Refer to chapter 3, Working With Family Databases, to learn how to perform a database check/repair.

Internet menu

Menu item	Description
Search Ancestry.com	Connects you to Ancestry.com and automatically searches for data on the individual who is currently highlighted. Refer to chapter 12, Searching for Information on the World Wide Web, to learn how to search Ancestry.com.
Search Ancestry World Tree	Connects you to Ancestry.com and automatically searches the Ancestry World Tree for data on the individual who is currently highlighted. Refer to chapter 12, Searching for Information on the World Wide Web, to learn how to search the Ancestry World Tree.
Search Ancestry Message Boards	Connects you to Ancestry.com and automatically searches the message boards for data on the individual who is currently highlighted. Refer to chapter 12, Searching for Information on the World Wide Web, to learn how to search Ancestry.com.

Menu item	Description
Ancestry.com Home Page	Connects you to the Ancestry.com home page.
Create Web Page	Lets you create a webpage from a family database. Refer to chapter 13, Publishing Your Data on the World Wide Web, to learn how to create a webpage.
Favorite Sites	Opens the list of your favorite websites. Refer to chapter 12, Searching for Information on the World Wide Web, to learn how to maintain a list of your favorite websites.
Search Favorite Sites	Opens a list of searchable websites from your list of favorite sites. Refer to chapter 12, Searching for Information on the World Wide Web, to learn how to maintain a list of your favorite websites.

CHAPTER 2

Installation and Setup

This chapter describes how to install Ancestry Family Tree on your computer and how to define user preferences. User preferences allow you to customize the way Ancestry Family Tree works and how you interact with it.

In this chapter

• Installing Ancestry Family Tree
• Defining user preferences

Installing Ancestry Family Tree

Ancestry Family Tree is available on CD-ROM. Or, if you have access to the World Wide Web, you can download Ancestry Family Tree at no charge from Ancestry.com.

To install Ancestry Family Tree from a CD-ROM

1. Insert the CD-ROM in your CD-ROM drive.

2. Wait while the installation program starts automatically.

3. Follow the instructions presented by the installation program.

To download Ancestry Family Tree from Ancestry.com

1. Go to Ancestry.com on the World Wide Web (http://www.ancestry.com/).

2. Find the **Free Family Tree Software** link.

3. Click the link and follow directions to download Ancestry Family Tree at no charge.

Defining user preferences

You can set a number of user preferences that affect the behavior of Ancestry Family Tree—for example, the preferred format for date entry and whether to append identification numbers to names. However, you don't have to set any preferences to use Ancestry Family Tree. The default preferences—those that exist when you install the software—may well suffice for many users. And you can change the preferences at any time while using Ancestry Family Tree.

Open the **Preferences** form by doing one of the following:

- In the **Tools** menu, click **Preferences**, or

- press Shift+Ctrl+P on your keyboard.

The **Preferences** form will be displayed.

```
Preferences                                                    [X]

  | Compiler |  | Fonts |  | Multimedia |  | Formats |
    | General |        | Database |      | InfoBox |

  ┌ Append to Names ─────────┐   ☑ Use LDS Data  ☑ Show on Reports
  │  ⦿ Nothing               │   ☑ Verify New Names
  │  ○ RIN (Record ID Number)│   ☑ Capitalize Surnames
  │  ○ ID                    │   ☐ Edit Marriage when Created
  │  ○ AFN                   │   ☑ Shade Reports  ☐ Hide in Preview
  └──────────────────────────┘   ☑ Use List when Navigating
  ┌ Notes Btn while editing indiv ┐  ☐ Reenable Tips  ☐ Disable Tips
  │  ○ Notes Screen          │   ┌ Double-Click on Pedigree/Family ┐
  │  ⦿ Notes Selector Screen │   │  ○ Selects Primary Individual   │
  └──────────────────────────┘   │  ○ Edits Individual             │
  ┌ Notes Btn while browsing ┐    │  ⦿ Edits Primary/Selects Primary│
  │  ⦿ Notes Screen          │    └─────────────────────────────────┘
  │  ○ Notes Selector Screen │
  └──────────────────────────┘   ┌ Data Entry ──────────────┐
  ┌ Date Entry ──────────────┐    │  ○ Case as Entered       │
  │  ⦿ U.S.  ○ European      │    │  ⦿ Capitalize First Character │
  └──────────────────────────┘    │  ☑ Use Quick Entry       │
                                  └──────────────────────────┘
    [ Colors... ]  [ Password... ]

        [    OK    ]   [ Cancel ]   [ Apply ]   [ Help ]
```

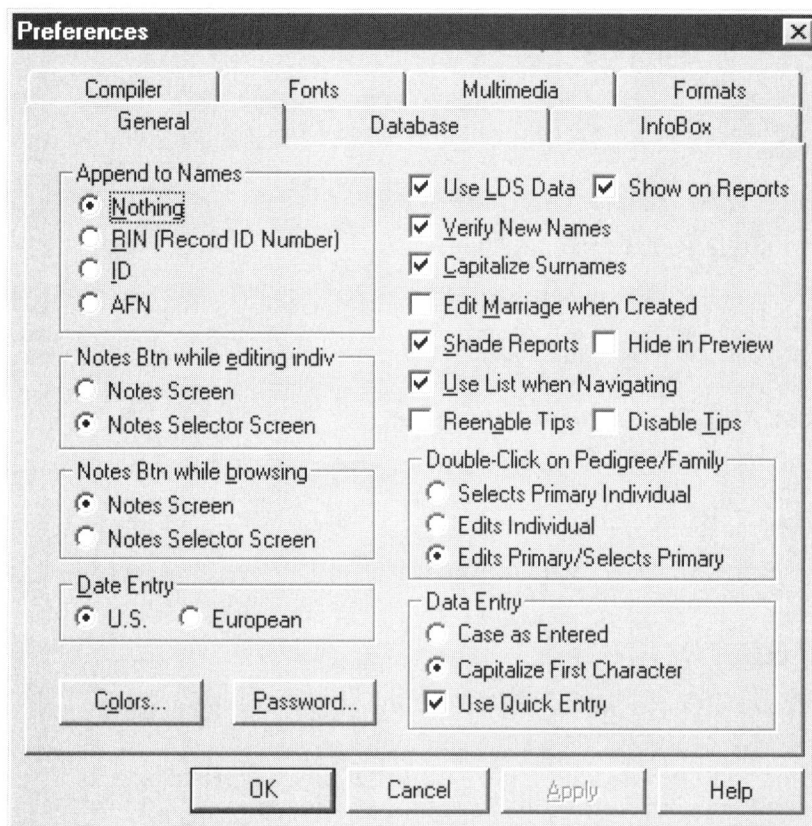

Defining general preferences

The "general" preferences options allow you to select from a wide range of preferences that affect the general behavior of Ancestry Family Tree.

To access general preferences options

On the **Preferences** form, click the **General** tab.

The **General** page of the Preferences form will be displayed.

To define ID number preference

Under **Append to Names**, click a button to indicate the type of identification number that will follow each name in the database. (The number will appear on-screen as you view the database in Ancestry Family Tree and on printed reports.) The following options are available:

Nothing   No identification number will appear.

RIN   (Record Identification Number) The RIN (generated automatically by Ancestry Family Tree for each individual in a database) will appear.

ID   An identification number that you define will appear. (You assign such a number to an individual using the Add/Edit Individual form.)

AFN   (Ancestral File™ Number) The Ancestral File number, if present, will appear. This number identifies an individual within the Ancestral File database maintained by The Church of Jesus Christ of Latter-day Saints. If you have downloaded data from Ancestral File, these numbers will be present.

To define Notes form preference

1. Under **Notes Btn while editing indiv**, click a button to determine whether the Notes form or the Notes Selector form appears when you click the Notes button on the Add/Edit individual form. (The Notes form allows you to enter a new note for the individual; the Notes Selector form allows you to select existing notes for the individual. Refer to chapter 6, Working with Notes, to learn how to create notes.) The options are:

   Notes Screen   The Notes form appears when you click the Notes button on the Add/Edit individual form.

   Notes Selector Screen   The Notes Selector form appears when you click the Notes button on the Add/Edit individual form.

2. Under **Notes Btn while browsing**, click a button to determine whether the Notes form or the Notes Selector form appears while you are browsing in the Pedigree view, the Family view, or the Search for Individual form. (For example, you can view the type of notes form you select here by right-clicking a name in the Pedigree view and selecting Notes from the pop-up menu.)

To define date entry preference

The options under **Date Entry** determine how Ancestry Family Tree will interpret dates as you enter them. Click one of the following options:

U.S.   The U.S. convention is month/day/year; therefore, if you enter 5/6/02, for example, Ancestry Family Tree will interpret the date as 6 May 2002.

European   The European convention is day/month/year; therefore, if you enter 5/6/02, Ancestry Family Tree will interpret the date as 5 June 2002.

To define double-click behavior in Pedigree view and Family view

You can use the options under **Double-Click on Pedigree/Family** to determine what happens when you double-click an individual in the Pedigree view or the Family view. Click one of the following options:

Selects Primary Individual   Double-clicking an individual will make that person the primary individual in the view.

Edits Individual   Double-clicking an individual will open the Edit Individual form.

Edits Primary/Selects Primary   Double-clicking the primary individual will open the Edit Individual form for that individual; double-clicking any other individual will make that person the primary individual.

To define data entry preferences

The options under **Data Entry** allow you to select preferences that affect how Ancestry Family Tree renders data as you enter it.

1. The **Case as Entered** and **Capitalize First Character** options let you determine how data is capitalized as you enter it.

   - Click **Case as Entered** to cause data to be capitalized exactly the way you enter it. For example, if you enter the name as "john q. Farley," you will see "john q. Farley" and it will be stored that way in the record.

   - Click **Capitalize First Character** to cause the first character of each word to be capitalized automatically. For example, if you enter the name as "john q. Farley," you will see "John Q. Farley" and it will be stored that way in the record. (The *j* and the *q* are capitalized for you.)

     Note: If you select the **Capitalize First Character** option, you can force a character to lowercase after entering it by backspacing and re-typing the lowercase character. Ancestry Family Tree will then retain the lowercase character.

2. The **Use Quick Entry** option enables Ancestry Family Tree to fill in the remainder of a name or place name automatically from a list of names you have already entered.

   - If you are entering a **name**, you can use the spacebar to speed the entry of multiple names. For example, if you have entered the name Bradley Russell, you can quickly re-enter this name as follows: As you type the *B,* you will see the first name in your database that starts with *B;* then, as you type the *r,* you will see the first name that starts with *Br,* which will probably be Bradley. If this is the case, you will notice that the remainder of the name, *adley,* is highlighted. At this point, if you press the spacebar, the cursor will jump past *adley* and add a space. You will now see Bradley and be positioned to enter the next name. As you type *Rus* or some portion of the name Russell, you will eventually see the full name and can then press the spacebar to accept it. It may take only three or four keystrokes to enter the name using this method.

   - If you are entering a **place**, you can use the comma (,) to speed entry of multiple place names. For example, if you have already entered the place names *Jonesboro, Jefferson,* and *Alabama* separately but never combined as *Jonesboro, Jefferson, Alabama,* you would first start entering *Jonesboro;* after a few keystrokes you will see a matching name. At this point you do not have to finish typing the name. Instead you can enter a comma to accept the name. A comma and a space will be placed at the end of the name, and you will be ready to enter the county. When you start entering *Jefferson,* you will see the full name after a couple of keystrokes and can again accept this name with a comma. You can then start entering *Alabama* and enter it as well with very few keystrokes.

   - If you need to enter an abbreviated form of a word that is suggested, use the Delete key on your keyboard to remove the remainder. For example, if you have already entered *Smithfield* but not *Smith,* you will notice that as you enter *Smi Smithfield* is suggested. You would finish entering the word *Smith;* the undesired portion, *field,* would be highlighted. At this point you would press the Delete key to remove the highlighted portion of the word.

- If, after typing a few characters of a name, you realize that the desired name is not going to be suggested (because there are many similar names in the database), you can press Alt+Down Arrow on your keyboard to open a list of names. You can scroll through this list using the up and down arrow keys, the PgUp and PgDn keys, and the Home and End keys. If you find the name you are looking for, highlight it and press the Enter key to accept it. If you want to close the list without accepting the highlighted name, use Alt+Up Arrow or press Tab. (Do not use the Esc key; if you do, all editing on the current form will be lost.)

The **Use Quick Entry** option is enabled by default. Uncheck the **Use Quick Entry** box if you don't want to use this option.

To define other general preferences

1. The following two check boxes determine whether LDS ordinance data can be entered and whether it will appear on reports.

   - The **Use LDS Data** check box determines whether you can enter data regarding LDS temple ordinances for every individual. If this box is checked, Ancestry Family Tree data entry forms will provide fields that let you to enter dates and places (LDS temples) of LDS baptism, endowment, sealing to parents, and sealing to spouse ordinances.

     Uncheck the box if you don't want to be able to enter LDS ordinance data.

   - The **Show on Reports** check box (available only if the Use LDS Data box is checked) determines whether LDS ordinance data will appear on printed Pedigree charts, Family Group records, and Individual Summary reports.

     Uncheck the box if you don't want LDS ordinance data to appear on these reports.

2. The **Verify New Names** option causes Ancestry Family Tree to query you after you enter a name that you have not previously entered in the database. This query allows you to verify the validity of the new name.

   If you select this option, a form similar to the one shown below will be displayed each time you enter a new name in an Ancestry Family Tree form.

   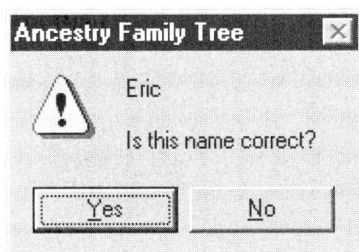

   Uncheck the box if you don't want to use this option.

3. The **Capitalize Surnames** option determines whether surnames will automatically be displayed in all-uppercase letters in the Pedigree and Family views. If you do not select this option, surnames will be displayed exactly as you enter them.

Entering surnames with an initial capital letter and allowing Ancestry Family Tree to capitalize them for you is recommended because, if you share your data with others, they will have the option of displaying surnames in either format.

Uncheck the box if you don't want Ancestry Family Tree to display surnames in all-capital letters.

4. The **Edit Marriage When Created** option determines whether you are prompted to enter marriage information immediately whenever you enter other information that implies the likelihood of a marriage—for example, when you add a parent to an individual.

   Check the box if you want to cause the Marriage form to be opened automatically when you enter information that implies the likelihood of a marriage.

5. Some of the reports that Ancestry Family Tree can print allow shading to enhance their appearance and readability. The **Shade Reports** option enables this feature. The **Hide in Preview** option causes the shading to be hidden when you preview a report on-screen.

   Uncheck the Shade Reports box if you don't want shading to appear on reports that allow this feature.

   If you find the shading to be distracting when you preview reports on-screen, check the Hide in Preview box to suppress shading in the report preview.

   Note: Regardless of the option you select here, you can also turn on (or turn off) the shading option when defining the preferences for an individual report type, and you can select the color of the shading as well. (Refer to chapter 11, Creating Reports and Charts, to learn how to create reports and define preferences for individual types of reports.)

6. In the Pedigree view and the Family view, a left arrow appears next to the primary person if that person has descendants. The **Use List When Navigating** option determines whether a list of the individual's descendants will appear when you click the descendants arrow.

   If you click the descendants arrow, one of three things will happen:

   • If you have been moving along the ancestral line *from* a particular descendant, the view will go back to the child you last viewed; *otherwise,*

   • if the Use List When Navigating box is checked, the list of descendents will pop up and you will be allowed to select a descendant to go to; or,

   • if the Use List When Navigating box is not checked, the view will go to the oldest child with descendants or to the oldest child if no children have descendants.

   Check the Use List When Navigating box to cause the Descendents List to be opened when you click the descendents arrow (unless you have been moving along the ancestral line *from* a particular descendant).

7. Tip screens contain hints that will aid you in using the various Ancestry Family Tree forms. By default, a tip screen will appear the first time you open a form in an

Ancestry Family Tree session. (A tip screen that has already been shown will not appear again in the same session.) The **Disable Tips** option allows you to prevent tip screens from appearing. The **Reenable Tips** option allows you to view tip screens again after you have disabled them.

Check the Disable Tips box if you want to prevent tip screens from being displayed (until you check the Reenable Tips box).

Check the Reenable Tips box if you want to allow tip screens to be displayed again.

Selecting the colors used in Ancestry Family Tree views

You can assign different colors to various parts of the Pedigree view and Family view. In doing so, you can select from a group of basic colors or create your own custom colors.

To select the colors used in Ancestry Family Tree views

1. On the **General** page of the **Preferences** form, click the **Colors** button.

   The **Choose Colors** form will be displayed. You can use it to determine the colors used for names, backgrounds, etc., in the Pedigree and Family views.

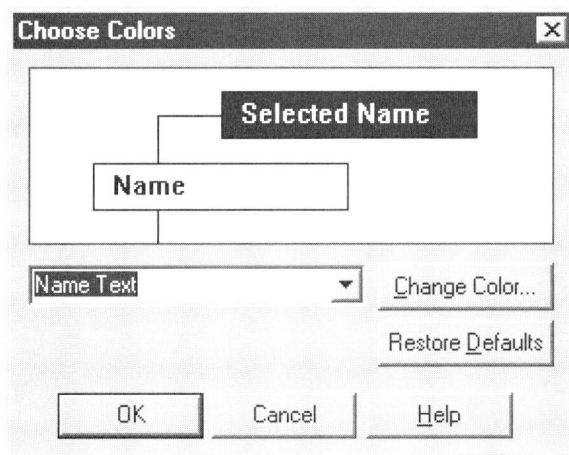

2. Click the arrow button to the right of the drop-down box and select the part of the view for which you want to define the color. The options are:

Name Text	Define the color of the name text.
Name Background	Define the color of the name text background.
Selected Name Text	Define the color of the text for a name when you select it in the view.
Selected Name Background	Define the color of the text background for a name when you select it in the view.
Pedigree window	Define the color of the window background.

3. Click the **Change Color** button.

   The **Color** form will be displayed. It lets you select and assign one of 48 basic colors for the part of the view you selected; it also lets you create custom colors that you can assign.

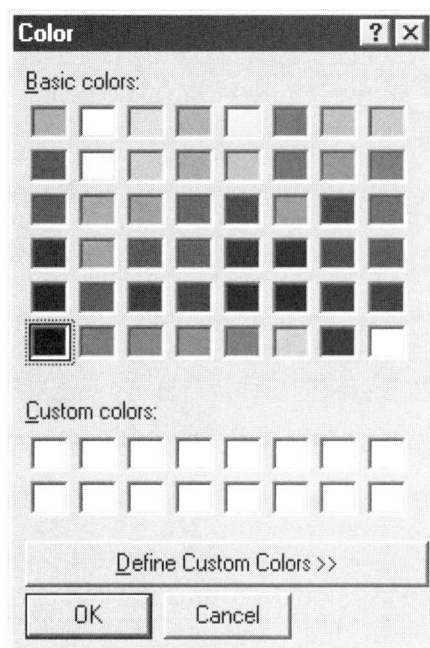

4. Under **Basic colors**, select the color you want to use and then click the **OK** button to close the Color form and return to the Choose Colors form.

    The display sample on the Choose Colors form is updated to show the color you selected.

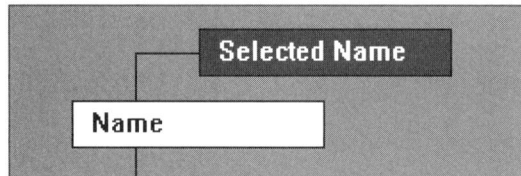

5. Repeat steps 2–4 to assign different colors to other parts of the views.

6. On the **Choose Colors** form, click the **OK** button to close the form and update the views with the selected colors.

To create custom colors for the Ancestry Family Tree views

1. Perform steps 1–3 in "To select the colors used in Ancestry Family Tree views," above.

2. On the **Color** form, click the **Define Custom Colors** button.

    The Color form expands to include the custom color design controls.

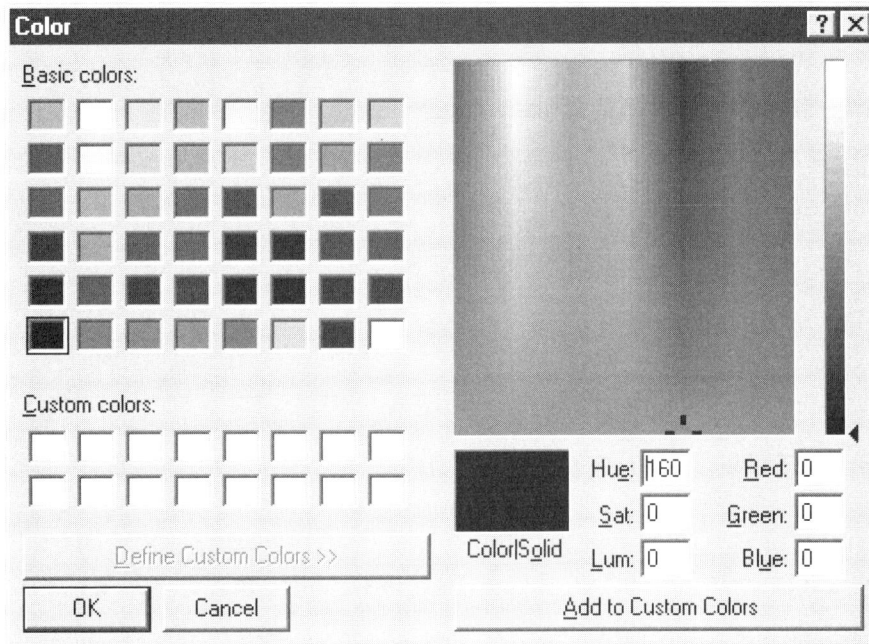

3. Select an empty box under **Custom colors** and then do one of the following:

   • Click the crosshairs [crosshairs icon] in the custom color box and drag it until you see the color you want in the **Color|Solid** box, or

   • enter numbers in the **Hue**, **Sat** (saturation), and **Red**, **Green**, **Blue** boxes to define the custom color.

4. Click and drag the arrow [arrow icon] next to the luminosity scale, or enter a number in the **Lum** (luminosity) box to determine the luminosity of the color.

5. Click the **Add to Custom Colors** button.

   The custom color is added to the Color form under **Custom colors**. You will be able to select this color in the future by opening the Color form.

6. Repeat steps 3–5 if you want to create additional custom colors.

7. Under **Custom colors**, select the color you want to use and then click the **OK** button to close the Color form and return to the Choose Colors form

8. On the **Choose Colors** form, click the **OK** button to close the form and update the views with the selected colors.

To restore the default colors to the views

On the **Choose Colors** form, click the **Restore Defaults** button to restore the default colors for the views.

Defining a password for Ancestry Family Tree

You can define a password that any user will be required to enter before he or she is allowed to enter or change any data in a database. (The password will not be required to start Ancestry Family Tree or to open a database—only to change or enter data.)

To define a password

1. On the **General** page of the **Preferences** form, click the **Password** button.

    The **Change Password** form will be displayed.

    ```
    Change Password

        Password: [            ]

        [  OK  ]   [ Cancel ]
    ```

2. Enter a password of your choosing in the **Password** box.

    Note: The password is case-sensitive. Therefore, if you enter *Fortune* as the password, for example, a user must enter *Fortune* when required—not *fortune* or *FORTUNE*.

3. Click the **OK** button to save the password and close the Change Password form.

    Beginning with the next Ancestry Family Tree session, the user will be presented with the **Enter Password** form the first time he or she attempts to enter or modify data (or attempts to view the password).

    ```
    Enter Password

        Password: [            ]

        [  OK  ]   [ Cancel ]
    ```

    If the correct password is entered, the user will not be required to enter a password again until the next session. The user will be allowed three attempts to enter the correct password. If the correct password is not entered within three attempts, the user will not be allowed to save any entered or changed data in the current session. At the next Ancestry Family Tree session, the user will again be required to enter the password.

    If the correct password is not entered, the user will be presented with the following dialogue box when attempting to save the database:

    ```
    Ancestry Family Tree                    [X]

       /!\   You are not authorized to perform this function.

                    [  OK  ]
    ```

    After this form is closed, any open data entry form will be closed and the user will not be able to enter or change data.

To change the password

1. On the **General** page of the **Preferences** form, click the **Password** button.

   The **Enter Password** form will be displayed.

2. Enter the current password and then click the **OK** button.

   The **Change Password** form will be displayed.

3. Enter the new password and then click the **OK** button.

   The new password will be saved.

To delete the password

1. On the **General** page of the **Preferences** form, click the **Password** button.

   The **Enter Password** form will be displayed.

2. Enter the current password and then click the **OK** button.

   The **Change Password** form will be displayed.

3. Delete all the characters of the current password and then click the **OK** button.

   The password is deleted; a password will no longer be required to enter or modify data.

To recover a password

To learn your password if you've forgotten it, find and open the "AncestryFamilyTree.ini" file (located in the Windows directory) in Notepad and then search for "PedPwd="; it will be followed by the password.

Defining database preferences

The database preferences options let you define various preferences for the family database that is currently open.

To access database preference options

On the **Preferences** form, click the **Database** tab.

The **Database** page of the Preferences form will be displayed.

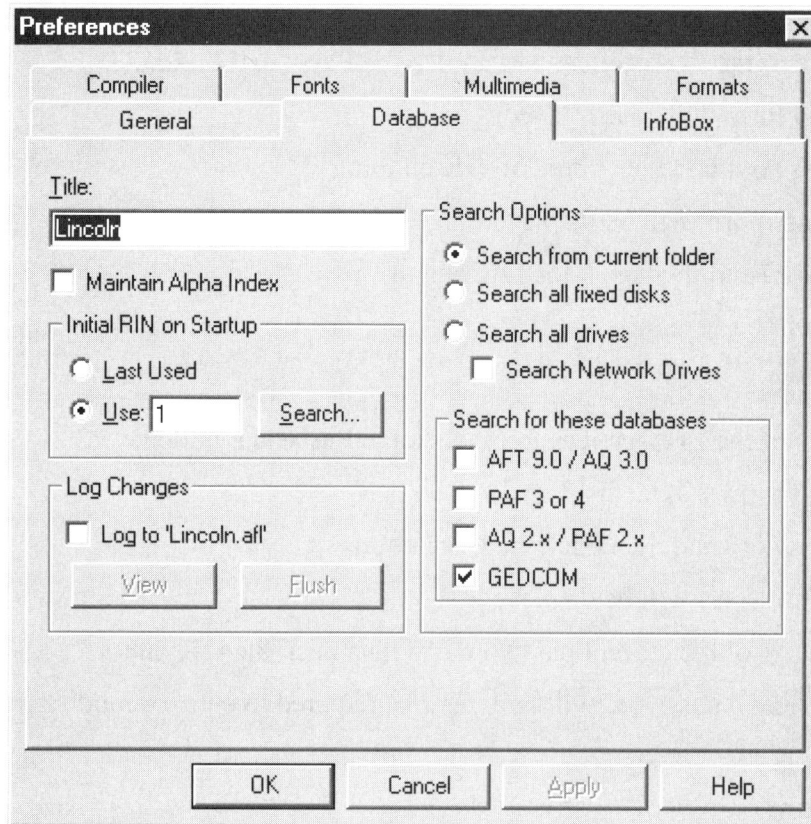

To define the title of the database

In the **Title** box, enter the title that you want to use for the current database. (The database's *title* is separate from its *name*. The title you define here will appear in the Ancestry Family Tree title bar next to the application's name:

Ancestry Family Tree - [Lincoln Family Tree]

The database's name is its file name—for example, Lincoln.aft. By default, the database's title is the same as its name.)

To update the alphabetical index automatically

The **Maintain Alpha Index** box determines whether the database's alphabetical index of individuals (shown in the Name List view) will be updated every time you add or delete an individual or change the name of an individual. Using this option will slow down the process of updating the database. (If you don't select this option, the index will be updated the first time you click the Name List tab after adding or deleting an individual.)

Check the box if you want the index to be updated automatically.

To define the startup primary individual

The options under **Initial RIN on Startup** let you determine which individual in the database will appear as the primary individual whenever the database is opened.

- Click the **Last Used** option to cause the last individual who appeared as the primary individual to appear as the primary individual the next time the database is opened, or

- click the **Use** option and in the adjacent box enter the RIN of the individual whom you want to appear as the primary individual whenever the database is opened. (If you don't know the individual's RIN, you can search for the individual by clicking the **Search** button. Refer to chapter 9, Searching the Database, to learn how to search the database for an individual.)

Maintaining a database log

A database *log file* records database activity. The **Log to [log file name].afl** box determines whether a log file will be maintained for the database. If turned on, the log file will record the addition, modification, and deletion of all individual records and marriage records. It will also record all linking and unlinking of individuals to marriages.

To turn on the database log file

1. Check the **Log to [log file name].afl** box to cause a log file to be maintained. The log file will be saved in the same folder as the database. It will have the same name as the database and the suffix *.afl.*

   Log file entries appear as follows:

   > 3-12-01 11:29 Mod Ind 1
   >
   > 3-12-01 11:35 Mod Nts 15
   >
   > 3-12-01 11:41 Unl Ch 62 10
   >
   > 3-12-01 11:41 Unl Sp 63 10
   >
   > 3-12-01 11:41 Del Mar 10

   Each entry records the date and time, followed by information. The first entry above shows that the individual with RIN 1 was modified. The second entry shows that notes were modified for RIN 15. The last three entries all show the deletion of MRIN 10: First the only child of the marriage, RIN 62, was unlinked from marriage 10, then the only spouse in the marriage, RIN 63, was unlinked, and finally the marriage itself was deleted.

   Maintaining a log file is useful for reviewing your work if you have made a mistake. More importantly, if you are coordinating research efforts with someone else, you can review the log file to see exactly what records have been affected by your entries; you need only forward the changed records to your associate. This can save hours that might be devoted to reconciling your work with your associate's.

To view the database log file

1. Open the **Preferences** form and click the **Database** tab.

2. Click the **View** button to view the contents of the log file.

3. To clear all of the data currently in the log file, click the **Flush** button.

Selecting search options

Search options determine what drives and folders will be searched when you search your computer for family databases. (Refer to chapter 4, Working with Individuals in a Database, to learn how to search your computer for databases.)

To select search options

1. Under **Search Options**, select one of the following options:

   Search from current folder   Searches the current folder and all of its sub-folders.

   Search all fixed disks   Searches all folders on all hard drives on your computer. (Removable disks, such as floppy disks, will not be searched.)

   Search all drives   Searches all folders on all drives connected to your computer, including removable disks.

2. The **Search Network Drives** box determines whether network drives will be searched for databases.

   If your computer is connected to a network and you want to search other computers on the network, click the Search Network Drives box.

3. The boxes under **Search for these databases** allow you to determine what types of family databases will be included in the search. The options are:

   AFT 9.0/AQ 3.0   The search will include Ancestry Family Tree 9.0 and Ancestral Quest 3.0 databases.

   PAF 3 or 4   The search will include Personal Ancestral File 3 and 4 databases.

   AQ 2.x/PAF 2.x   The search will include Ancestral Quest 2.x and Personal Ancestral File 2.x databases.

   GEDCOM   The search will include GEDCOM files.

   Select any combination of these options.

Defining information box preferences

Ancestry Family Tree's Pedigree view displays summarized information about an individual in an *information box* when the cursor passes over a field containing an individual's name or when you click on such a field. In the Family view the information box appears constantly in the upper-left corner. You can select options that affect the behavior of these boxes.

There are two types of information boxes in the Pedigree view: *floating* and *locked*. Floating information boxes appear when the cursor passes over a field containing an individual's name; when the cursor moves on, the information box disappears. A locked information box appears when you click on a field containing an individual's name and remains until you click on the field a second time, when it disappears.

To access the information box preference controls

Click the **InfoBox** tab on the **Preferences** form.

The **InfoBox** page will be displayed.

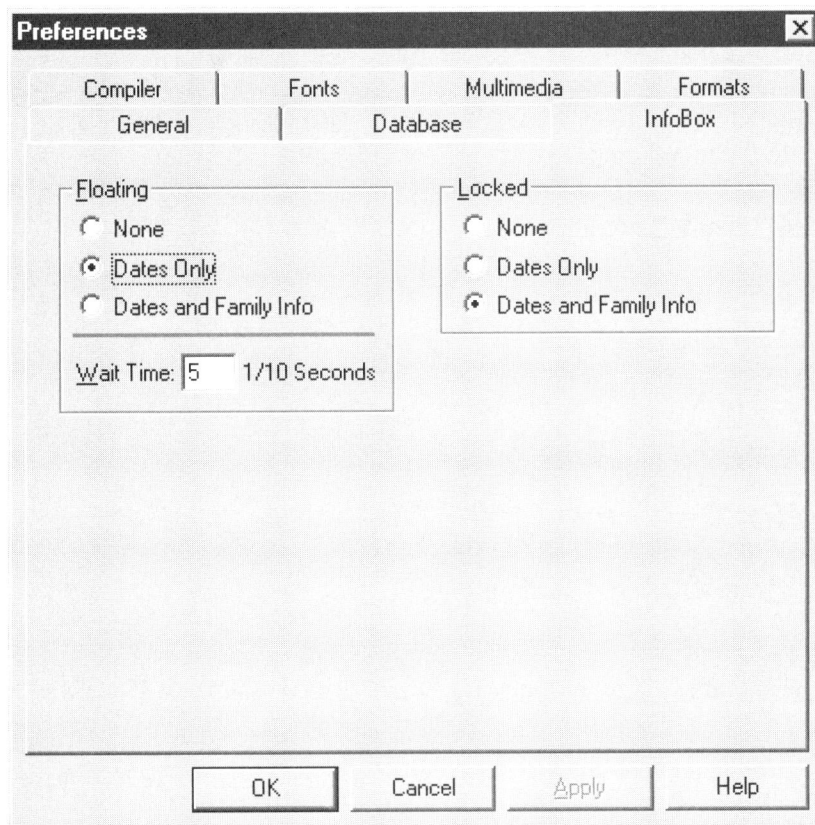

To determine the behavior of information boxes

1. Under **Floating** and **Locked**, select one of the following options for each type of information box:

   None　　　　　　　　The information box will never appear.

   Dates Only　　　　　The information box will contain only the dates and places of birth (or alternate event if no birth date exists), marriage, and death. If Use LDS Data is selected on the General tab of the Preferences form, LDS ordinance codes will appear as well (uppercase codes meaning that ordinances are complete and lowercase codes meaning that the ordinance has been submitted).

   Dates and Family Info　In addition to dates, the information box will contain all spouses and all children born to each spouse. You can then double-click on a spouse or child to make him or her the primary individual.

2. The **Wait Time** box lets you specify how much time should elapse after the cursor enters the name field until the floating information box appears. The number entered

here represents tenths of a second; therefore, the default value of 5 causes the floating information box to appear after five-tenths of a second.

Enter a number if you want to change the wait time for floating information boxes. (You can enter any amount up to 600/10, or 60 seconds.)

Entering compiler data

You can enter data about the compiler of a database (the person who maintains the database). The information you enter will appear in the Compiler field in printed reports and in GEDCOM export files. This information is stored separately for every database, so you will need to enter it for each database you maintain.

To access the compiler data entry controls

Click the **Compiler** tab on the **Preferences** form.

The **Compiler** page will be displayed.

To enter compiler data

Enter your name, address, telephone number, Ancestral File number, and e-mail address in the appropriate boxes.

Defining font preferences

You can select the text fonts and font properties (style, size, etc.) used on-screen in the Pedigree and Family views. There are two viewing modes for which you can select

Pedigree and Family view fonts and font properties: the *maximized* view and the *sized* view. You are seeing the maximized view when Ancestry Family Tree occupies the entire monitor screen, and you are seeing the sized view when Ancestry Family Tree occupies less than the entire monitor screen. You are allowed to select fonts for these modes separately because the sized view requires a TrueType font. (TrueType fonts are scalable to adjust to the dimensions of the sized Ancestry Family Tree view.) The maximized view, however, benefits from a rasterized (non-TrueType) font, which will be rewritten more rapidly than a TrueType font as you view and edit data.

You can also select the text fonts and font properties used for notes as they appear on the **Notes** form (when you are viewing and entering notes on-screen) and as they appear when printed on reports.

To access the font preferences controls

Click the **Fonts** tab on the **Preferences** form.

The **Fonts** page will be displayed.

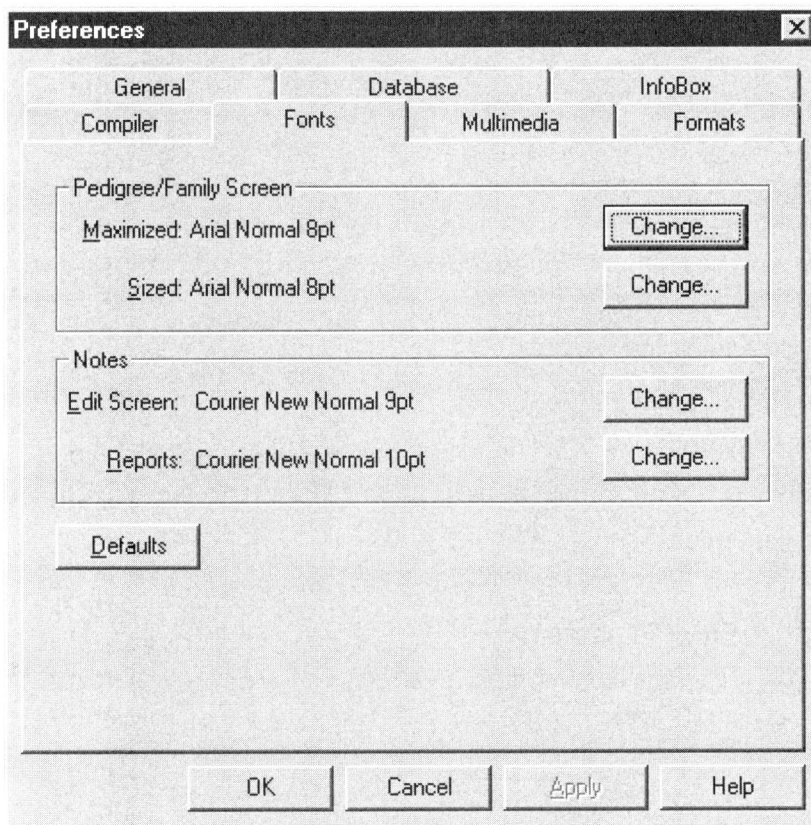

Preferences			✕
General	Database	InfoBox	
Compiler	Fonts	Multimedia	Formats

Pedigree/Family Screen

Maximized: Arial Normal 8pt   Change...

Sized: Arial Normal 8pt   Change...

Notes

Edit Screen: Courier New Normal 9pt   Change...

Reports: Courier New Normal 10pt   Change...

Defaults

OK   Cancel   Apply   Help

To define fonts for the Pedigree and Family views

1. Under **Pedigree/Family Screen**, click the **Change** button adjacent to **Maximized** or **Sized** to change the font or font properties for the maximized or sized Pedigree/Family view.

   The **Font** form will be displayed.

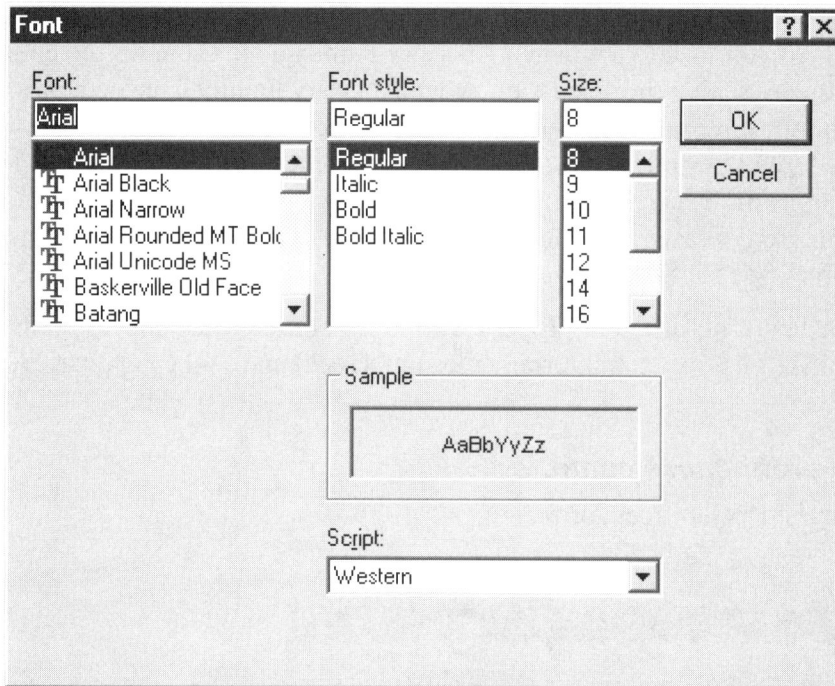

2. Under **Font**, select the font you prefer.

   Note: If you are selecting a font for the maximized Pedigree/Family view, a non-TrueType font is preferable because it will be rewritten faster as you view and edit data. If you are selecting a font for the sized Pedigree/Family view, you can only select TrueType fonts.

3. Under **Font style**, select the font style you prefer.

4. Under **Size**, select the point size of the font.

   Note: If you are selecting a font for the sized Pedigree/Family view, the size selection will be ignored because the font size will be adjusted automatically to fit the sized view.

5. Click the **OK** button to close the Font form and return to the Preferences form.

   The Preferences form displays the font you selected.

To define fonts for notes

1. Under **Notes** on the **Fonts** page of the **Preferences** form, click the **Change** button adjacent to **Edit Screen** or **Reports** to change the font or font properties for notes as they appear on the Notes form (Edit Screen) or on printed reports.

   The **Font** form will be displayed.

2. Refer to steps 2–5 in "To define fonts for the Pedigree and Family views," above, to define note fonts.

To restore the default fonts

On the **Fonts** page of the **Preferences** form, click the **Defaults** button to restore all of the font settings to those defined for Ancestry Family Tree by default.

Defining multimedia preferences

You can define a number of preferences that determine how Ancestry Family Tree's multimedia features behave. These preferences include the amount of time each slide show image will be displayed, background color, etc. (Refer to chapter 8, Working with Media Collections, to learn how to use the multimedia features described here.)

To access the multimedia preferences controls

Click the **Multimedia** tab on the **Preferences** form.

The Multimedia page will be displayed.

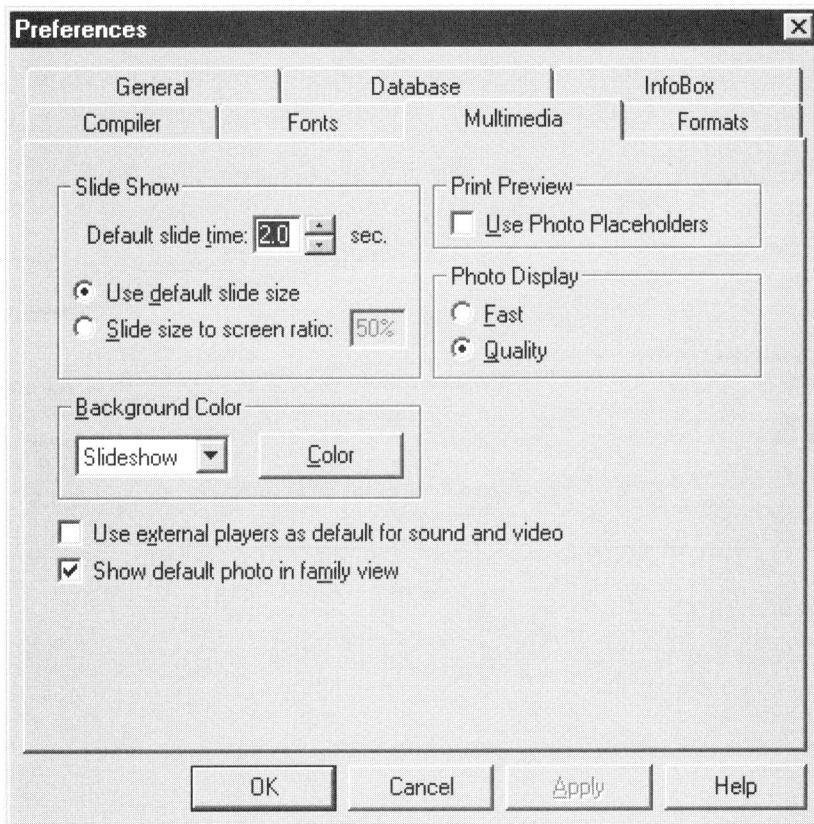

To define slide show preferences

1. The **Default slide time** box determines how long (in seconds) each slide show image will be displayed.

   Click the arrow buttons to the right of the box to adjust the number of seconds upward or downward, or enter the number of seconds in the box.

   Note: You can define the display time for specific slide show images in the Edit Photo form. Refer to chapter 8, Working with Media Collections, to learn how to use the Edit Photo form.

2. Select one of the following options to determine the size of the slide show images:

Use default slide size	Each image will be displayed in its original dimensions. (If the image is too large to fit entirely on the screen, it will be reduced to fit.)
Slide size to screen ratio	Each image will be re-sized to fit the percentage of the monitor screen specified in the adjacent box. Therefore, each image will be the same size.

3. If you selected **Slide size to screen ratio** above, enter a number representing the size of the slide show image in relation to the monitor screen size. For example, if you enter 70, the slide show images will be 70 percent of the size of the monitor screen.

To define the background color for slide shows and scrapbooks

1. Under **Background Color**, click the arrow button to the right of the box and select **Slideshow** or **Scrapbook**.

2. Click the **Color** button.

   The **Color** form will be displayed. It lets you select and assign one of 48 basic colors for the slide show or scrapbook background. It also lets you create custom colors that you can assign.

3. Under **Basic colors**, select the color you want to use and then click the **OK** button to close the Color form and return to the Choose Colors form

4. To create custom colors, refer to the steps in "To create custom colors for the Ancestry Family Tree views," above.

To use image placeholders in report previews

The **Use Photo Placeholders** box determines whether a placeholder will be displayed when a report is previewed. When you are previewing reports that contain photo images, you might not want to wait for the image to be read from your computer's disk. Using a placeholder (which appears as a gray box) will speed up the preview.

Click the box to cause placeholders to be used when previewing reports that contain photo images.

To determine photo image display quality

The options under **Photo Display** determine whether Ancestry Family Tree will display images quickly or will display a higher-quality image (which will take longer to display).

Click one of the following options: **Fast** or **Quality**.

To use external players for sound and video

The **Use external players as default for sound and video** box determines whether Ancestry Family Tree's player or a different player will be used to play sound and video files. Ancestry Family Tree comes with a player that will play .wav, .mid, and .rmi sound files and .avi video files. If you have installed a more advanced player for these or other files, you can cause Ancestry Family Tree to use it instead.

Check the box to use a different player for these files. Ancestry Family Tree will check the Windows registry for the player you have registered and use it. (Even if you don't use this option, Ancestry Family Tree will check for another player if you use multimedia files other than wav, .mid, and .rmi sound files and .avi video files.)

To show the default photo image in the Family view

The **Show default photo in family view** box determines whether the default photo image (if there is one) in the media collection for the highlighted individual will be displayed in the Family view. You can create a media collection for each individual in the database. One photo image in each collection is designated the default image—the image that will appear in Family view for the highlighted individual. (Refer to chapter 8, Working with Media Collections, to learn how to create a media collection for an individual.)

Check the box to cause the default photo image in an individual's media collection to appear when the individual is highlighted in the Family view.

Defining name, place name, and date format preferences

You can define preferences that determine how names and place names are condensed when necessary to fit the space provided on-screen and on reports and charts. There are also several options that determine how dates are formatted when they appear on-screen and on printed reports.

To access the format preferences controls

Click the **Formats** tab on the **Preferences** form.

The **Formats** page will be displayed.

Preferences ☒

| General | Database | InfoBox |

| Compiler | Fonts | Multimedia | Formats |

Clipping Method (Names, Places)

○ Truncate   Condense: Robert Allen David Jones

◉ Initials   To: Robert A D Jones

Place Level Importance

Condense:

Årjäng, Lungsund, Värmland, Sweden

[Largest, smallest, next smallest ▼]

To: Å, L, V, Sweden

or: Årjäng, L, V, Sweden

or: Årjäng, Lungsund, V, Sweden

Date Display Styles

Order: ○ MDY ◉ DMY

Day: ◉ 3   ○ 03

Month: [Aug ▼]

Separators:

◉ Space   ○ Dash '-'

○ Slash '/'   ○ Dot '.'

Bef 3 Aug 1886

☐ Include 'Reference' when printing sources

[OK] [Cancel] [Apply] [Help]

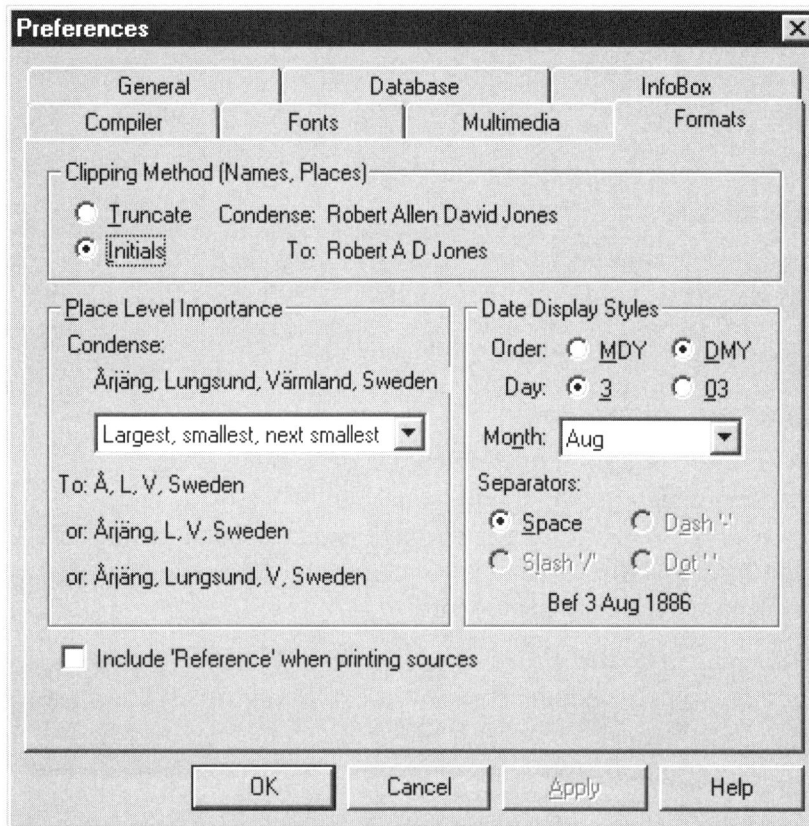

To determine how names and place names are condensed

The options under **Clipping Method (Names, Places)** determine how names and place names are condensed if there is not enough room to display them on-screen or on reports. Select one of the following options:

Truncate   Show as much of a name or place name as possible and omit the portion that will not fit.

Initials   Use initials where necessary to make the name or place name fit.

Note: As you click each of the options, examples on the form change to show you how each condensing method affects names (examples under Clipping Method) and place names (examples under Place Level Importance).

To define place level importance when condensing

The options available in the **Condense** box determine what parts of a place name will be condensed and in what order. For example, selecting the *Smallest, Largest, Next Smallest* option ensures that the smallest geographical area in the place name will have priority to be spelled out entirely; then the largest geographical area; then the next smallest; and finally the next largest. Therefore, the next largest geographical area is most likely to be condensed, the next smallest is second most likely to be condensed, etc. This selection works in concert with the Clipping Method option you select.

Click the arrow button to the right of the Condense box and select an option from the list. You can select each option in turn and observe how it affects the place name examples displayed below to find one that you prefer.

To select the date display style

1. Under **Date Display Styles**, select one of the two options available for the **Order** to determine whether dates will be displayed in the order *month, day, year* (**MDY**) or *day, month, year* (**DMY**).

    Note: As you select date display style options, the date example below the Date Display Styles controls will change to show you how the options affect date formatting.

2. Select one of the two options available for **Day** to determine whether days of the month that are less than 10 will have a leading zero.

3. Select one of the options available in the **Month** box to specify how the month will be formatted. The options are numeric (**8**), numeric with leading zero (**08**), abbreviated name with initial capital (**Aug**), and abbreviated name with all-capital letters (**AUG**).

    Select the option you prefer.

4. If you selected a numeric format for the month, you can select an option to specify how the elements of the date will be separated under **Separators**. Select **Space**, **Slash**, **Dash**, or **Dot**.

To include a reference number when printing source citations

If you have entered reference numbers for any of your source citations, you can choose to have them printed on reports. The **Include 'Reference' when printing sources** box determines whether the reference number will be printed. (The reference number is entered on the Source Citation form. Refer to chapter 7, Working with Sources and Source Citations, to learn how to create source citations.)

Check the box to cause source citation reference numbers to be printed on reports.

Saving your preferences

The preferences you define will be applied to each family database you work with using Ancestry Family Tree.

To save your preferences

After you have defined your preferences, click the **OK** button on the **Preferences** form to close the form and save the preferences.

CHAPTER 3

Working with Family Databases

After you've installed Ancestry Family Tree, you need to know how to start it and then use it to create family databases. This chapter describes how to open Ancestry Family Tree and create databases.

In this chapter

• Starting Ancestry Family Tree
• Creating a new family database
• Backing up and restoring a database
• Checking and repairing a database
• Closing a database

Starting Ancestry Family Tree

After you have installed Ancestry Family Tree, you can start it

- by using the Start menu or
- by clicking the desktop icon.

To open Ancestry Family Tree

1. Click the **Start** menu button in the lower left-hand corner of the screen.
2. Click the **Ancestry Family Tree** menu item.

Alternately, you can double-click the Ancestry Family Tree icon on your computer's desktop.

- If Ancestry Family Tree locates family databases that currently exist on your computer, it will open the family database that you have worked in most recently.
- If you have not yet created any family databases or if Ancestry Family Tree cannot locate any databases that currently exist on your computer, the **Welcome** form shown below will be displayed.

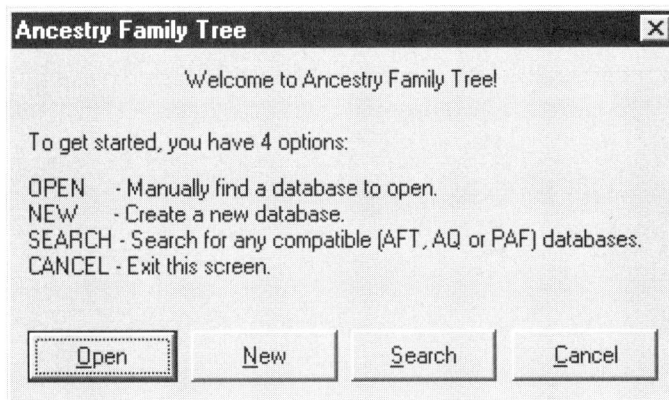

Creating a new family database

After you have installed Ancestry Family Tree and know how to open it, the next step is to create a family database. This section describes how to

- Create a new database using Ancestry Family Tree
- Create a new database by importing a GEDCOM file

Creating a new database using Ancestry Family Tree

If you have not yet created any Ancestry Family Tree family databases, the **Welcome** form shown above will be displayed.

To start at the Welcome form

1. Click the **New** button.

   The **Get Started** form, shown below, will be displayed.

   ```
   ┌──────────────────────────────────────────────────┐
   │ Get Started with Ancestry Family Tree            │
   ├──────────────────────────────────────────────────┤
   │                                                  │
   │      You are about to create a family tree using │
   │      Ancestry Family Tree. When creating a family│
   │      tree, you typically begin with yourself.    │
   │      Please enter your name, or the name of the  │
   │      person whose family tree you are creating.  │
   │                                                  │
   │                                                  │
   │  Surname:              Given Names:              │
   │  ┌─────────────────┐   ┌───────────────────────┐ │
   │  │                 │   │                       │ │
   │  └─────────────────┘   └───────────────────────┘ │
   │                                                  │
   │                                                  │
   │                                                  │
   │              ┌──────────────┐                    │
   │              │ Start My Tree │                   │
   │              └──────────────┘                    │
   └──────────────────────────────────────────────────┘
   ```

2. Enter your surname and given name(s) or those of another person whose family tree you are creating in the **Surname** and **Given Names** boxes. This is the database's *initial person* or *root person*.

   Note: You can skip this step and enter the initial person later.

3. Click the **Start My Tree** button.

   The **Add New Individual** form will be displayed. It contains any name information that you entered in the Get Started form. Ancestry Family Tree will automatically name the new database with the surname you entered in the Get Started form and save it in the My Documents folder on your computer's C: drive.

Add New Individual

Edit Ditto Tools

Surname: Hopkins

Given Names: Andrew Joseph

RIN: 190

Gender: ○ Male ○ Famle ● Unknown   Nickname:

Title: (Prefix)   (Suffix)

Birth: Place:

Christening: Place:

Death: Place:

Burial: Place:

LDS Ordinances

☐ Live Baptism   Baptism:

Endowment:

Sealed to Parents:

Multiple Parents / Parent Relationships...

ID #:

Save   More...   Address...   Notes...   Sources...   Media...   Cancel   Help

4. If you are ready to enter data for the initial person, you can do it now. Refer to chapter 4, Working with Individuals in a Database, to learn how to enter data for an individual.

5. Click the **Save** button to save the new database.

   The **Pedigree** view of the new database will be displayed with the initial person shown in the primary position.

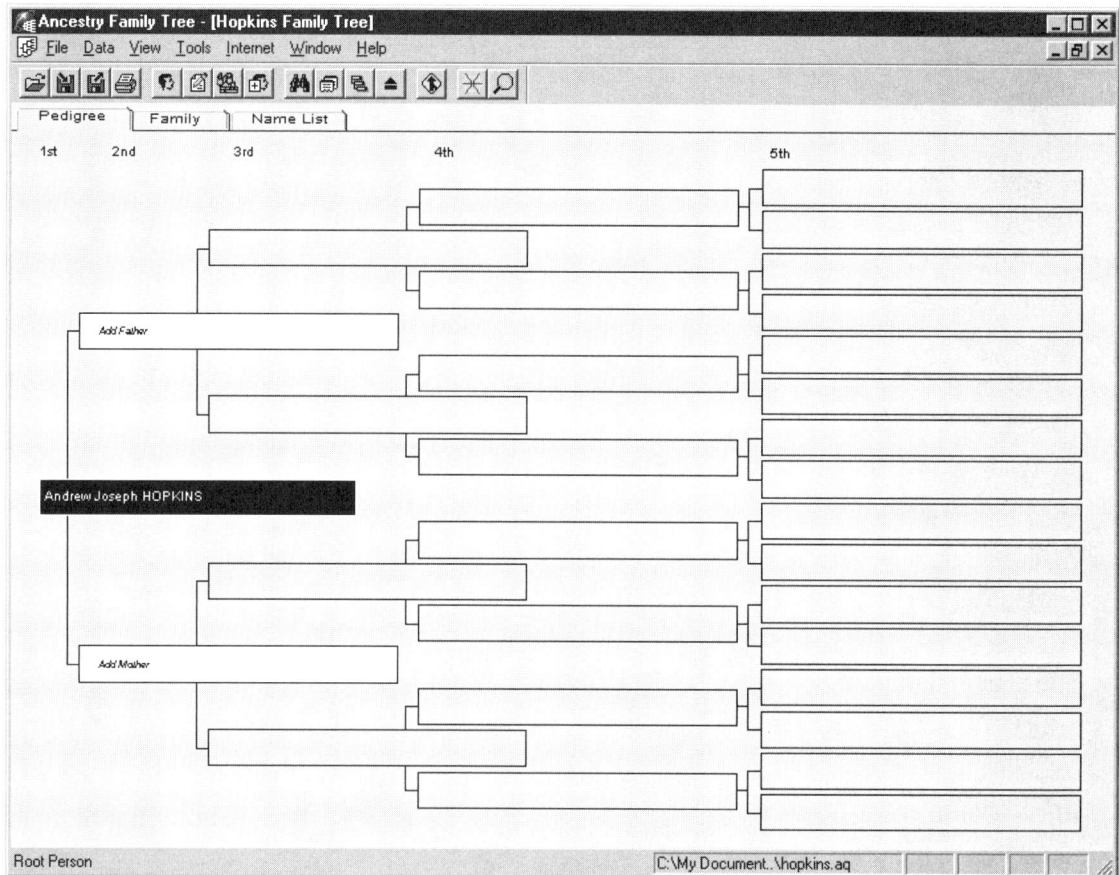

6. To add and edit information for individuals in the database, refer to chapters 4, 5, 6, 7, and 8.

To create a new database if Ancestry Family Tree is already running

1. In the **File** menu, click **New**.

    The **Create New Family File** form will be displayed.

Create New Family File

Save in: Ancestry Family Tree

- Chapters
- Graphics
- Lincoln
- Edwards.aft
- Leopold.aft

File name:

Save as type: AFT 9.0 (*.aft)

Create

Cancel

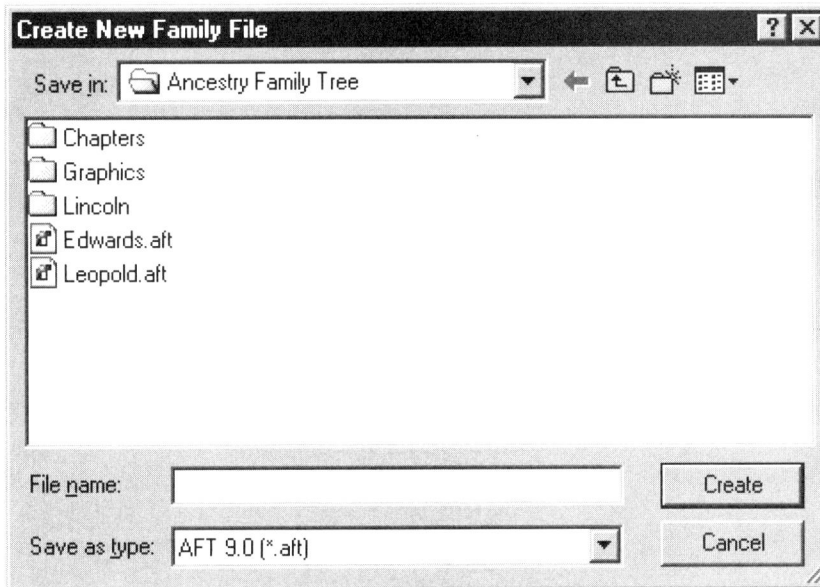

2. Use the controls described below to locate the folder in which you want to save the new database.

- Look in: Hopkins   Click the drop-down button to the right of the **Look In** box to view the contents of the drives and folders on your computer.

- Click the Up One Level button to view the contents of the folder one level above the folder you are currently viewing.

- Click the New Folder button to create a new sub-folder in the current folder.

- Enter a name for the new database in the **File name** box.

3. Click the **Create** button.

The **Pedigree** view of the new database will be displayed.

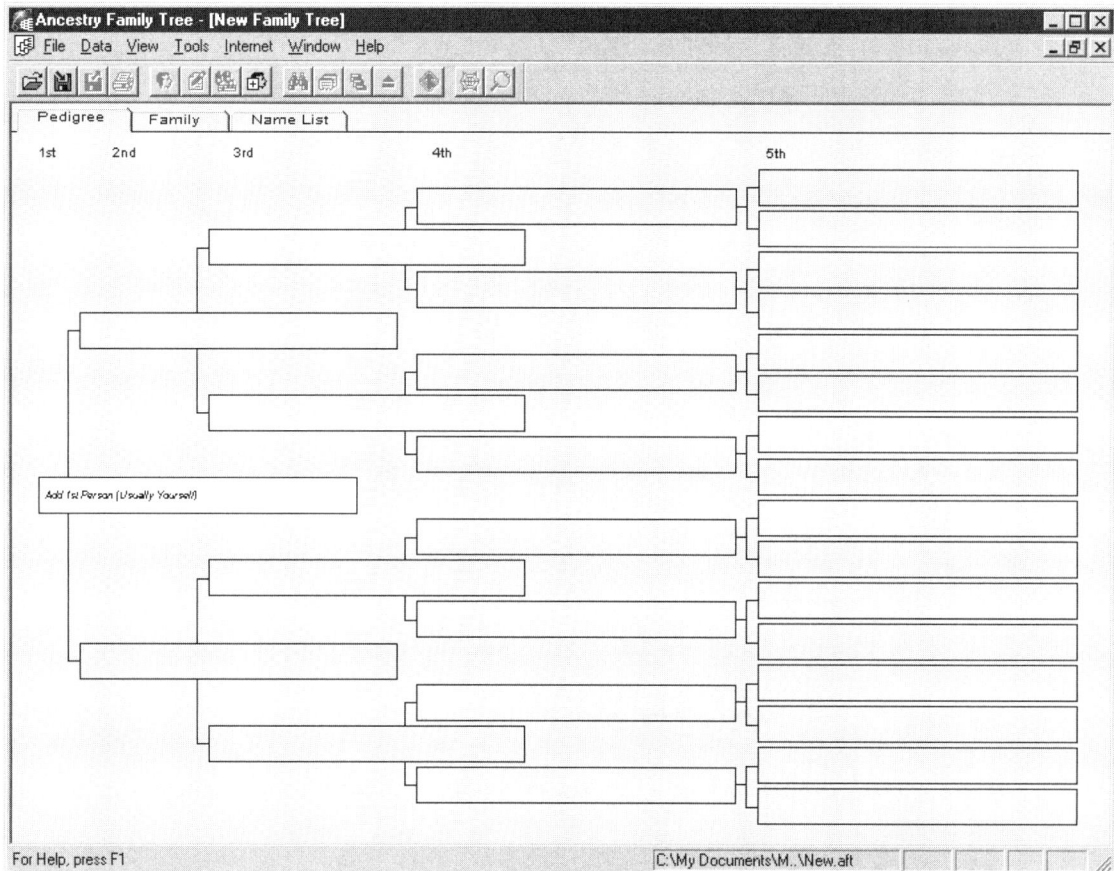

4. To continue working with the database, refer to chapters 4, 5, 6, 7, and 8.

Creating a new database by importing a GEDCOM file

You can import data compiled by other researchers and saved in the GEDCOM format. GEDCOM stands for Genealogical Data Communication; it is a data format standard that allows genealogical data created and stored by different genealogy software programs to be shared among their users.

Using Ancestry Family Tree, you can import GEDCOM files from several types of sources:

- Directly from other researchers—they may e-mail their GEDCOM files to you or give them to you on a floppy disk or CD-ROM.

- From sites on the World Wide Web. Individual family history researchers and larger organizations often allow you to download their family history data in GEDCOM format directly from their websites. Ancestry.com, for example, lets you import data from its World Family Tree, a collection of family history data contributed by researchers from all over the world. This option requires Web browser software on your computer and access to the Web through an Internet service provider.

- An Online Family Tree™ hosted by Ancestry.com on the World Wide Web. Ancestry Family Tree users can export databases to Ancestry.com as Online

Family Trees; you can import them if you are given access by the person who created the Online Family Tree. The imported Online Family Tree will be saved as an Ancestry Family Tree file. This option also requires Web browser software on your computer and access to the Web through a Web provider.

To import a GEDCOM file

1. Close any databases that are currently open.

2. In the **File** menu, click **Import**.

   The **Create New Family File** form will be displayed.

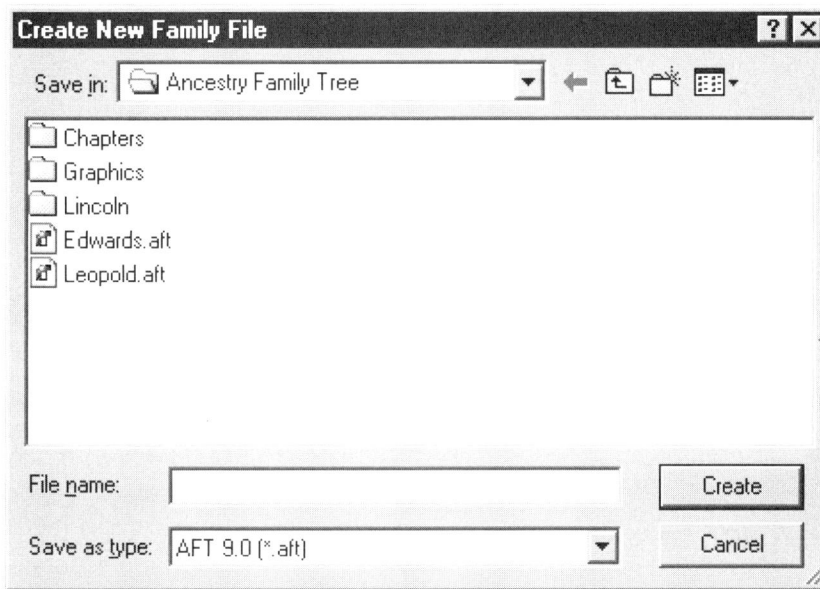

3. Use the controls described below to locate the folder in which you want to save the new database.

   - Click the drop-down button to the right of the **Look In** box to view the contents of the drives and folders on your computer.

   - Click the Up One Level button to view the contents of the folder one level above the folder you are currently viewing.

   - Click the New Folder button to create a new sub-folder in the current folder.

In the **File name** box, enter a name for the new database.

Click the **Create** button.

   The **Import GEDCOM File** form will be displayed.

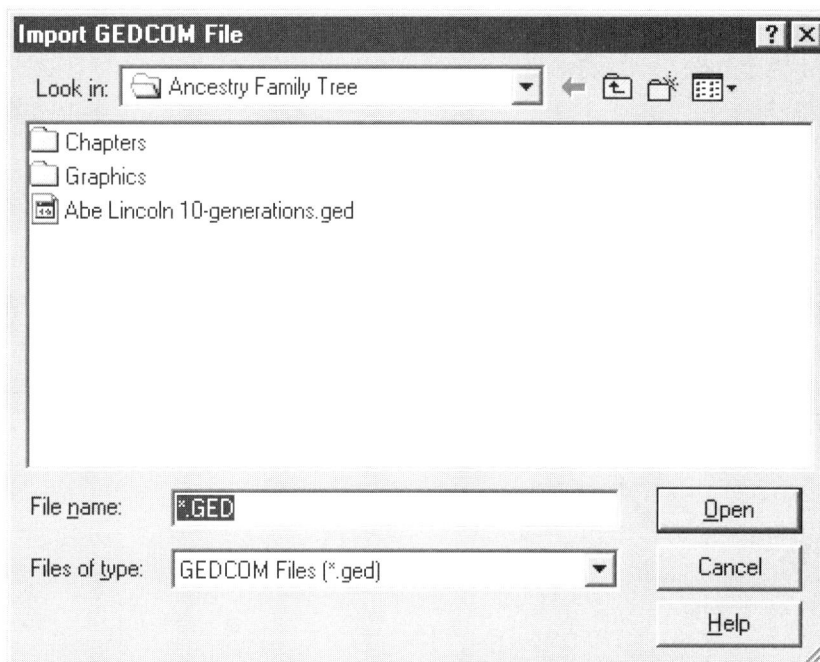

Locate the GEDCOM file you want to import, and highlight it in the list of files.

Click the **Open** button.

The **GEDCOM Import** form will be displayed.

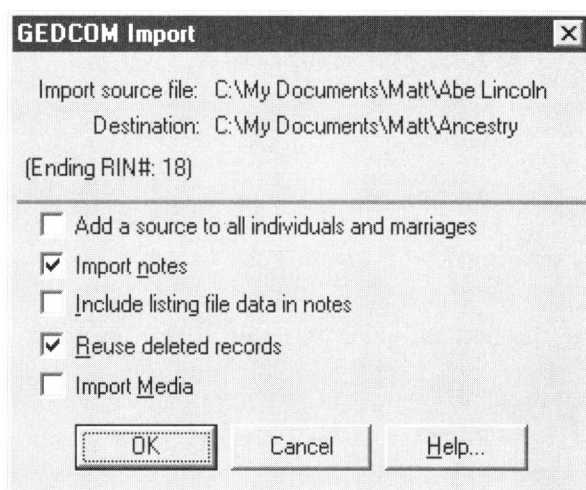

The GEDCOM Import form allows you to select import options that affect the resulting Ancestry Family Tree database. Refer to the table below to learn about the purpose of each option and then check the appropriate boxes.

Option	Description
Add a source to all individuals and marriages	If you check this box, Ancestry Family Tree will create a new source citation and attach it to every individual record and marriage record that is imported from this GEDCOM file. You will be able to edit this source citation during the import process. (Refer to chapter 7, Working with Sources

Option	Description
	and Source Citations, to learn about source citations.)
	This option is useful because it allows you to identify the source of every individual and marriage record imported from the GEDCOM file. You might want to indicate the name of the GEDCOM file, where or from whom you got the file, the date on which you imported it, etc.
Import notes	If checked, any notes in the GEDCOM file will be added to the new database.
Include listing file data in notes	Any data in the GEDCOM file that cannot be imported properly into your database will be copied to an exception report called the *listing file*. If you check this box, listing file data will also be added to the notes for each affected individual. This option is recommended because it is much easier to locate the errors and decide how to resolve them when they are noted in the individuals' notes. (Refer to chapter 6, Working with Notes, to learn about notes.)
Reuse deleted records	Leave this check box blank if you are importing into a new database.
Import media	If you check this box, any multimedia objects embedded in the GEDCOM file will be added to your database. (Refer to chapter 8, Working with Media Collections, to learn about multimedia objects.)
	If you don't check this box, these objects will be ignored.

Click the **OK** button.

> **Note:** If you checked the **Add a source to all individuals and marriages** box, the **Source Citation** form will be displayed. Refer to chapter 7, Working with Sources and Source Citations, to learn how to use the Source Citation form. After you have created the new source citation and saved it, proceed to the following step.

The **GEDCOM Import** confirmation form will be displayed.

```
GEDCOM Import      [X]

189 Individuals Imported
113 Marriages Imported

[    OK    ]
```

Click the **OK** button to close the form and complete the import process.

The **Pedigree** view of the new database will be displayed.

4. To add and edit information for individuals in the database, refer to chapters 4, 5, 6, 7, and 8.

Closing a database

After you have created a family database, you can close it at any time. When you do, Ancestry Family Tree will automatically save the database for you.

To close a family database

1. In the **File** menu, click **Exit**, or

click the Close button ☒ in the upper right-hand corner of the Ancestry Family Tree application window.

Backing up and restoring a database

You should keep a backup copy of every family database. A backup copy allows you to restore information that was in a database if the original database somehow becomes corrupted or deleted, or if you have made changes to a database that you no longer want and wish to start again with the database as it existed at the last backup. When you use a backup file to restore a database, the database will be restored with the data that it contained when the backup file was created.

To back up a database

1. Open the database you want to back up.

2. In the **File** menu, click **Backup**.

   The **Back Up Database To** form will be displayed.

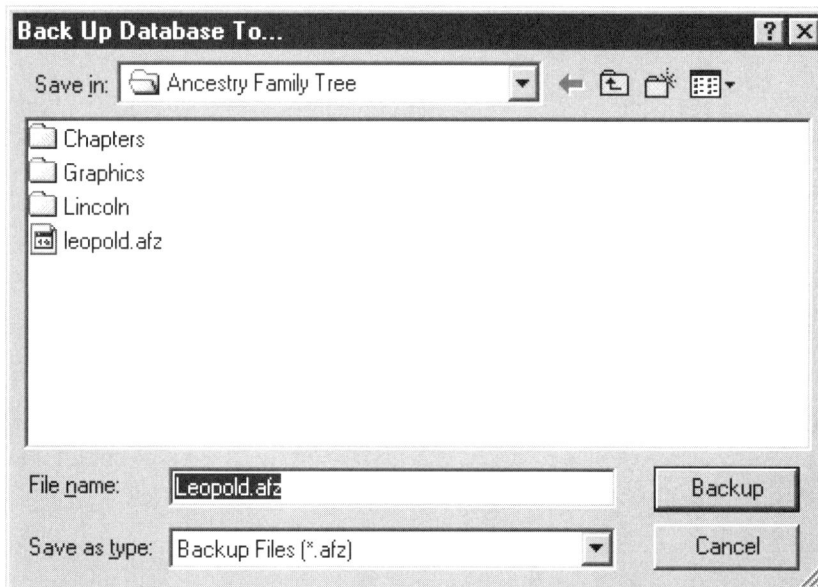

The **File name** box contains the name of the database with an extension of *.afz*. This extension identifies the backup copy of the database.

If you want to give the backup file a different name, enter it in the **File name** box in place of the current name. You must use the extension *.afz,* however.

3. Use the controls described below to locate the directory in which you want to save the backup copy.

- Look in: Hopkins ▼ Click the drop-down button to the right of the **Look In** box to view the contents of the drives and folders on your computer.

- Click the Up One Level button to view the contents of the folder one level above the folder you are currently viewing.

- Click the New Folder button to create a new sub-folder in the current folder.

Click the **Backup** button.

- If there is no backup copy of the database with the same name in the directory you selected, the backup file is created and the **Backup** form will be displayed.

> **Backup** ☒
>
> ⓘ   Backup complete
>
> [OK]

Click the **OK** button to close the Backup form and return to the Ancestry Family Tree view.

- If a backup file for the database already exists in the directory you selected, the **Save As** form will be displayed.

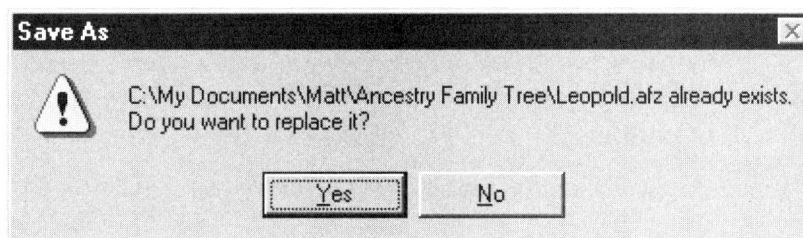

> **Save As** ☒
>
> ⚠   C:\My Documents\Matt\Ancestry Family Tree\Leopold.afz already exists.
> Do you want to replace it?
>
> [Yes]   [No]

Click the **Yes** button to replace the old backup copy and return to the Ancestry Family Tree view, or click the **No** button to close the Save As form and return to the Back Up Database To form (where you can cancel the backup, select a new directory, or give the backup file a different name).

Note: Periodically, Ancestry Family Tree will prompt you to back up a database if it has not been backed up recently. You can then back up the database or choose not to back it up.

To restore a database from a backup copy

Note: When restoring a database, you can start with all databases closed, or you can open the database you want to restore. You can even restore a database while working in a different database.

1. In the **File** menu, click **Restore**.

   The **Restore Database From** form will be displayed.

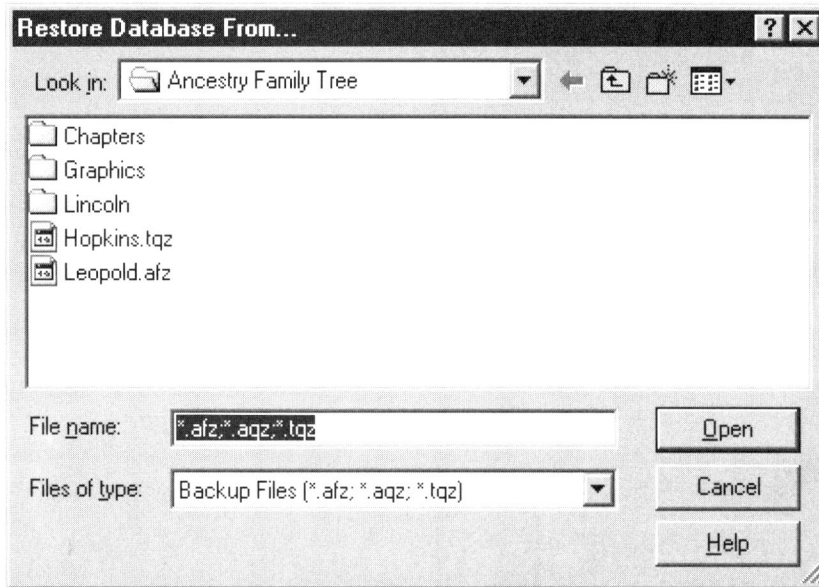

2. Use the controls described below to locate the folder in which the backup copy is stored.

   - Click the drop-down button to the right of the **Look In** box to view the contents of the drives and folders on your computer.

   - Click the Up One Level button to view the contents of the folder one level above the folder you are currently viewing.

3. Select the backup file you want and then click the **Open** button.

   The **Save As** form will be displayed.

Save As

Save in: Ancestry Family Tree

Chapters
Graphics
Lincoln

File name: hopkins.aq

Save as type: AFT 9.0 (*.aft)

Restore

Cancel

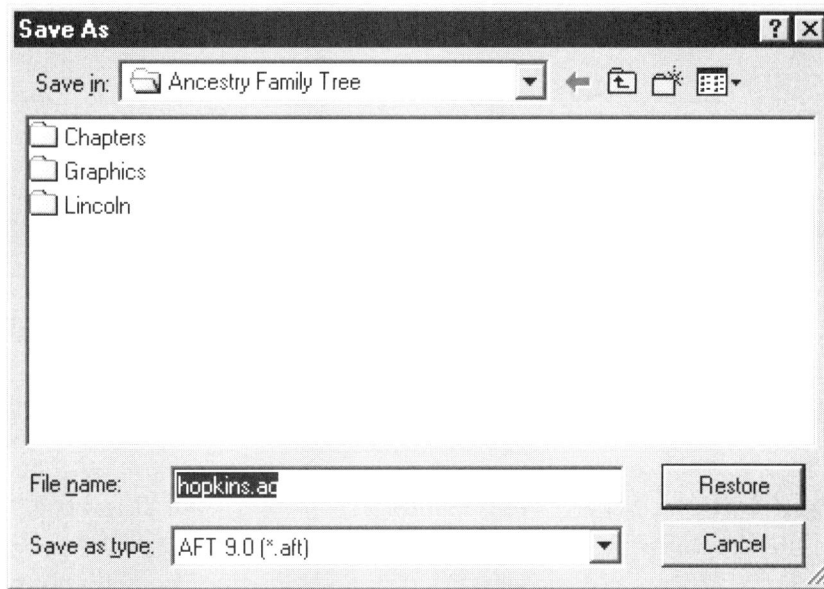

Locate the folder in which you want the database to be restored and then click the **Restore** button.

- If the database currently exists in the folder you selected, the **Save As** form will be displayed.

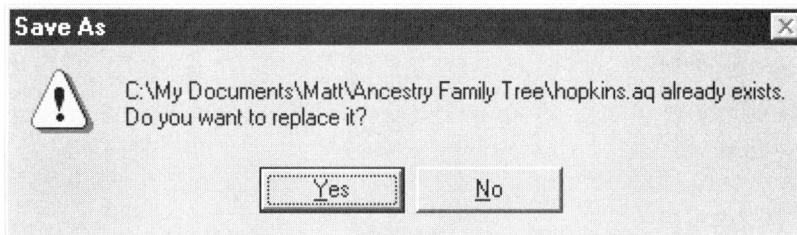

Save As

C:\My Documents\Matt\Ancestry Family Tree\hopkins.aq already exists. Do you want to replace it?

Yes   No

Click the **Yes** button to replace the current version of the database (or click the **No** button to cancel the restore procedure).

If you clicked **Yes**, a form similar to the one below will be displayed.

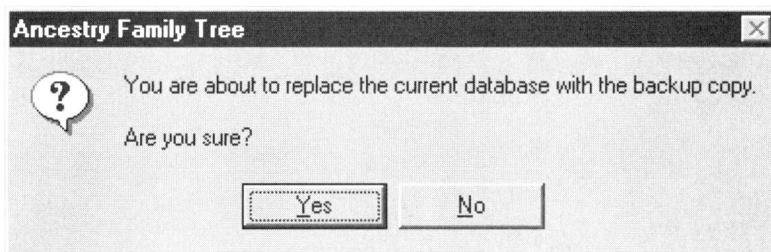

Ancestry Family Tree

You are about to replace the current database with the backup copy.

Are you sure?

Yes   No

Click the **Yes** button to replace the current version of the database (or click the **No** button to cancel the restore procedure).

If you clicked **Yes**, the **Restore** form will be displayed.

Restore ☒

(i) Restore complete of C:\My Documents\Matt\Ancestry Family Tree\hopkins.aq

[OK]

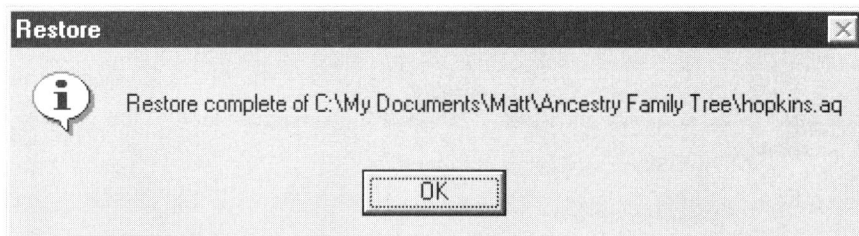

Click the **OK** button to close the form and view the restored database.

- If the database does not exist in the directory you selected, the **Restore** form will be displayed.

Click the **OK** button to close the form and view the restored database.

Checking and repairing a database

Family databases sometimes accumulate "problems"—for example, the MRIN for a deleted marriage record might still exist in the database, or a source citation might not be linked to a source. Such problems might not be apparent to you, but correcting them is important to maintaining the integrity of a database. Ancestry Family Tree can check a database for internal problems, report any that it finds, and, if you choose, attempt to repair the problems.

To check a database for problems

1. Open the database you want to check.

2. Back up the database. Refer to "Backing up and restoring a database," above, to learn how to back up a database.

   Caution: The check/repair process can result in damage to a database, so it is very important to back up any database you want to check.

In the **Tools** menu, click **Database Check/Repair**.

The **Check/Repair** form will be displayed.

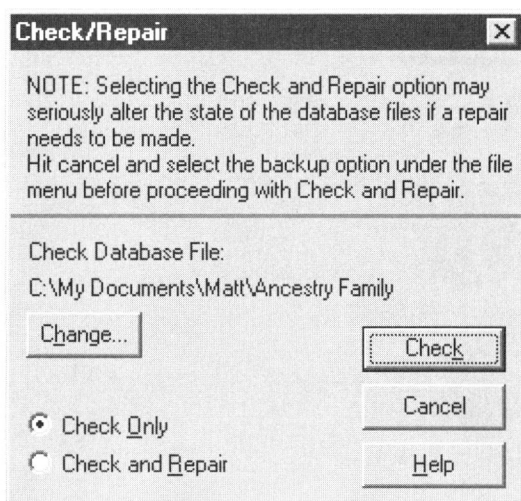

Check/Repair ☒

NOTE: Selecting the Check and Repair option may seriously alter the state of the database files if a repair needs to be made.
Hit cancel and select the backup option under the file menu before proceeding with Check and Repair.

Check Database File:

C:\My Documents\Matt\Ancestry Family

[Change...]   [Check]

                         [Cancel]

◉ Check Only
○ Check and Repair   [Help]

At this point you can click the **Change** button to select a different database to check. If you do, be sure the database has been backed up recently.

Click the **Check Only** option to have Ancestry Family Tree check the database and generate a report of the results.

The **Save As** form will be displayed.

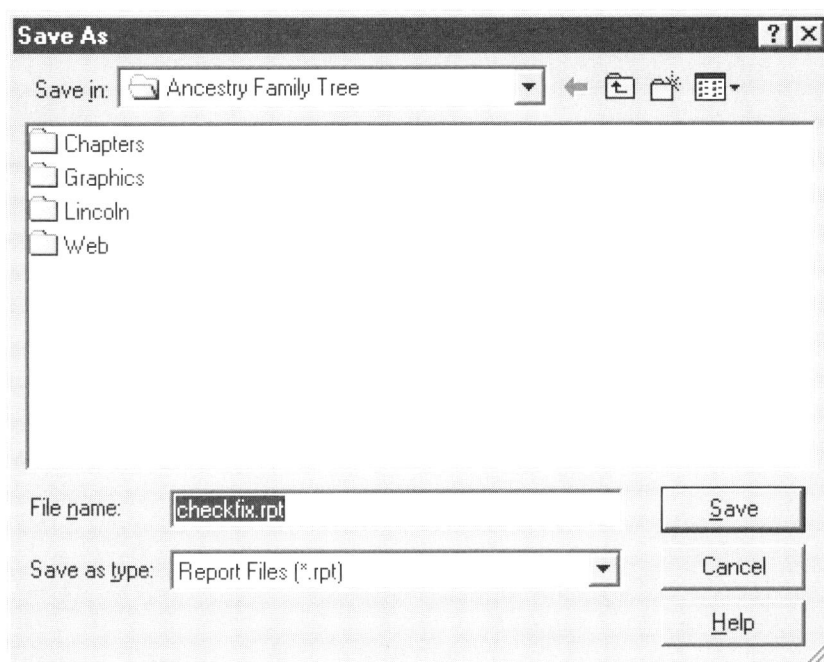

Locate the folder in which you want the check report to be saved and then click the **Save** button.

The check procedure is performed. If the check report is not too large, it will automatically be opened in Notepad. If it is too large to be opened in Notepad, open it using a word processing application.

To check a database for problems and have Ancestry Family Tree attempt to repair them

1. Perform steps 1–3 in "To check a database for problems," above.

Click the **Check and Repair** option to have Ancestry Family Tree check the database, generate a report of the results, and attempt to repair any problems that it finds.

The **Database Problem** form will be displayed.

Database Problem   ☒

If there is a problem with the selected database file. Ancestry Family Tree will attempt to repair these problems but it is highly recomended that a backup be made first.

See HELP for important additional details before proceeding.

| Backup | Check Repair | Cancel | Help |

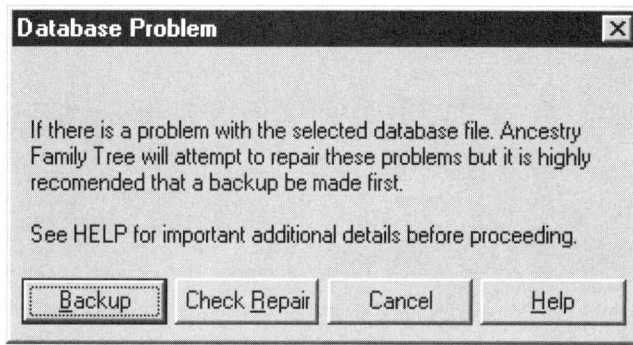

If you have not yet backed up the database, you can do it at this point by clicking the **Backup** button. Otherwise, click the **Check Repair** button.

The **Save As** form will be displayed.

Locate the folder in which you want the check/repair report to be saved and then click the **Save** button.

The check and repair procedure is performed. If the check report is not too large, it will automatically be opened in Notepad. If it is too large to be opened in Notepad, open it using a word processing application.

Copying a database

You can copy an existing database and save it with a new name.

To copy a database

1. Open the database that you want to copy.

2. In the **File** menu, click **Copy**.

The **Save As** form will be displayed.

Using the Save As form, locate the folder in which you want to save the new database and then enter a name for it in the **File Name** box with the suffix *.aft*.

Click the **Copy** button.

The original database will be saved with the new name and can be opened in the Ancestry Family Tree view. (The original database will be closed but will still exist on your computer.)

Deleting a database

You can delete an existing database.

1. In the **File** menu, click **Delete**.

The **Delete Family Database** form will be displayed.

Do one of the following:

- Highlight the database that you want to delete, click the **Delete** button, and then proceed to step 3, or

- click the **Search** button to search the indicated disk or folder. When the search is complete, the **Results from Search** form will be displayed.

  Note: The type of database file that is included in the search (for example, GEDCOM, Ancestry Family Tree, Personal Ancestral File, etc.) is determined by the settings on the Database page of the Preferences form. Refer to chapter 2, Installation and Setup, to learn about these settings.

Databases:	Name:	Individuals:	Marriages:
C:\My Do..\Abe Lincoln 10-generations.ged		91 KB	
C:\My Documents\Matt\Anc..\Edison.aft.aq	Edison	19	12
C:\My Documents\Matt\Ance..\GEDTest.aft	GEDTest	189	113
C:\My Documents\Matt\Ances..\Edison.ged		4 KB	
C:\My Documents\Matt\Ances..\Hopkins.aq	Hopkins	2	0
C:\My Documents\Matt\Ancest..\export.ged		6 KB	
C:\My Documents\Matt\Ancestr..\Lincoln.aft	Lincoln	190	113
C:\My Documents\Matt\Ancestry ..\New.aft	New	189	112

Results from search of C:\My Documents\Matt\Ancestry Family Tree

[Open] [Cancel]

- Highlight the database you want to delete and then click the **Open** button.

  The **Delete Database** form will be displayed.

  Delete Database

  Are you sure?

  [Yes] [No]

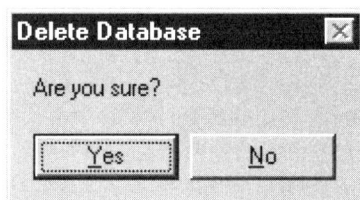

Click the **Yes** button to delete the database (or click the **No** button to cancel the deletion).

CHAPTER 4

Working with Individuals in a Database

This chapter describes how to work with individuals in family databases. For every person represented in a database there is an individual record; each individual record has a unique Record Identification Number (RIN). The concept of "working with" individuals ranges from entering such basic information as their names and the dates and places of events to creating additional events and identifying the relationships among individuals.

In this chapter

• Opening an existing family database
• Adding an individual to the database
• Entering data for an individual
• Editing an individual record
• Arranging the order of multiple parents, spouses, or children
• Unlinking an individual
• Deleting an individual from the database
• Identifying relationships among individuals
• Calculating dates from other information
• Determining the Soundex code for a name

Opening an existing family database

This section describes how to find and open family databases that currently exist on your computer. You can go directly to the database you want to work with and then open it, or you can search your computer for all family databases that are currently stored on it. (To learn how to create a family database, refer to chapter 3, Working with Family Databases.)

To open an existing family database

1. Start Ancestry Family Tree.

2. Do one of the following:

   - In the **File** menu, click **Open**, or

   - click the **Open** button on the button bar. 🗁

   The **Open Family Database** form will be displayed.

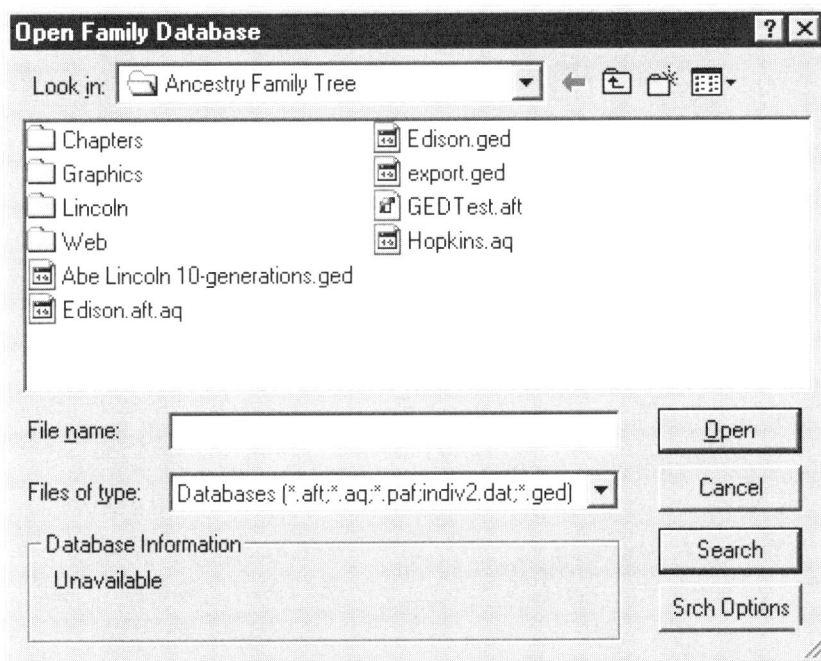

Open Family Database	? ✕

   Look in: Ancestry Family Tree

   - Chapters
   - Graphics
   - Lincoln
   - Web
   - Abe Lincoln 10-generations.ged
   - Edison.aft.aq
   - Edison.ged
   - export.ged
   - GEDTest.aft
   - Hopkins.aq

   File name:

   Files of type: Databases (*.aft;*.aq;*.paf;indiv2.dat;*.ged)

   Database Information
   Unavailable

   Open
   Cancel
   Search
   Srch Options

3. Use the controls described below to locate the disk drive or folder where the database you want to open is located.

   - Look in: Hopkins Click the drop-down button to the right of the **Look In** box to view the contents of the drives and folders on your computer.

   - Click the 🔼 button to view the contents of the folder one level above the folder you are currently viewing.

4. Select the database you want to open and then click the **Open** button.

The database will be displayed with the view (**Pedigree**, **Family**, or **Name List**) that you last used when viewing it.

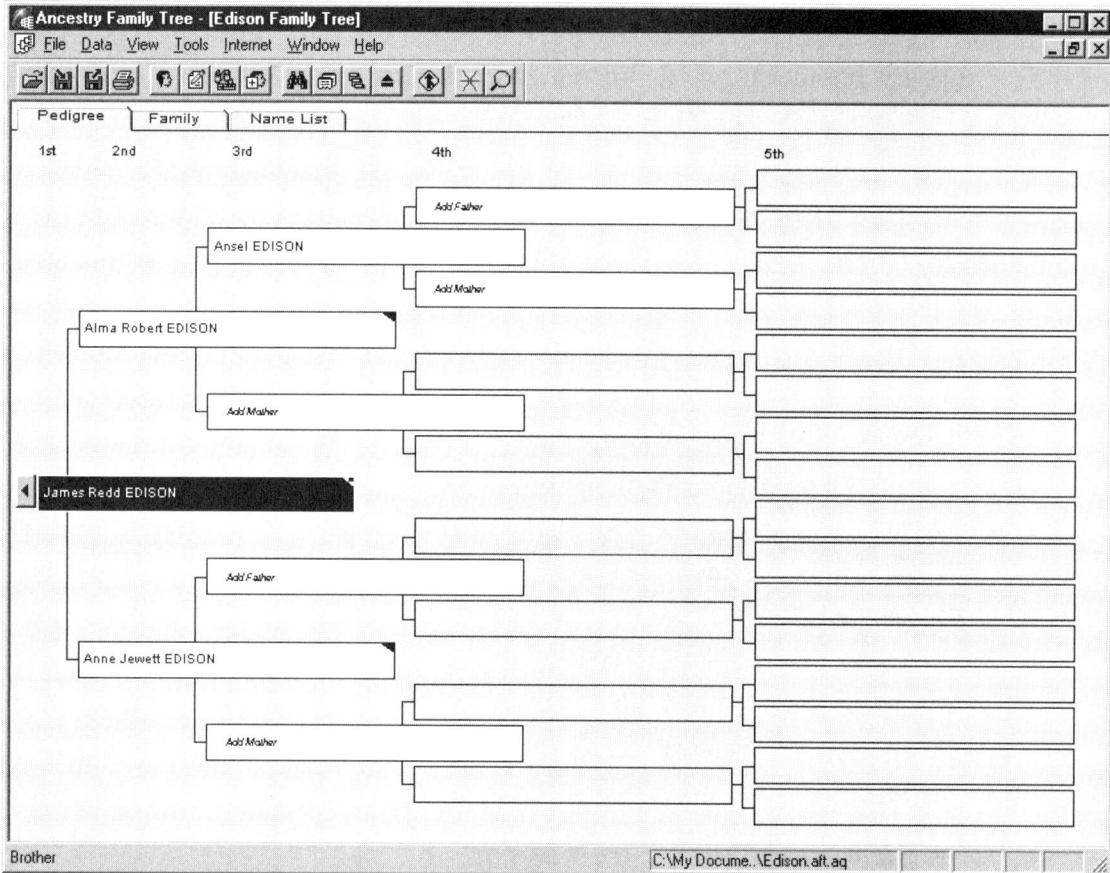

Searching for databases on your computer

You can search your computer for family databases of various types that are currently stored on it.

To search for databases on your computer

1. Do one of the following:

    - In the **File** menu, click **Open**, or

    - click the Open button on the button bar. 📂

    The **Open Family Database** form will be displayed.

2. Locate the disk drive or folder that you want to search.

    Note: The type of database file that is included in the search (for example, GEDCOM, Ancestry Family Tree, Personal Ancestral File, etc.) is determined by the settings on the Database page of the Preferences form. Refer to chapter 2, Installation and Setup, to learn about these settings.

3. Click the **Search** button.

Ancestry Family Tree will search the indicated disk or folder. When the search is complete, the **Results From Search** form will be displayed.

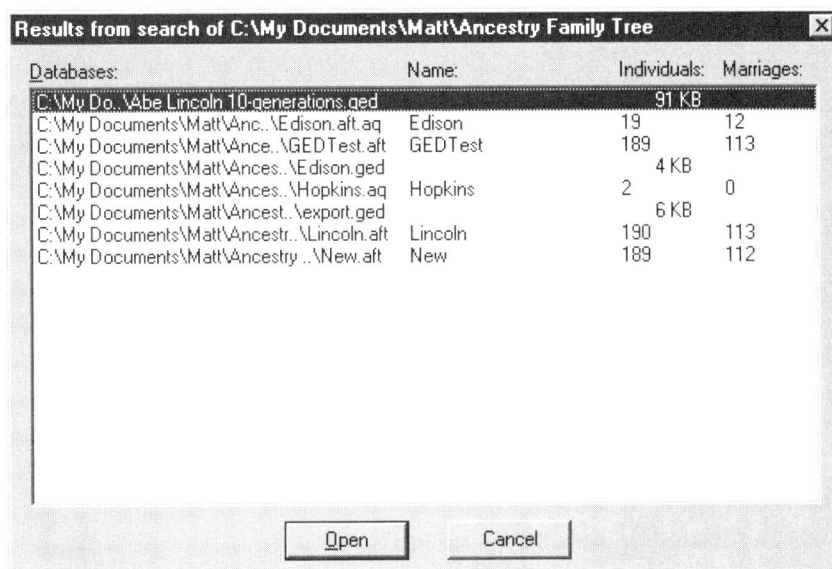

4. Highlight the database you want to open and then click the **Open** button.

   The database will be displayed with the view (**Pedigree**, **Family**, or **Name List**) that you last used when viewing it.

Adding an individual to the database

While you can import individual records into Ancestry Family Tree from a number of sources (refer to chapter 10, Importing and Exporting Files and Merging Records), Ancestry Family Tree also allows you to enter the names of individuals in a family database and define their relationships. It also allows you to enter and store detailed information about each individual. This section describes how to:

- add an individual to the database based on relationship, and

- add an "unlinked" individual.

Adding an individual based on relationship

You can add a new individual to the database by entering his or her name based on the person's relationship to an individual who already exists in the database: as the mother, father, spouse, or child of the existing individual. The new individual will be added as a relation to the existing individual who is currently highlighted in the Ancestry Family Tree view. You can also search for an individual already in the database who will be added as a relation to the existing individual.

To add an individual based on relationship to an existing individual

5. In the **Pedigree** view or the **Family** view, highlight the individual to whom the new individual is related.

6. Do one of the following:

- In the **Data** menu, click **Add Father**, **Add Mother**, **Add Spouse**, or **Add Child**, or

- click the Add Individual button on the button bar.  🔲

  A form similar to the one shown below will be displayed.

James Redd EDISON	☒

  Select type of individual:
  - ○ Father
  - ○ Mother
  - ○ Spouse
  - ○ Child
  - ⊙ New unlinked individual

  [Add New]
  [Find Existing]
  [Cancel]

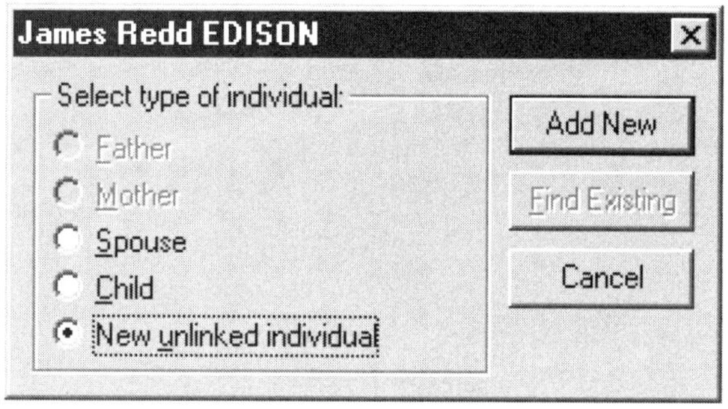

  Click **Father**, **Mother**, **Spouse**, or **Child**. (Note that some options may not be allowed—for example, Mother and Father are not enabled if the existing individual already has a mother and father in the database.)

An **Add Individual** form similar to the one shown below will be displayed.

Note: The **LDS Ordinances** section of the form will be displayed only if the Use LDS Data box is selected on the General page of the Preferences form. Refer to chapter 2, Installation and Setup, to learn about user preferences.

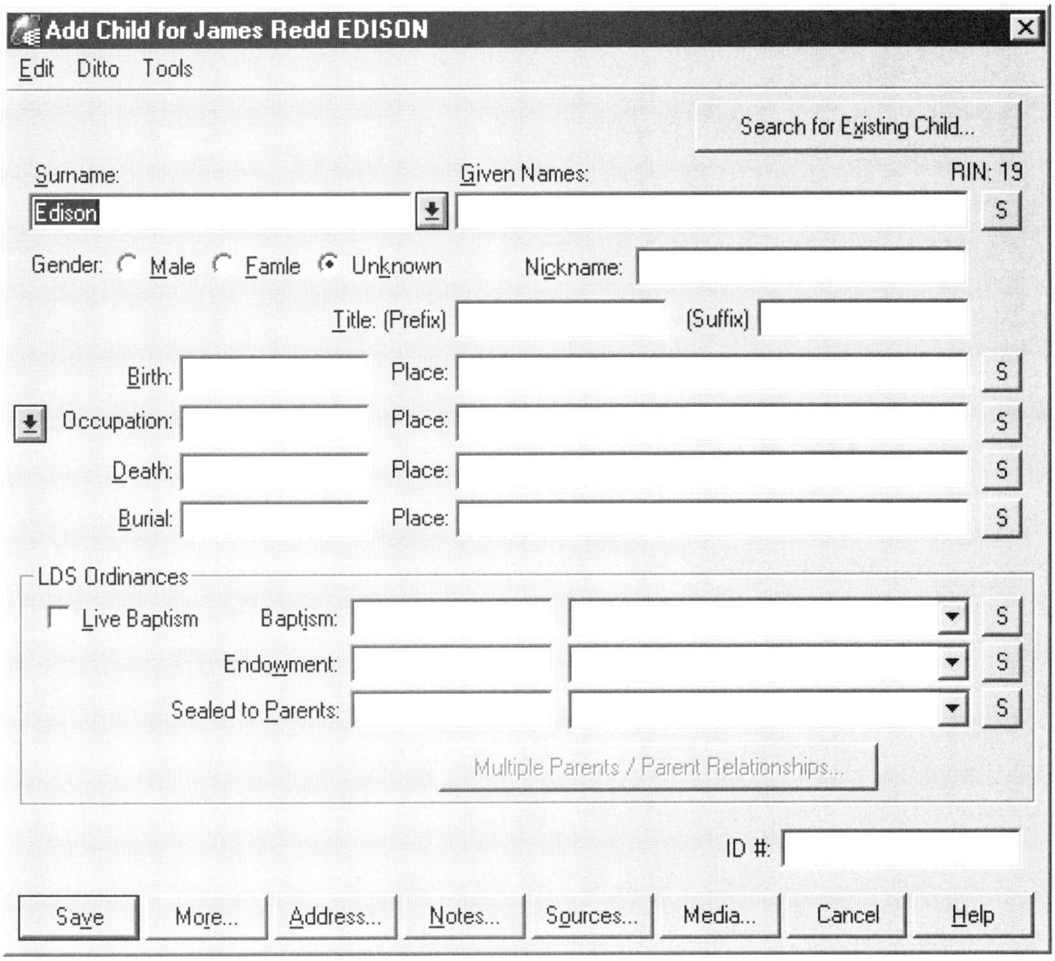

![Screenshot of the "Add Child for James Redd EDISON" dialog window]

```
Add Child for James Redd EDISON                                    [X]
Edit  Ditto  Tools

                                      Search for Existing Child...

Surname:                    Given Names:                    RIN: 19
[Edison]                [▼]  [                            ]    [S]

Gender:  ○ Male  ○ Famle  ◉ Unknown    Nickname: [            ]

                    Title: (Prefix) [          ]   (Suffix) [        ]

        Birth: [        ]    Place: [                        ]  [S]
[▼]  Occupation: [        ]    Place: [                        ]  [S]
        Death: [        ]    Place: [                        ]  [S]
        Burial: [        ]    Place: [                        ]  [S]

─ LDS Ordinances ─────────────────────────────────────────────
   □ Live Baptism    Baptism: [        ] [                ][▼] [S]
               Endowment: [        ] [                ][▼] [S]
           Sealed to Parents: [        ] [                ][▼] [S]

                    Multiple Parents / Parent Relationships...

                                            ID #: [            ]

 [Save]  [More...]  [Address...]  [Notes...]  [Sources...]  [Media...]  [Cancel]  [Help]
```

7. Proceed to "Entering data for an individual," below, to learn how to enter data using this form.

To search for and add an existing related individual

1. On the **Add Individual** form, click the **Search for** . . . button in the upper-right corner. (The label on this button will vary depending upon the type of relationship to be added that you chose earlier.)

   [Search for Existing Child...]

   A **Find** form similar to the one shown below will be displayed.

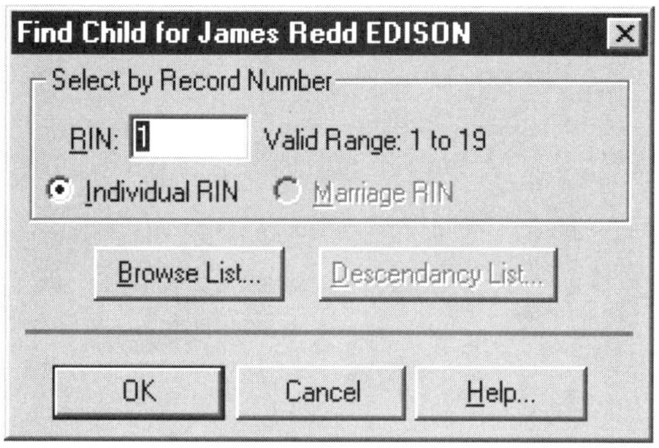

Find Child for James Redd EDISON

Select by Record Number

RIN: 1   Valid Range: 1 to 19

● Individual RIN   ○ Marriage RIN

Browse List...   Descendancy List...

OK   Cancel   Help...

2. Refer to chapter 9, Searching the Database, to learn how to use this form to find an individual in the database.

Adding an "unlinked" individual

You can enter an "unlinked" individual who is not related to any other person in the database and therefore is not linked to any other person (until you choose to link the person to others in the database).

To add an unlinked individual

1. Do one of the following while in the **Pedigree** view or the **Family** view:

   - In the **Data** menu, click **Add Individual**, or

   - click the Add Individual button 🔳 on the button bar.

   A form similar to the one shown below will be displayed.

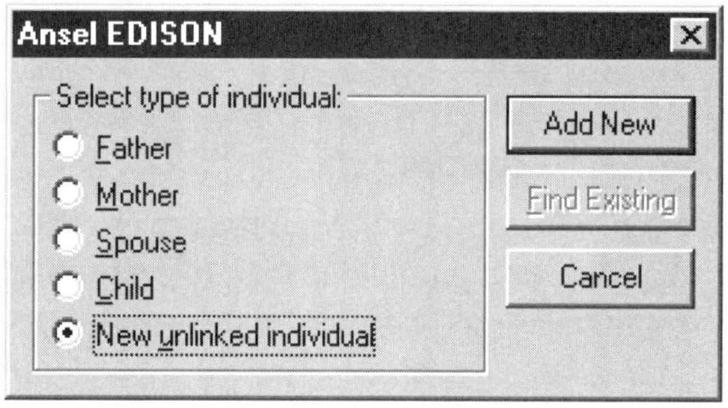

Ansel EDISON

Select type of individual:

○ Father
○ Mother
○ Spouse
○ Child
● New unlinked individual

Add New
Find Existing
Cancel

2. Click the **New unlinked individual** option.

   An **Add Individual** form similar to the one shown above will be displayed.

3. Proceed to "Entering data for an individual," below, to learn how to enter data using this form.

Entering data for an individual

The **Add Individual** and **Edit Individual** forms allow you to enter information specific to each individual. You can enter the individual's name, of course, and date and place data for specific events such as birth and death. If you checked the Use LDS Data box on the General page of the Preferences form, you can also enter LDS ordinance data.

Finally, you can assign an ID number of your own choosing to the individual. The Individual form can also be the starting point from which you enter other data about the individual such as contact information, notes, sources, and multimedia (image and sound) files.

To enter name data for the individual

1. Type the appropriate names in the **Surname**, **Given Names**, and **Nickname** boxes. (The Surname box may contain the surname of the new individual's relation; you can delete it and enter a different name if necessary.) You can omit any name that you do not know.

    Hint: As the cursor moves through boxes on this form that allow you to enter names, places, and certain other information, a drop-menu button ⬇ will appear to the right of the box. You can click it to see a list of names or places already in the database, then click the word you want to enter (if it appears in the list) to insert it in the box.

2. Indicate the individual's gender by clicking one of the following option buttons: **Male**, **Female**, or **Unknown**.

3. Use the **Title: (Prefix)** and **(Suffix)** boxes to specify honorifics and other information, such as Dr., Jr., etc., if they exist.

To enter event data for the individual

1. In the **Birth [or alternate birth event]**, **Death**, and **Burial** boxes, enter the dates of those events (if known).

    Enter the dates known for the individual in the appropriate boxes.

    *   The preferred format for date entry is DD/MMM/YYYY (for example, 12 Aug 1956).

    *   You can enter the date in numeric form (for example, 1/30/1900 or 1-30-1900) or with the month spelled out.

    *   You must enter four digits for the year.

    *   You may enter a partial date (for example, June 1946 or just 1946).

    Note: A drop-menu button ⬇ appears to the left of the *alternate birth event* box.

⬇	Christening:	

    You can click the drop-menu button to view a list of alternate events and select a different alternate birth event for which you want to enter date and place data, or you can define a new type of alternate event. The alternate birth event is useful if you don't know a date or place of birth but you do have related information, such as the date or place of blessing or christening. Entering an alternate birth event allows alternate birth event data to be printed on reports if there is no birth data. Refer to "Creating an additional event," below, to learn how to select, add, or modify types of additional (alternate) events.

2. Use the **Place** box adjacent to each event box to indicate where the event took place, if known.

   Note: Enter place information from smallest level to largest, separating each level with a comma. For example, if the individual was born in the city of Oakland, in the county of Alameda, in California, you would enter: Oakland, Alameda County, California, USA. It is important to enter place information in this format because Ancestry Family Tree's place search feature depends on comma separation to distinguish between city, county, state, and country in place fields. (Refer to "Searching for an individual using filters" in chapter 9, Searching the Database, to learn how to search for individuals based on place and other information.)

   For each event, you can enter up to 120 characters of place information.

To create and select sources and source citations

For the individual's name and for each event, you can create or select a source and source citation by clicking the corresponding button ⑤. (A *source* is the origin, or source, of the information you enter. A *source citation* refers to a specific part of a particular source.) Refer to chapter 7, Working with Sources and Source Citations, to learn how to create and select sources and source citations.

To enter an ID number

The **ID #** box allows you to assign an identification number of your own choosing to the individual. The number can contain up to 40 alphanumeric characters in any combination.

Enter an alphanumeric identification number in the box if you want to assign one.

Using menu commands

The **Edit**, **Ditto**, and **Tools** menus on the Add Individual or Edit Individual form provide a number of tools to help you enter and edit individual information. Refer to the table below to learn about the menu commands.

Edit menu

Menu command	Description
Undo	Undo the previous action. For example, if you inadvertently delete text, you can select the Undo command to restore it.
Cut	Delete the highlighted text and place it on the clipboard.
Copy	Copy the highlighted text to the clipboard.
Paste	Paste cut or copied text from the clipboard.
Delete	Delete the highlighted text.

Ditto menu

Menu command	Description
Ditto Last Record	Pastes the data from the last individual record you saved into the corresponding field. For example, if you place the cursor in the

Menu command	Description
	Birth Place box and then click Ditto Last Record, the birth place from the previous individual record will be inserted into the Birth Place box.
Ditto Father Ditto Mother	Pastes the data from the current individual's father or mother into the corresponding field. For example, if you place the cursor in the Birth Place box and then click Ditto Father, the birth place from the father's record will be inserted into the Birth Place box.
Ditto Older Sibling	Pastes the data from the current individual's next older sibling into the corresponding field. (Both individuals must have birth dates.)
Ditto Down	Pastes the data from a previous field on the form into a corresponding type of field. For example, if you place the cursor in the Burial date box and then click Ditto Down, the date in the Death date box will be inserted into the Burial date box.

Tools menu

Menu command	Description
Character Map	Opens the standard Windows character map, which lets you enter extended characters (those other than the standard alphanumeric characters used in English, including characters with diacritical marks).
Date Calculator	Opens the Date Calculator form. Refer to "Calculating dates from other information," below, to learn how to use the date calculator.

To use the character map

1. Click **Notes** on the Add Individual or Edit Individual form, then choose an event. Go to **Tools**, and choose **Character Map**.

   The **Character Map** form will be displayed.

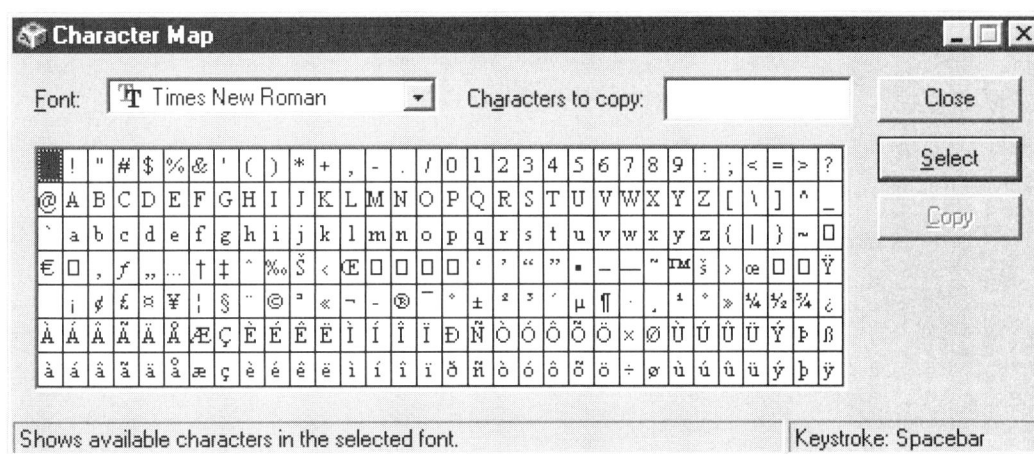

2. Click the character you want to place in the notes; click the **Select** button; and then click the **Copy** button.

3. On the **Notes** form, place the cursor at the point where you want the character to be inserted.

4. On the **Edit** menu of the **Notes** form, click **Paste**.

   The character is pasted into the Notes form.

   Note: Before you select and copy other characters from the Character Map form, clear the previously selected character from the **Characters to copy** box by highlighting it and pressing the DEL key on your keyboard.

5. Click the **Close** button to close the Character Map form.

Creating an additional event

In addition to entering date and place data for birth, death, and burial events, you can enter date and place data for additional events of your choice. You can select from a list of existing additional event types, define new types of additional events, or modify existing types of additional events.

To select an existing type of additional event

1. Do one of the following:

   - On the **Add Individual** or **Edit Individual** form, click the drop-menu button ▣ to the left of the alternate birth event box.

	Birth: [_____]
▣	Christening: [_____]
	Death: [_____]
	Burial: [_____]

   - On the **Additional Individual Information** form, click the **Add** button. (Refer to "Entering additional information for an individual," below, to learn how to use the Additional Individual Information form.)

   - The **Select Event** form will be displayed. It contains a list of additional event types.

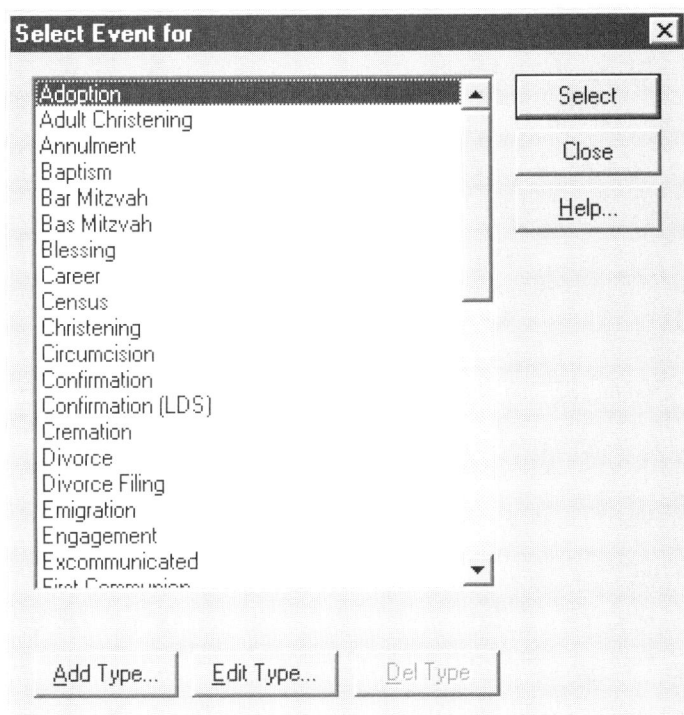

2. Highlight the appropriate event type in the list and then click the **Select** button.

- If you opened the Select Event form from the Add Individual or Edit Individual form, the Select Event form will close immediately and the name of the event will appear on the Add Individual or Edit Individual form.

  Enter event data and source information as described in "To enter event data for the individual" and "To create and select sources and source citations," above.

- If you opened the Select Event form from the Additional Individual Information form, the Additional Event form will be displayed. (Refer to "Entering additional information for an individual," below, to learn how to use the Additional Event form.)

To create a new type of additional event

1. Do one of the following:

- On the **Add Individual** or **Edit Individual** form, click the drop-menu button ⬇ adjacent to the alternate birth event box.

- On the **Additional Individual Information** form, click the **Add** button. (Refer to "Entering additional information for an individual," below, to learn how to use the Additional Individual Information form.)

The **Select Event** form will be displayed. It contains a list of additional event types.

2. On the **Select Event** form, click the **Add Type** button.

The **Define Other Event** form will be displayed.

```
┌─ Define Other Event ──────────────────── [X] ─┐
│                                                 │
│          Title: [                          ]    │
│                                                 │
│     Short title: [            ]                 │
│                                                 │
│    Abbreviation: [   ]                          │
│   ┌─ Date ──────────────────┐                   │
│   │ ⦿ None  ○ Single  ○ Range │  □ Use Description │
│   └──────────────────────────┘                  │
│   ┌─ Sentence Usage ─────────────────────┐      │
│   │  Verb Construct: [                  ] │      │
│   │                                       │      │
│   │  Place Preposition: [       ]         │      │
│   │                                       │      │
│   │  Sample:  He  Yuma, Arizona.          │      │
│   └───────────────────────────────────────┘      │
│                                                 │
│      [  OK  ]    [ Cancel ]    [ Help... ]      │
│                                                 │
└─────────────────────────────────────────────────┘
```

3. The Define Other Event form contains fields that allow you to enter information regarding the type of event and how information will be entered for that type of event. Refer to the table below to learn about the purpose of each field and then enter the appropriate information in the fields.

Field	Description
Title	Enter a name for the event. This name will appear in the list of other events on the Select Event form and on reports (if there is enough space).
Short Title	Enter a shortened version of the name. It will appear on most reports.
Abbreviation	Enter a one-character abbreviation for the event name. It will appear on reports if space is very limited.
Date	The options under **Date** determine how dates will be entered for this type of event. The options are: • **None:** Select if a date does not apply to the event type—for example, a chronic illness. The form for this event type will not include a date field. • **Single:** Select if the event typically occurs on a specific date—for example, retirement. The form for this event type will include a date field.

Field	Description
	• **Range:** Select if the event typically occurs over a span of time—for example, a career or military service. The form for this event type will include date *from* and *to* fields.

4. The controls under **Sentence Usage** allow you to define a book report sentence based on this event. The sentence always begins with the pronoun "he" or "she" based on the gender defined for the individual. The next part of the sentence is a verb construct that you can enter or edit. You can also enter a place preposition. A description, date or range of dates, and place are filled in for you with the description, date(s), and place you enter when you add an additional event of this type to an individual's record using the Additional Event form. (Refer to "Entering additional information for an individual," below, to learn how to use the Additional Event form.)

Referring to the sample sentence near the bottom of the Define Other Event form is a good way to understand how the sentence should be constructed. The verb construct and place preposition that you enter are added to the sample sentence as you enter them. For example, for a new event type titled "Career," you might enter the verb construct "was employed as a" and the place preposition "in." The resulting book report passage might read "He was employed as a haberdasher Mar 1913-24 Nov 1917 in Billings, Montana."

Refer to the table below to learn about the purpose of each field and then enter the appropriate information in the fields

Field	Description
Use Description	If checked, you will be able to enter a description of the event in the Additional Event form. A description entered in the Additional Event form will appear in a book report passage about the event. (The Additional Event form is used to add an additional event to the individual's record. Refer "Entering additional information for an individual," below, to learn about the Additional Event form.)
Verb Construct	Enter the form of verb you want to appear in a book report passage about this type of event. For example, the event type titled "Adoption" contains the verb construct "was adopted" by default.
Place Preposition	Enter the preposition that will appear in a book report passage about this type of event—for example, "in," "at," or "on."

5. Click the **OK** button to save the new additional event type and add it to the list of additional event types.

To modify an existing type of additional event

1. Do one of the following:

    • On the **Add Individual** or **Edit individual** form, click the drop-menu button ⬇ adjacent to the alternate birth event box.

Birth:		
Christening:		
Death:		
Burial:		

- On the **Additional Individual Information** form, click the **Add** button. (Refer to "Entering additional information for an individual," below, to learn how to use the Additional Individual Information form.)

The **Select Event** form will be displayed. It contains a list of additional event types.

2. On the **Select Event** form, click the **Edit Type** button.

The **Define Other Event** form will be displayed. You are not allowed to change the title of the event, but you can modify all of the other event attributes, such as short title, verb construct, etc. Refer to "To create a new type of additional event," above, to learn how to work with the other event attributes.

Define Other Event

Title: Census

Short title: Census

Abbreviation: CS

Date
- None • Single - Range   ☑ Use Description

Sentence Usage

Verb Construct: was counted in a census

Place Preposition: in

Sample: He was counted in a census [DESCRIPTION] 29 Feb 1980 in Yuma, Arizona.

OK   Cancel   Help...

3. Click the **OK** button to save the modified event type.

Entering LDS ordinance data

If you checked the Use LDS Data box on the General page of the Preferences form, the Add Individual or Edit Individual form contains boxes that allow you to enter LDS ordinance data. (If the Use LDS Data box is not checked, these boxes will not appear.)

To enter LDS ordinance data

1. The **Baptism**, **Endowment**, and **Sealed to Parents** boxes allow you to enter the dates of those ordinances.

   Enter the dates known for the individual in the appropriate boxes.

   - The preferred format for date entry is DD/MMM/YYYY (for example, 12 Aug 1956).

   - You may enter the date in numeric form (for example, 1/30/1900 or 1-30-1900) or with the month spelled out.

   - You must enter four digits for the year.

   - You may enter a partial date (for example, June 1946 or just 1946).

2. If the individual was baptized while living (and thus not by proxy in a temple), check the **Live Baptism** box. Doing so will allow you to enter a place of baptism in the place box adjacent to the Baptism box.

3. You can use the place box adjacent to the Baptism, Endowment, and Sealed to Parents boxes to indicate the LDS temple in which each ordinance was performed, if known.

   Click the arrow button to the right of the box and select the temple in the list.

   Note: If you checked the **Live Baptism** box, a drop-menu button will appear to the right of the baptism place box.

   You can enter the place of baptism in the box, or you can click the button to see a list of places already in the database, then click the word you want to enter (if it appears in the list) to insert it in the box.

4. For each ordinance, you can define a source or a source citation by clicking the corresponding button . (A *source* is the source, or origin, of the information you enter. A *source citation* refers to a specific part of a particular source.) Refer to chapter 7, Working with Sources and Source Citations, to learn how to create and select sources and source citations.

Entering additional information for an individual

You can select additional events for which you want to enter date and place data (in addition to birth, death, and burial information defined on the Add Individual or Edit

Individual form). You can also edit existing event types, create new types of events, and enter aliases, physical description, and other non-event personal data.

On the **Add Individual** or **Edit Individual** form, click the **More** button.

The **Additional Individual Information** form will be displayed.

To enter data for additional events

1. Click the **Add** button.

   The **Select Event** form will be displayed. It contains a list of event types.

Select Event for

Adoption
Adult Christening
Annulment
Baptism
Bar Mitzvah
Bas Mitzvah
Blessing
Career
Census
Christening
Circumcision
Confirmation
Confirmation (LDS)
Cremation
Divorce
Divorce Filing
Emigration
Engagement
Excommunicated
First Communion

Select   Close   Help...

Add Type...   Edit Type...   Del Type

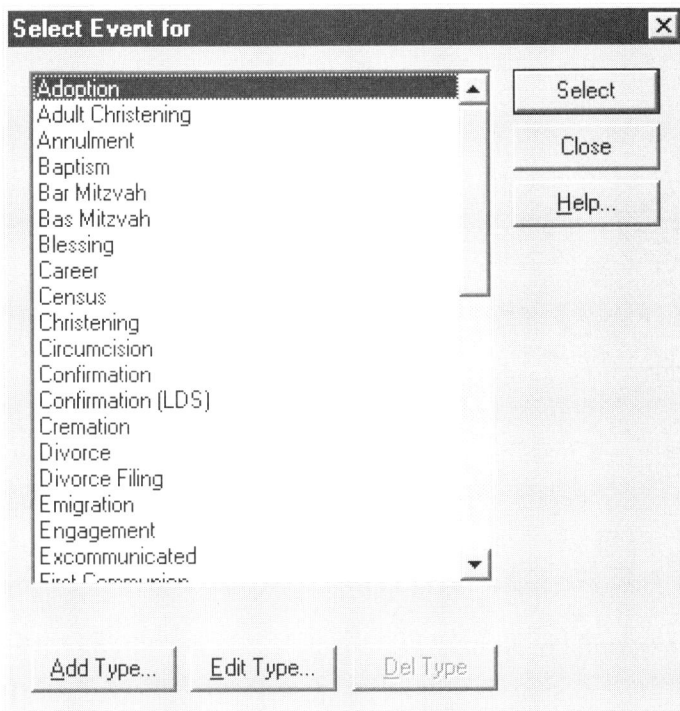

2. In the list of event types, highlight the type of event you want to select and then click the **Select** button.

    An Additional Event form similar to the one shown below will be displayed.

Occupation - James Redd EDISON

Date: 6 Mar 1885   To: 15 Sep 1893

Place:

Description:

Source...   ☐ Event is Confidential

OK   Cancel   Help...

Note: The information you enter in the Additional Event form can appear in a book report in the form of a sentence that is constructed automatically. (Refer to chapter 11, Creating Reports and Charts, to learn how to create book reports.) For example, for the additional event titled "Occupation," the default construction of the book report sentence (assuming the individual is a male) is "He was employed [description] [date] in [place]." On the book report the description, date, and place are filled in for you with the information you enter in this form—for example, "He was employed as a haberdasher Mar 1913-24 Nov 1917 in Billings, Montana."

3. In the **Date** box, enter the date of the event (if known). Depending on the type of event, there may be a **To** box as well. If both boxes are present, you can enter a range of dates—for example, **Date:** Mar 1913 **To:** 24 Nov 1917.

- The preferred format for date entry is DD/MMM/YYYY (for example, 12 Aug 1956).

- You can enter the date in numeric form (for example, 1/30/1900 or 1-30-1900) or with the month spelled out.

- You must enter four digits for the year.

- You may enter a partial date (for example, June 1946 or just 1946).

4. In the **Place** box, enter the place of the event.

   Note: When you click in the Place box, a drop-menu button will appear to the right of the box. You can click the button to see a list of places already in the database, then click the place you want to enter (if it appears in the list) to insert it in the box.

5. If the form contains a **Description** box, you can enter a description of the event. Referring to the Define Other Event form (see "To create a new type of additional event," above) for the type of event you are adding to the individual is a good way to understand how the description should be entered. For example, the event type titled "Occupation" contains the verb construct "was employed" by default. Therefore, you might want to enter the occupation of someone who sold men's clothing as "as a haberdasher"; the book report passage would read "He was employed as a haberdasher . . ."

   Note: The Description box appears on this form only if the Use Description box on the Define Other Event form (which is used to create this type of event) is checked. Refer to "To create a new type of additional event," above, to learn how to use the Define Other Event form.

6. Clicking the **Source** button allows you to define a source or source citation for the event. Refer to chapter 7, Working with Sources and Source Citations, to learn how to create or select a source or source citation.

7. Check the **Event Is Confidential** box if you want to designate the event as confidential. This gives you the option of excluding the event (and all other confidential events) from reports and GEDCOM export files when you generate them.

8. Repeat steps 1–7 above to create other additional events for the individual.

Note: Refer to "Creating an additional event," above, to learn how to add or edit types of additional events.

To edit existing additional events

1. On the **Additional Individual Information** form, highlight the event you want to edit in the **Other Events** list and then click the **Edit** button.

   An event form containing the data for the event will be displayed.

2. Refer to steps 3–7 under "To enter data for additional events, " above, to edit the data in the form.

To delete existing additional events

1. On the **Additional Individual Information** form, highlight the event you want to delete in the **Other Events** list and then click the **Delete** button.

   A warning dialog box similar to the one shown below will be displayed.

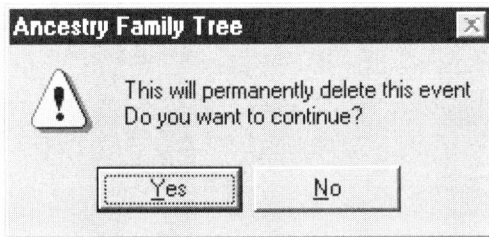

2. Click **Yes** to delete the event (or **No** to retain the event).

To enter alias, physical description, etc.

The Additional Individual Information form contains several fields that allow you to enter additional information regarding the individual. Entering information such as married name and aliases in these fields (rather than elsewhere, such as in the notes for the individual) causes that information to be printed on reports in specific places where you will know to look for it. Refer to the table below to learn about the purpose of each field and then enter the appropriate information in the fields.

Field	Description
Married Name	Enter the individual's married name if it is different from the birth name. It will appear on Family Reunion Contacts reports. Do not enter aliases or other changes of name here.
AFN	Every individual in the Ancestral File™ database of the LDS church is given an ID number called the Ancestral File Number (AFN). If you import records from the Ancestral File into any Ancestry Family Tree database, each individual's AFN is automatically entered in this field. You can also enter an AFN into this field yourself if needed.
AKA	(Also Known As) Enter any name change that occurred in an individual's lifetime (other than married name)—such as those resulting from immigration, stage names, and aliases. These names will be printed in the AKA field on the Individual Summary report.
Cause of Death	A cause of death entered in this field will not be printed on any report, but it can be used in a filtered search to produce a list of all individuals with matching information. Therefore, it is essential that you enter the cause of death in exactly the same way for all similar occurrences. For example, if you enter "cancer" for one person and "carcinoma" for another, both will not be found if you perform a search for one or the other of those words. (Refer to chapter 9, Searching the Database, to learn how to search using

Field	Description
	filters.)
Physical Description	A physical description entered in this field will be printed on the Individual Summary report. You can also perform a filtered search for any text in this field to find all persons with the same physical characteristics. (Refer to chapter 9, Searching the Database, to learn how to search using filters.)

3. Click the **OK** button to save the additional information and return to the Add Individual or Edit Individual form.

    Note: On the Add Individual or Edit Individual form an asterisk appears on the More button to indicate that there is additional information for the individual.

Defining sources and source citations for an individual's name or events

A *source* is the source, or origin, of the information you enter—a birth certificate or published family history, for example. For the individual's name and for each of various events (birth, death, burial, and one or more additional events), and for a marriage, you can create a new source or select a source that already exists in the database. Then cite one or more specific parts of that source as source citations.

Refer to chapter 7, Working with Sources and Source Citations, to learn how to create and select sources and source citations.

Adding contact information for an individual

You can use Ancestry Family Tree as a family address book by entering contact information for individuals in a database. The contact information you enter can also be used to generate address labels and contact lists.

To add contact information for an individual

1. On the **Add Individual** or **Edit Individual** form, click the **Address** button.

    The **Contact Information** form will be displayed.

```
Contact Information of James Redd EDISON          [X]

      Contact Name: [                                    ]

      Street Address: [                                  ]
                      [                                  ]
                      [                                  ]

              City: [                                    ]

             State: [                                    ]

   Zip/Postal Code: [                                    ]

           Country: [                                    ]

             Phone: [                                    ]

             Email: [                                    ]

         Home Page: [                                    ]

       [   OK   ]      [  Cancel  ]      [  Help...  ]
```

2. Refer to the table below to learn the purpose of the unique fields on the Contact Information form.

Field	Description
Contact Name	The primary purpose of this field is for generating a list report called a Family Reunion Contacts list. The Family Reunion Contacts list report allows you to print a phone list, address list, or e-mail list to a text file. You can then open the text file in a word processing application and print it if necessary—for example, to print address labels. (Refer to chapter 11, Creating Reports and Charts, for more information on creating list reports.)
	You don't have to enter a name in the Contact Name field. If you do not, Ancestry Family Tree will use the birth name entered in the Surname and Given Names fields of the Individual form as the contact name by default; or, if you enter a married name for the individual on the Additional Individual Information form, it will be used as the surname. However, if you want to print some other name on address labels and contact lists, you can enter it here; it will be used instead of the birth name (or married name). For example, you might want to enter the contact name for one spouse in a married couple as "Mr. and Mrs. Carl Krebsbach" and enter no contact information for the other spouse.
	Note: If you do not want to contact the individual, enter one of the following: *No Contact* or *NC*. The individual will not be included in address labels or contact lists.
Home Page	If the individual has a site on the World Wide Web, you can enter the URL address in the **Home Page** box.

3. Enter the appropriate information in the remaining boxes.

4. Click the **OK** button to save the contact information for the individual.

Adding additional parents for an individual

You can add additional parents for an individual who already has a mother and/or father in the database. For example, you can add adoptive parents or guardians who would be designated as parents along with the biological parents. If there are multiple sets of parents for an individual, one set of parents will always be the *primary parents*. The primary parents will appear on-screen and in reports as the individual's parents. By default, the first parents entered for an individual are the primary parents; however, you can specify other parents as the primary parents. You can also specify the nature of the individual's relationship to each set of parent(s)—for example, whether the individual is a biological child or an adopted child.

To add additional parents to an individual

1. In the **Pedigree** view or the **Family** view, highlight the individual for whom you want to add parents.

2. In the **Data** menu, click **Add Parents**. (The Add Parents menu item is available only if one or more parents already exist for the individual.)

   The **Parents** form will be displayed.

3. Click the **New** button.

   The **Add Parents** form will be displayed.

```
Add Parents for James Redd EDISON                    [X]

         [     Search for Existing Parents...         ]

Father:    [  Add Father...  ]      [  Find Father...  ]

Mother:    [  Add Mother...  ]      [  Find Mother...  ]

                 [    Edit Marriage    ]

     [   OK   ]      [  Cancel  ]      [  Help...  ]
```

4. Do one of the following:

- To find an existing married couple to add as parents, click the **Search for Existing Parents** button.

   The **Find Marriage** form will be displayed. To learn how to use the Find form to locate a marriage record, refer to "Searching for a marriage" in chapter 9, Searching the Database.

- To add a new individual to the database as a parent, click the **Add Father** or **Add Mother** button.

   The **Add Father** or **Add Mother** form will be displayed. To learn how to use the Add form, refer to "Entering data for an individual," above.

- To find an existing individual to add as a parent, click the **Find Father** or **Find Mother** button.

   The **Find** form will be displayed. To learn how to use the Find form to locate an individual in the database, refer to "Searching the entire database" in chapter 9, Searching the Database.

If you have located an existing marriage and returned to the Add Parents form, the names of the couple will appear on the form, as shown in the example below.

```
Add Parents for James Redd EDISON                    [X]

         [     Search for Existing Parents...         ]

Father:    [        Jeremiah ANDREWS        ]

Mother:    [         Amelia MORTON          ]

                 [   Edit Marriage - 4   ]

     [   OK   ]      [  Cancel  ]      [  Help...  ]
```

- At this point you can modify the marriage record—for example, you might want to add the facts of an adoption to the marriage notes. *To modify the marriage record,* click the **Edit Marriage** button.

The **Marriage** form for the married couple will be displayed. To learn how to use the Marriage form, refer to "Entering data for a marriage" in chapter 5, Working with Marriages.

- You can also modify the record of either individual parent. *To modify an individual parent's record,* click the appropriate button on the form.

  The **Edit Individual** form will be displayed. To learn how to use the Edit Individual form, refer to "Entering data for an individual," above.

If you have added an individual as a parent, or located an existing individual to add as a parent and returned to the Add Parents form, the individual's name will appear on the form. At this point you can modify the individual's record—to note the facts of a guardianship, for example. *To modify the individual's record,* click the appropriate button on the form.

The **Edit Individual** form will be displayed. To learn how to use the Edit Individual form, refer to "Entering data for an individual," above.

5. Click the **OK** button to close the Add Parents form and add the married couple or individual to the Parents form as additional parent(s).

To arrange the order of multiple parents

You can rearrange the order of the parents in the list.

To do so, highlight the parents you want to move and then click the up or down arrows adjacent to the list to move them up or down in the list.

To specify the primary parent(s)

Highlight the primary parent(s) in the Parents list on the **Parents** form and click the **Make Primary** button. The primary parents are denoted in the list by an asterisk. (The primary parents are those who will appear on-screen and in reports as the individual's parents. The first parents defined for an individual are the primary parents by default.)

To specify the nature of the individual's relationship to the parent(s)

1. In the **Parents** list on the **Parents** form, highlight the set of parents whose relationship to the individual you want to specify.

2. In the **Relationship to Father** and **Relationship to Mother** boxes, click the arrow button to the right of the box and select the appropriate relationship type from the list. The options are **Biological**, **Adopted**, **Guardian**, and **Sealing** (if Use LDS Data is selected in Preferences).

The relationship for the first set of parents defined for an individual is Biological by default. The relationship for additional parents is Adopted by default.

3. In the **Status of Relationship** box, click the arrow button to the right of the box and select the appropriate status from the list. The options are **Verified**, **Challenged**, and **Disproved**.

4. If Use LDS Data is selected on the General page of the Preferences form, the **Sealed to Parents** boxes allow you to enter the date of sealing and the LDS temple in which the sealing occurred.

   - Enter the date of sealing in the left-hand box.

     - The preferred format for date entry is DD/MMM/YYYY (for example, 12 Aug 1956).

     - You can enter the date in numeric form (for example, 1/30/1900 or 1-30-1900) or with the month spelled out.

     - You must enter four digits for the year.

     - You may enter a partial date (for example, June 1946 or just 1946).

   - In the right-hand box, click the arrow button to the right of the box. From the list displayed, select the LDS temple in which the sealing occurred. If the temple is not in the list, you can enter a five-character abbreviation indicating which temple was used for the sealing.

To edit the notes for the individual

1. On the **Parents** form, click the **Notes** button.

   The **Notes** form for the individual will be displayed.

2. Refer to the steps in "Creating notes for an individual" in chapter 6, Working with Notes, to learn how to use the Notes form. For example, you might want to enter information about an adoption in the individual's notes.

Editing parent links

You can modify how parents are linked to an individual. You can *unlink* parents from an individual (remove the parent-child relationship), or you can change the nature of the individual's relationship to the parent(s)—for example, whether the individual is a biological child or an adopted child.

To unlink parents from an individual

1. In the **Pedigree** view or the **Family** view, highlight the individual whose parent links you want to modify.

2. In the **Data** menu, click **Edit Parent Links**. (The Edit Parent Links menu item is available only if one or more parents already exist for the individual.)

   The **Parents** form will be displayed.

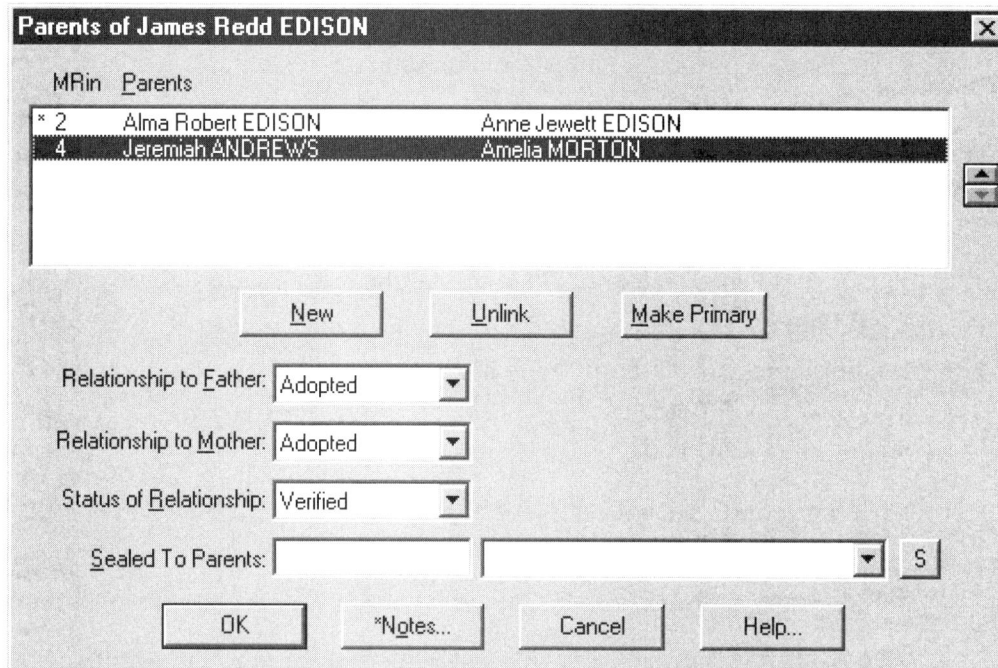

3. In the **Parents** list, highlight the parent(s) whom you want to unlink from the individual and then click the **Unlink** button. (The marriage record for the unlinked parents will still exist, and they will still be linked to their remaining children.)

A warning dialog box similar to the one shown below will be displayed.

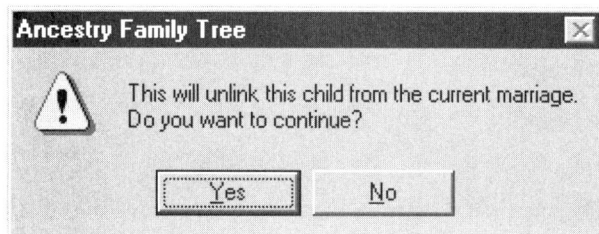

4. Click the **Yes** button to unlink the parents (or click the **No** button to abort the unlink procedure).

If you click the Yes button, the parent(s) are unlinked from the individual and are removed from the Parents list on the individual's Parents form.

To modify the nature of the individual's relationship to the parent(s)

1. In the Parents list, highlight the set of parents whose relationship to the individual you want to modify.

2. Modify the entries in the **Relationship to Father**, **Relationship to Mother**, **Status of Relationship**, and (if Use LDS Data is selected in Preferences) **Sealed to Parents** boxes as necessary. To learn how to use these boxes, refer to "Adding additional parents for an individual," above.

Editing an individual record

After you have entered an individual into a database, you might need to change existing data or add to it.

To edit an individual record

1. Highlight the individual whose record you want to edit.

2. Do one of the following:

   - In the **Data** menu, click **Edit** Individual,

   - double-click on the individual (if Edits Individual or Edits Primary/Selects Primary is selected on the General page of the Preferences form), or

   - right-click on the individual and click **Edit** in the pop-up menu (not applicable to the Name List view).

   The **Edit Individual** form for the selected individual will be displayed.

3. Refer to "Entering data for an individual," above, to learn how to use the Edit Individual form.

Arranging the order of multiple parents, spouses, or children

For individuals who have multiple sets of parents, multiple spouses, or multiple children, you can adjust the order in which the multiple relations appear.

To adjust the order of multiple sets of parents

1. In the **Pedigree** view or the **Family** view, place the individual for whom you want to rearrange sets of multiple parents in the primary position.

2. In the **Data** menu, click **Order** and then click **Parents** in the sub-menu.

   The **Parents** form will be displayed.

3. In the list of parents, highlight the set of parents that you want to move in the list.

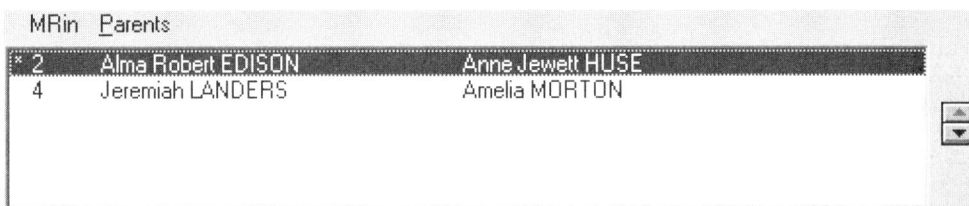

MRin	Parents	
* 2	Alma Robert EDISON	Anne Jewett HUSE
4	Jeremiah LANDERS	Amelia MORTON

4. Click the up or down arrow to the right of the list to move the set of parents up or down in the list.

5. Click the **OK** button to close the Parents form.

To adjust the order of multiple spouses

1. In the **Family** view, place the individual for whom you want to rearrange the order of multiple spouses in the primary position.

2. In the **Data** menu, click **Order** and then click **Spouses** in the sub-menu.

   The **Spouse Order** form will be displayed.

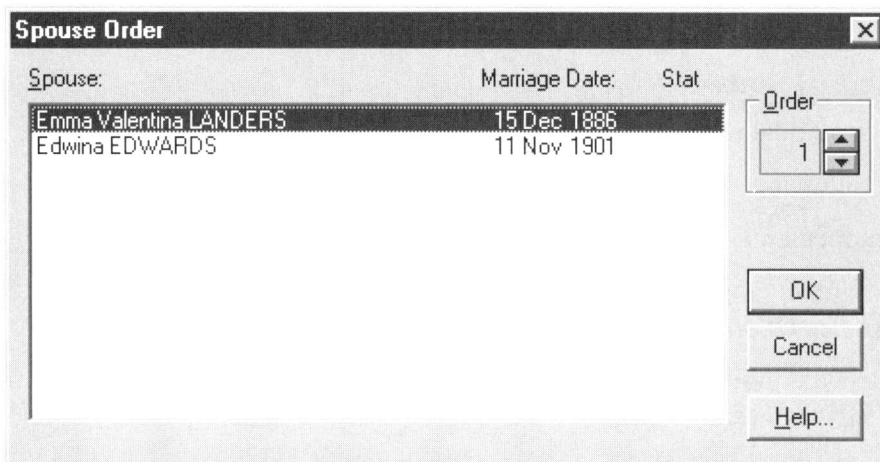

3. In the **Spouse** list, highlight the spouse that you want to move in the list.

4. Click the up or down arrow to the right of the list to move the spouse up or down in the list.

5. Click the **OK** button to close the Spouse Order form.

To adjust the order of multiple children

1. In the **Family** view, place the individual for whom you want to rearrange the order of multiple children in the primary position.

2. In the **Data** menu, click **Order** and then click **Children** in the sub-menu.

   The **Child Order** form will be displayed.

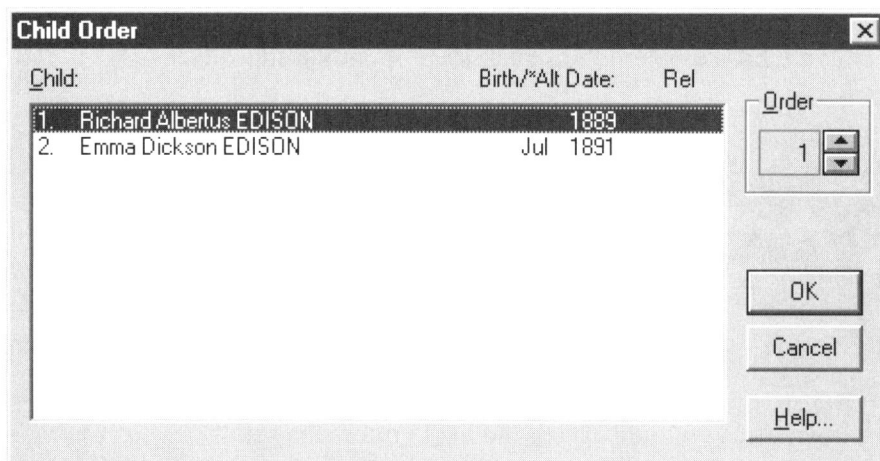

3. In the **Child** list, highlight the child that you want to move in the list.

4. Click the up or down arrow to the right of the list to move the child up or down in the list.

5. Click the **OK** button to close the Child Order form.

Unlinking an individual

You can "unlink" an individual from all of his or her relationships. (The unlinked individual will not be removed from the database.) For example, you could unlink a father for whom there is a spouse and children in the database; his relationship to the former wife and children would no longer exist in the database. (A marriage record will still exist but with the father unknown.)

Note: You cannot use the Unlink Individual command to unlink a single remaining parent from his or her children. In such a case you would have to delete the marriage record or unlink each child from the parent.

1. In the **Family** view, highlight the individual whom you want to unlink. (You can highlight one of the parents of the primary individual, a child of the primary individual, or a spouse of the primary individual; the individual to be unlinked cannot be in the primary position.)

2. Do one of the following:

   - In the **Data** menu, click **Unlink Individual**, or

   - right-click the individual and then click **Unlink** in the pop-up menu.

   A confirmation form similar to the one shown below will be displayed.

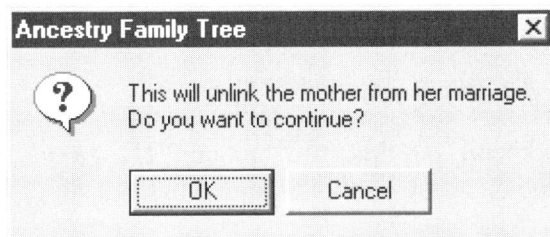

Ancestry Family Tree	✕
❓ This will unlink the mother from her marriage. Do you want to continue?	
OK Cancel	

3. Click the **OK** button to unlink the individual (or click the **Cancel** button to abort the unlink).

Deleting an individual from the database

You can delete any individual from a database if you find it necessary—for example, you might find that an individual record you have created is a duplicate of an existing one.

To delete an individual from the database

1. In the **Pedigree** view or the **Family** view, highlight the individual whom you want to delete.

2. In the **Data** menu, click **Delete Individual**.

   A warning dialog box similar to the one shown below will be displayed.

> **Ancestry Family Tree**
>
> ⚠ Oliver MCLAIRD
>
> This individual will be removed from disk and unlinked from any existing relations.
>
> Individual is linked to 1 marriage(s).
>
> [OK]   [Cancel]

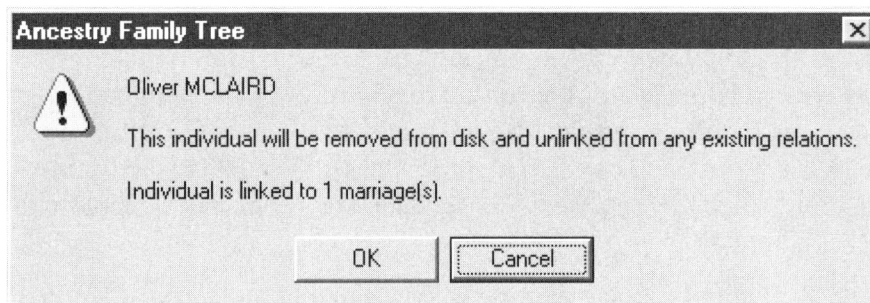

3. Click the **OK** button to delete the individual record from the database (or click the **Cancel** button to cancel the deletion).

Identifying relationships among individuals

Ancestry Family Tree provides several tools to help you identify relationships among individuals in a database. This section describes how to

- view the relationship of every individual to a specific individual,

- determine the blood relationship between two individuals, or

- view all descendants of a specific individual.

Viewing the relationship of every individual to a specific individual

The Relationship Indicators tool can show you how every individual in a database is related to a specific individual. You begin by specifying this "root person." The Family view then shows how every other person in the database is related to that individual.

To view the relationship of all individuals to a specific person

1. In the **Tools** menu, click **Relationship Indicators**.

   The **Set Relationship Indicators** form will be displayed, and the **Show Relationships in Family View** box is checked by default. (The box must be checked to cause relationships to appear.)

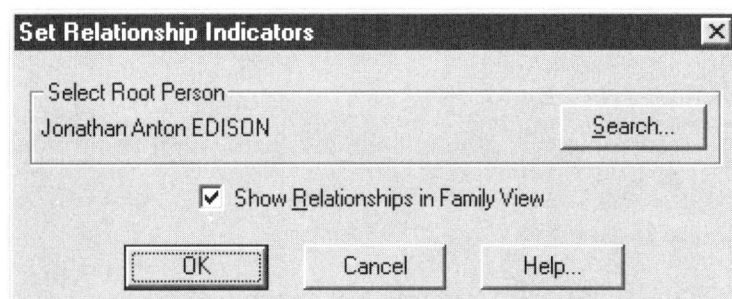

> **Set Relationship Indicators**
>
> Select Root Person
> Jonathan Anton EDISON   [Search...]
>
> ☑ Show Relationships in Family View
>
> [OK]   [Cancel]   [Help...]

2. Click the **Search** button to locate the root person.

   Tip: The individual currently highlighted in the Pedigree view, Family view, or Name List view will appear as the root person by default. Therefore, you can avoid having to search for the root person by highlighting that individual before you select Relationship Indicators in the Tools menu.

The **Find Individual** form will be displayed. Refer to "Searching the entire database" in chapter 9, Searching the Database, to learn how to search for an individual.

3. After you have located the individual who will be the root person, click the **OK** button to select the individual as the root person and close the Set Relationship Indicators form. That individual will be retained as the root person (even after the database is closed and re-opened) until a new root person is specified.

The **Family** view displays the relationship of every individual to the root person. (Relationships are shown only in the Family view.) The relationship appears directly above the box containing an individual's name, as shown in the example below.

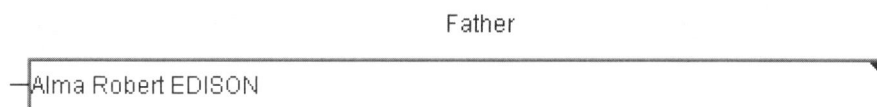

Father

— Alma Robert EDISON

Determining the relationship between two individuals

The Relationship Examiner can determine how (or if) any two individuals in a database are related to one another by blood. You select two individuals; Ancestry Family Tree can then determine the common ancestors of the individuals and, for each individual, indicate the line of descent to each common ancestor.

To determine the blood relationship between two individuals

1. In the **Tools** menu, click **Relationship Examiner**.

The **Relationship Examiner** form will be displayed.

2. Under **First Person**, click the **Search** button to specify the first individual.

   Tip: The individual currently highlighted in the Pedigree view, Family view, or Name List view will appear as the "First Person" by default. Therefore, you can avoid having to search for the first individual by highlighting that individual before you select the Relationship Examiner in the **Tools** menu.

   The **Find Individual** form will be displayed. Refer to "Searching the entire database" in chapter 9, Searching the Database, to learn how to search for an individual.

3. Under **Second Person**, click the **Search** button to specify the second individual.

   The **Find Individual** form will be displayed. Refer to "Searching the entire database" in chapter 9, Searching the Database, to learn how to search for an individual.

4. Click the **Examine** button.

   The **Relationship Examiner** form lists the common ancestors of the individuals under **Common Ancestors**.

5. Click the **Close** button to close the Relationship Examiner form and return to the Ancestry Family Tree view.

To view a full description of a relationship

1. Perform steps 2–4 in "To determine the blood relationship between two individuals," above.

2. In the **Common Ancestors** list, highlight a set of common ancestors.

   A full description of the relationship appears to the right of the **Common Ancestors** list.

To view the individuals' lines of descent to a common ancestor

1. Perform steps 2–4 in "To determine the blood relationship between two individuals," above.

2. In the **Common Ancestors** list, highlight a set of common ancestors.

   Under **Line of Descent to Common Ancestor** (for both the first individual and the second individual), the individual's line of descent to the highlighted common ancestor will be displayed.

Viewing the descendants of an individual

You can view a descendancy list for a selected individual. A descendancy list shows the parents, spouse(s), siblings, and children of the selected individual.

To view a descendancy list

1. In the Ancestry Family Tree view, highlight the individual for whom you want to view a descendancy list.

2. Do one of the following:

   - On the **Tools** menu, click **Descendancy List**.

   - Place the cursor over the individual, right click, and then select Descendancy from the pop-up menu.

   - On the keyboard, press Ctrl+D.

   - Click the Descendancy List button 🗗 on the button bar.

   The **Descendancy List** form will be displayed.

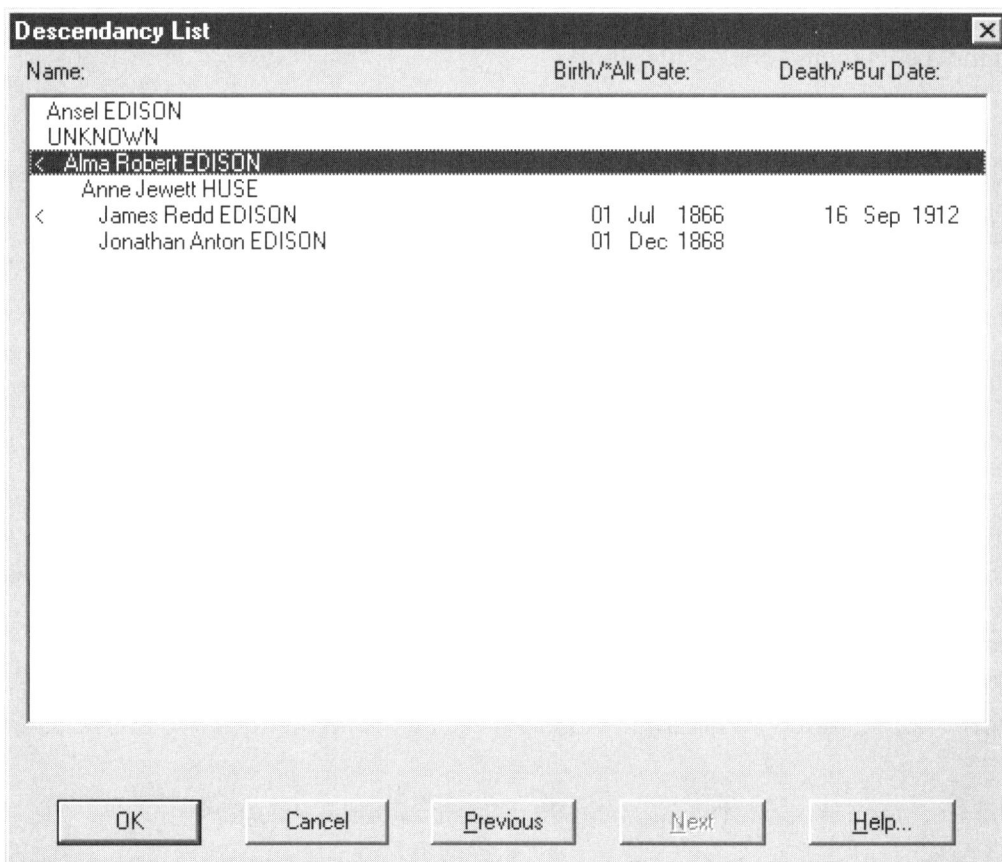

Descendancy List		☒
Name:	Birth/*Alt Date:	Death/*Bur Date:
Ansel EDISON		
UNKNOWN		
< Alma Robert EDISON		
Anne Jewett HUSE		
< James Redd EDISON	01 Jul 1866	16 Sep 1912
Jonathan Anton EDISON	01 Dec 1868	

OK	Cancel	Previous	Next	Help...

A < to the left of an individual's name indicates that the person has at least one descendant.

   - To view the parents, spouse(s), siblings, and children of any individual on the list, highlight the individual.

- To make an individual the primary individual in the current Ancestry Family Tree view, double-click the individual.

Calculating dates from other information

You can use Ancestry Family Tree's Date Calculator to determine the dates on which events occurred based on other information.

- If you know a start date and an end date, you can quickly determine the intervening number of years, months, and days.

- If you know a start date and know that a certain amount of time passed, you can determine the end date.

- If you know an end date and that a certain amount of time preceded that date, you can determine the start date.

For example, if you know an individual's death date and age at death, you can calculate his or her birth date.

To use the Date Calculator

1. In the **Tools** menu, click **Calculators**.

2. Click **Date Calculator** on the submenu.

Relationship Examiner...	
Calculators ▶	Date Calculator...
Edit Source List...	Soundex...
Edit Repository List...	

The **Date Calculator** form will be displayed.

Date Calculator

May 1933						
Sun	Mon	Tue	Wed	Thu	Fri	Sat
30	1	2	3	4	5	6
7	8	9	10	11	12	13
14	15	16	17	18	19	20
21	22	23	**24**	25	26	27
28	29	30	31	1	2	3
4	5	6	7	8	9	10

Difference

Years: 66

Months: 6

Days: 20

December 1999						
Sun	Mon	Tue	Wed	Thu	Fri	Sat
28	29	30	1	2	3	4
5	6	7	8	9	10	11
12	13	**14**	15	16	17	18
19	20	21	22	23	24	25
26	27	28	29	30	31	1
2	3	4	5	6	7	8

Start Date: 24 May 1933   Wednesday

End Date: 14 Dec 1999   Tuesday

Calculate   Clear Fields   Close   Help...

3. Enter two of the following three pieces of information:

   - Start date

   - Difference (years, months, days)

   - End date

   To enter a start date or end date, do one of the following:

   - Enter the date in the **Start Date** or **End Date** box, or

   - click the arrow buttons in the month bar to move ahead or back to the year and month of the event and then click the appropriate day of the month.

◄		December 1946			►	
Sun	Mon	Tue	Wed	Thu	Fri	Sat
24	25	26	27	28	29	30
1	2	3	4	5	6	7
8	9	10	11	12	13	14
15	16	17	18	19	20	21
22	23	**24**	25	26	27	28
29	30	31	1	2	3	4

   To specify an intervening period of time (difference), enter years, months, and/or days in the **Years**, **Months**, and **Days** boxes. (You don't have to enter all three; you can specify only one or two of these values. However, you cannot enter an amount greater than 366 in the Days box.)

4. Click the **Calculate** button to calculate the start date, difference, or end date.

   You can click the **Clear Fields** button to clear all of the fields and start again.

5. Click the **Close** button to close the Date Calculator form and return to the Ancestry Family Tree view.

Determining the Soundex code for a name

The Soundex index system was used to index the surnames of heads of household listed in the 1880, 1900, 1910, and 1920 federal censuses. (All members of each household are listed in the indexes under the head of household.) This index system assigned a code to each surname based on the consonant sounds in the name. If you are searching for an individual in one of these censuses, you might want to convert the person's name to its Soundex code so that you can use the Soundex index to locate him or her in the census.

To use the Soundex Code Calculator

1. In the **Tools** menu, click **Calculators**.

2. Click **Soundex** on the submenu.

Relationship Examiner...	
Calculators ▶	Date Calculator...
Edit Source List...	Soundex...
Edit Repository List...	

The **Soundex Code Calculator** form will be displayed.

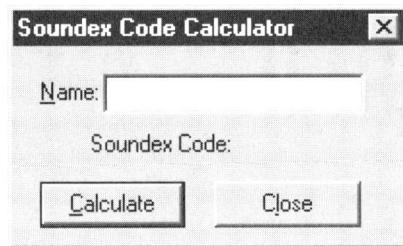

| Soundex Code Calculator ☒ |
| Name: [   ] |
| Soundex Code: |
| [Calculate] [Close] |

3. Enter the surname in the **Name** box and then click the **Calculate** button.

   The Soundex code will be displayed as shown below.

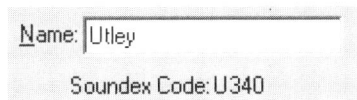

   Name: Utley

   Soundex Code: U340

4. Click the **Close** button to close the Soundex Code Calculator form and return to the Ancestry Family Tree view.

CHAPTER 5

Working with Marriages

A long with individual records, marriage records are the primary building blocks of an Ancestry Family Tree family database. For every mother and father represented in a family database, there is a marriage record (even if the two were never actually married); every marriage record is identified by a Marriage Record Identification Number (MRIN).

Ancestry Family Tree regards a marriage much as it does an individual: as an independent entity. Therefore, you can define notes, sources, and events for a marriage much as you can for an individual.

In this chapter

• Adding a marriage to a database
• Entering information for a marriage
• Editing a marriage
• Deleting a marriage from a database

Adding a marriage to a database

You must be in the **Family** view to work with marriage records. There are two ways to create a marriage:

- You can create a marriage by adding a spouse to an existing individual.

- You can create a marriage by adding a father and a mother to an individual.

Adding a spouse to an individual

You can create a marriage by adding a spouse to an existing individual. You can add the spouse as a new individual (a person who is not currently in the database); or, if the spouse is already in the database, you can find that individual and add him or her as the spouse. A marriage record will be created automatically for the two individuals.

To add a spouse to an individual

1. Click the **Family** tab to go to the **Family** view.

2. Make one of the individuals for whom you are creating the marriage the primary individual (or "root person"). In the Family view, the primary individual appears in the top left position.

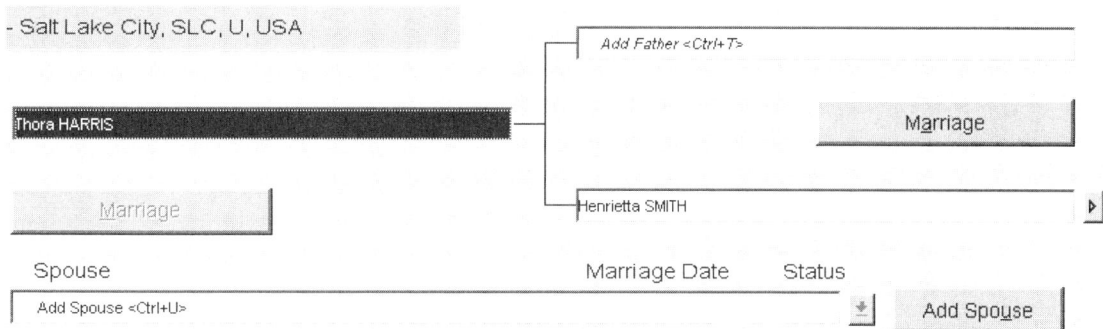

   Tip: Perhaps the easiest way to make the individual the primary individual in the Family view is to highlight him or her in the Name List view and then go to the Family view. The person you select in the Name List view will be the primary individual in the Family view. You can also highlight the individual in the Pedigree view and then go to the Family view to achieve the same result.

3. Do one of the following:

   - Click the **Add Spouse** button in the **Family** view, or

   - in the **Data** menu, click **Add Spouse**.

   The **Add Spouse** form will be displayed. This form will allow you to add the spouse as a new individual (if the spouse is not currently in the database); or you can search for an existing person in the database and add him or her as a spouse. (The **LDS Ordinances** section of the form will appear only if Use LDS Data is selected on the General page of the Preferences form.)

To add the spouse as a new individual

To learn how to add the spouse as a new individual, refer to "Adding an individual to the database" in chapter 4, Working with Individuals in a Database. This chapter describes the use of the Add form.

To search for and add an existing individual as the spouse

1. On the **Add Spouse** form, click the **Search for Existing Spouse** button.

   The **Find Spouse** form will be displayed.

2. Do one of the following:

- If you know the RIN of the individual you are searching for, enter it in the RIN box and then click the **OK** button.

  Both the Find Spouse and Add Spouse forms will close immediately and the view will return to the **Family** view. The individual you selected will be saved as the spouse of the primary individual.

- To search for the individual, click the **Browse List** button on the **Find Spouse** form.

  The **Search for Spouse** form will be displayed. This form allows you to search a list of all the individuals in the database. You can also use search filters to narrow your search for an individual by relationship or by information that exists for that individual. Note that, when you highlight an individual on the list, vital information for that individual is displayed on the right side of the form.

```
Search for Spouse for Thora HARRIS                                    [X]

12                                      ┌─Sort─────────────────────────┐
                                        │      ⦿ RIN        ○ Alpha     │
   1   EDISON, James Redd      b.1866   ├─Thora HARRIS─────────────────┤
   2   LANDERS, Emma Valentina b.1868   │   Sex: F         AFN:         │
   3   EDISON, Alma Robert     m.1860   │ ID No:                        │
   4   HUSE, Anne Jewett       m.1860   │                               │
   5   EDISON, Jonathan Anton  b.1868   │   Birth:                      │
   6   EDWARDS, Echo           b.1887   │     Alt:                      │
   7   BRADLEY, Jonathan                │                               │
   8   EDWARDS, Edwina                  │   Death:      Salt Lake City,SLC,Utah,USA
   9   EDISON, Richard Albertus b.1889  │   Burial:                     │
  10   ANDREWS, Jeremiah                │                               │
  11   MORTON, Amelia                   │   Baptism:                    │
  12   HARRIS, Thora                    │    Endow:                     │
  13   EDISON, Ansel                    │  Seal Par:                    │
  14   SMITH, Henrietta        b.1900   │                               │
  15   BERGER, Harrison                 │   Father:            B:        │
  17   EDISON, Emma                     │   Mother: Henrietta SMITH  B: 10 Jul 1900
  18   LANDERS, Emma Valentina m.1886   │   Spouse:            M:        │
                                        │   Spouse:            M:        │
                                        └───────────────────────────────┘
                                                        Advanced >>

   OK      Edit...    Notes...    Delete    Media...    Cancel    Help...
```

3. Use the option buttons under **Sort** to determine how individuals are listed: click **RIN** to list individuals in order by RIN, or click **Alpha** to list individuals alphabetically.

4. Do one of the following:

- Use the scroll bar at the right of the list to locate the individual you are searching for and then highlight the individual.

  Click the **OK** button to select the individual.

Both the Find Spouse and Add Spouse forms will close immediately and the view will return to the **Family** view. The individual you selected will be saved as the spouse of the primary individual.

- To search for the individual using database filters, click the **Advanced >>** button.

The **Search for Spouse** form is expanded to include a number of filtered search controls. To learn how to perform a filtered search, refer to "Searching for individuals using filters" in chapter 9, Searching the Database.

To save the individual as a spouse

- If you add the spouse as a new individual using the **Add Spouse** form, clicking the **Save** button on the Add Spouse form will save the spouse as a new individual in the database and as the spouse of the primary person.

- If you add an existing individual as the spouse, clicking the **OK** button on the **Find Spouse** form or the **Search for Spouse** form will save the individual as the spouse of the primary person.

Adding a father and mother to an individual

You can create a marriage by adding a father and a mother to an individual. You can add the father or mother as a new individual; or, if the father or mother is already in the database, you can find that individual and add him or her as the father or mother. A marriage record will be created automatically for the father and mother.

To add a father or mother to an individual

1. In the **Pedigree** view or the **Family** view, highlight the individual for whom you want to add a mother and/or father.

2. In the **Data** menu, click **Add Father** or **Add Mother**.

The **Add Individual** form will be displayed.

3. To learn how to enter data for the individual, refer to "Adding an individual to the database" in chapter 4, Working with Individuals in a Database. This chapter describes the use of the Add form.

Entering information for a marriage

After you have added a marriage to the database, you can enter notes, sources, and events associated with the marriage. If you checked the Use LDS Data box on the General page of the Preferences form, you can also enter LDS sealing data.

Entering event information for the marriage

To enter event information for the marriage

1. In the **Family** view, make one of the married individuals the primary person.

2. Do one of the following:

- Click the **Marriage** button on the **Family** view, or

* in the **Data** menu, click **Edit Primary Marriage**.

The **Marriage** form will be displayed. This form allows you to enter notes, sources, and event information associated with the marriage.

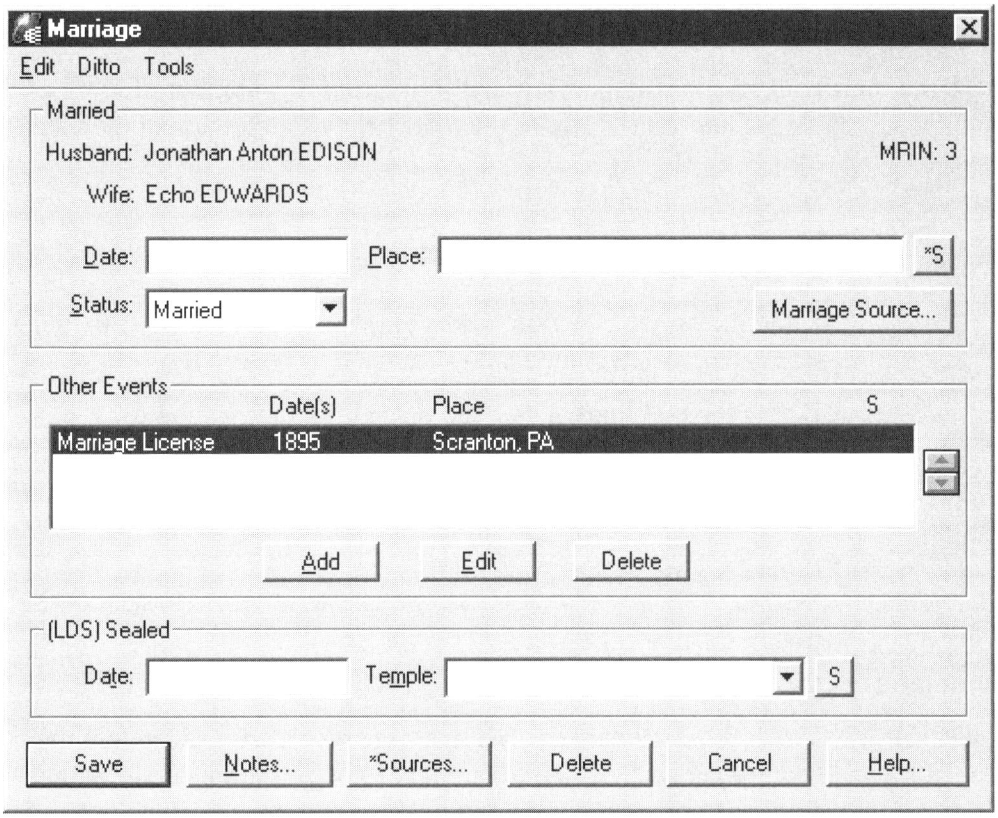

3. The **Date** box allows you to enter the date of the marriage.

   Type the date of the marriage in the box.

   * The preferred format for date entry is DD/MMM/YYYY (for example, 12 Aug 1956).

   * You may enter the date in numeric form (for example, 1/30/1900 or 1-30-1900) or with the month spelled out.

   * You must enter four digits for the year.

   * You may enter a partial date (for example, June 1946 or just 1946).

   Note: If a mother and father were never married, you can enter "Not married" in the date box instead of a date.

4. You can use the **Place** box to indicate where the marriage took place.

   Enter up to 120 characters of place information in the box.

   Note: When you click in the Place box, a drop-menu button ⊞ will appear to the right of the box. You can click the button to see a list of places already in the database, then click the place you want to enter (if it appears in the list) to insert it in the box.

5. Use the **Status** box to specify the status of the marriage. The options are *Married, Divorced,* and *Not Married.*

   Click the arrow button to the right of the box and select the status from the list.

Using menu commands

The **Edit**, **Ditto**, and **Tools** menus on the Marriage form provide a number of tools to help you enter and edit marriage data. Refer to the table below to learn about the menu commands.

Edit menu

Menu command	Description
Undo	Undo the previous action. For example, if you inadvertently delete text, you can select the Undo command to restore it.
Cut	Delete the highlighted text and place it on the clipboard.
Copy	Copy the highlighted text to the clipboard.
Paste	Paste cut or copied text from the clipboard.
Delete	Delete the highlighted text.

Ditto menu

Menu command	Description
Ditto Last Record	Pastes the data from the last marriage record you saved into the corresponding field. For example, if you place the cursor in the Date box and then click Ditto Last Record, the marriage date from the previous marriage record will be inserted into the Date box.
Ditto Down	Pastes the data from a previous field on the form into a corresponding type of field. For example, if you place the cursor in the (LDS) Sealed Date box and then click Ditto Down, the date in the Married Date box will be inserted into the (LDS) Sealed Date box.

Tools menu

Menu command	Description
Character Map	Opens the standard Windows character map, which lets you enter extended characters (those other than the standard alphanumeric characters used in English, including characters with diacritical marks).
Date Calculator	Opens the Date Calculator form. Refer to chapter 4, Working With Individuals in a Database, to learn how to use the date calculator.

To use the character map

1. On the **Tools** menu of the **Notes** form, click **Character Map**.

The **Character Map** form will be displayed.

2. Click the character you want to place in the notes; click the **Select** button; and then click the **Copy** button.

3. On the **Notes** form, place the cursor at the point where you want the character to be inserted.

4. On the **Edit** menu of the **Notes** form, click **Paste**.

   The character is pasted into the Notes form.

   Note: Before you select and copy other characters from the Character Map form, clear the previously selected character from the **Characters to copy** box by highlighting it and pressing the DEL key on your keyboard.

5. Click the **Close** button to close the Character Map form.

Entering LDS sealing data

If you checked the Use LDS Data box on the General page of the Preferences form, you can enter LDS sealing data for a marriage.

To enter LDS sealing data

1. On the **Marriage** form, under **(LDS) Sealed**, enter the date of the sealing in the **Date** box.

2. The **Temple** box lets you indicate the LDS temple in which the sealing was performed, if known.

   Click the arrow button to the right of the box and select the temple in the list.

Defining sources and source citations for the marriage

You can define sources and source citations to document the date and place of the marriage. You can also define sources and source citations to document the marriage itself; you might want to do this if you don't know the date or place of the marriage. If you checked the Use LDS Data box on the General page of the Preferences form, you can also enter sources and source citations for the LDS sealing.

To define sources and source citations for the marriage

1. On the **Marriage** form, do one of the following:

   - To define sources and source citations for the date and place of the marriage, click the $\boxed{S}$ button to the right of the **Place** box.

     The **Source Citation for Marriage** form will be displayed.

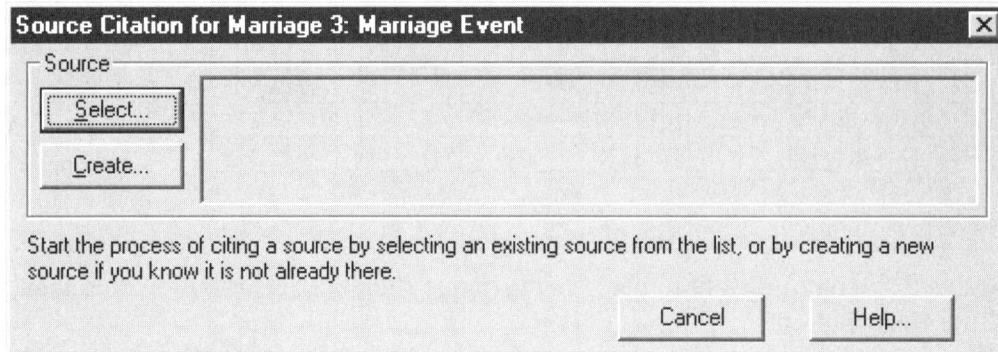

   Source Citation for Marriage 3: Marriage Event ☒

   ┌─ Source ─────────────────────────────────────┐

   $\boxed{\text{Select...}}$

   $\boxed{\text{Create...}}$

   Start the process of citing a source by selecting an existing source from the list, or by creating a new source if you know it is not already there.

   $\boxed{\text{Cancel}}$ $\boxed{\text{Help...}}$

   - To define sources and source citations for the marriage itself, click the **Marriage Source** button.

     The **Source Citation for Marriage** form will be displayed.

   - To define sources and source citations for the LDS sealing, click the $\boxed{S}$ button to the right of the **Temple** box.

     The **Source Citation for Marriage** form will be displayed.

2. To learn how to define sources and source citations, refer to chapter 7, Working with Sources and Source Citations.

Entering additional event information for the marriage

You can select additional events related to the marriage for which you want to enter date and place data, edit existing event types, and create new types of events.

To enter additional events for the marriage

1. On the **Marriage** form, click the **Add** button.

   The **Select Event for Marriage** form will be displayed. It contains a list of event types.

Select Event for Marriage of Jonathan Anton EDISON ... ☒

Annulment
Census
Divorce
Divorce Filing
Engagement
Marriage Contract
Marriage License
Marriage Notice
Marriage Settlement
Miscarriage
Mission
Separation

Select
Close
Help...

Add Type...   Edit Type...   Del Type

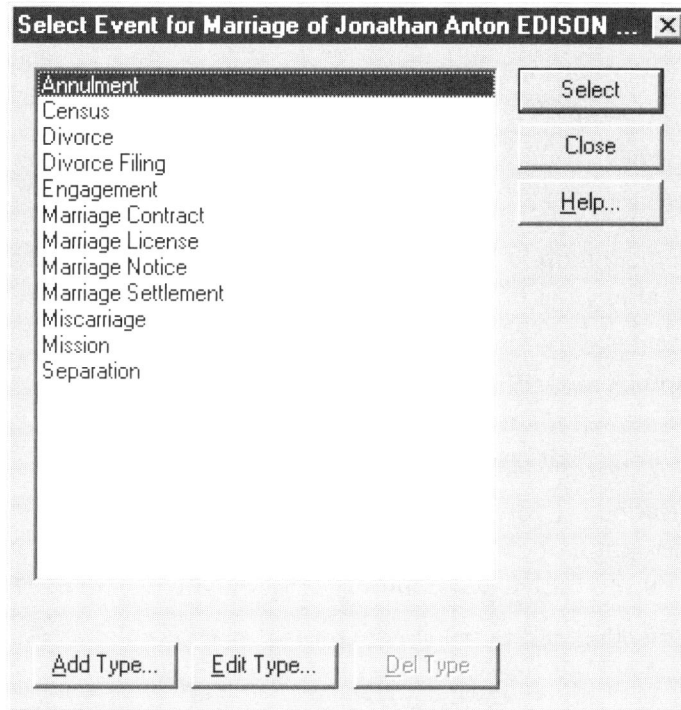

2. In the list of event types, highlight the type of event you want to select and then click the **Select** button.

A marriage event form similar to the one shown below will be displayed.

Annulment - Marriage of Jonathan Anton EDISON and... ☒

Date:
Place:
Description:

Source...   ☐ Event is Confidential

OK   Cancel   Help...

Note: The information you enter in this form can appear in book reports in the form of a sentence that is constructed automatically. For example, for the marriage event titled "Annulment," the default construction of the book report sentence (assuming the individual is a male) is "They had the marriage annulled [date] in [place]." On the book report the date and place are filled in for you with the information you enter in this form—for example, "They had the marriage annulled 17 Nov 1895 in Scranton, Pennsylvania."

3. In the **Date** and **Place** boxes, enter the date and place of the event (if known).

- The preferred format for date entry is DD/MMM/YYYY (for example, 12 Aug 1956).

- You can enter the date in numeric form (for example, 1/30/1900 or 1-30-1900) or with the month spelled out.

- You must enter four digits for the year.

- You may enter a partial date (for example, June 1946 or just 1946).

Note: When you click in the Place box, a drop-menu button ![button] will appear to the right of the box. You can click the button to see a list of places already in the database and then click the place you want to enter (if it appears in the list) to insert it in the box.

4. Clicking the **Source** button allows you to define a source or source citation for the event. Refer to chapter 7, Working with Sources and Source Citations, to learn how to define and select sources and source citations.

5. Check the **Event Is Confidential** box if you want to designate the event as confidential. This gives you the option of excluding the event (and all other confidential events) from reports and GEDCOM export files when you generate them.

6. Repeat steps 1–5 above to create other additional events for the marriage.

Note: Refer to chapter 4, Working with Individuals in a Database, to learn how to add or edit types of events.

To edit existing marriage events

1. On the **Marriage** form, highlight the event you want to edit in the **Other Events** list and then click the **Edit** button.

   An event form containing the data for the event will be displayed.

2. Refer to steps 3–5 in "To enter additional events for the marriage," above, to edit the data in the form.

To delete existing marriage events

1. On the **Marriage** form, highlight the event you want to delete in the **Other Events** list and then click the **Delete** button.

   A warning dialog box similar to the one shown below will be displayed.

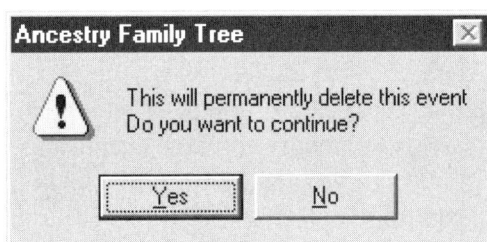

2. Click the **Yes** button to delete the event (or the **No** button to retain the event).

Creating notes for the marriage

Ancestry Family Tree allows you to enter everything you know about a marriage in the form of text *notes;* you can enter up to 60KB of information for each marriage. You might enter biographical information such as anecdotes, stories, journal entries, and quotes by the married individuals. You should also use the notes to record all the facts contained in all the sources you have for the marriage—for example, marriage announcement, marriage license, etc.

To create notes for a marriage

On the **Marriage** form, click the **Notes** button.

The **Notes for Marriage** form will be displayed. Refer to chapter 6, Working with Notes, to learn how to create notes for a marriage.

Editing a marriage

You can edit the information in an existing marriage record whenever you need to.

To edit a marriage record

1. In the **Family** view, place one of the married individuals in the primary position.

2. The marriage you edit will be for the *primary spouse*—the spouse whose name currently appears in the **Spouse** (or **Spouses** if there are multiple spouses) box in the Family view. If there are multiple spouses for the primary individual and you want to edit the marriage of a spouse who is not in the primary spouse position, click the arrow button to the right of the **Spouses** box and then highlight the spouse whose marriage to the primary individual you want to edit.

Spouses (2)	Wife of Grandson	Marriage Date	Status
Emma Valentina LANDERS		15 Dec 1886	⬇
Emma Valentina LANDERS		15 Dec 1886	
Edwina EDWARDS		11 Nov 1901	

3. Do one of the following:

   - In the **Data** menu, click **Edit Primary Marriage**, or

   - click the **Marriage** button. [Marriage]

   The **Marriage** form will be displayed.

4. Refer to the steps in "Entering information for a marriage," above, to learn how to use the Marriage form.

Deleting a marriage from a database

You can delete a marriage record from a database at any time.

To delete a marriage from the database

1. Open the Marriage record you want to delete as described in steps 1–3 in "Editing a marriage," above.

2. On the **Marriage** form, click the **Delete** button at the bottom of the form.

A warning dialog box similar to the one shown below will be displayed.

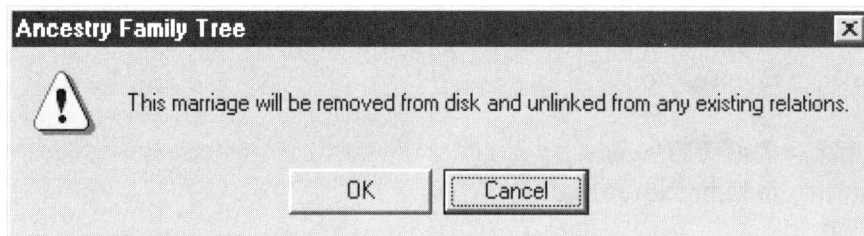

```
┌─────────────────────────────────────────────────────────────┐
│ Ancestry Family Tree                                    [x]  │
├─────────────────────────────────────────────────────────────┤
│                                                               │
│    ⚠     This marriage will be removed from disk and          │
│          unlinked from any existing relations.                │
│                                                               │
│              ┌────────┐    ┌────────────┐                     │
│              │   OK   │    │   Cancel   │                     │
│              └────────┘    └────────────┘                     │
└─────────────────────────────────────────────────────────────┘
```

3. Click the **OK** button to delete the marriage (or click the **Cancel** button to cancel the deletion).

   The record of the marriage will be permanently removed from the database. (The records of the married individuals will still exist.)

CHAPTER 6

Working with Notes

Ancestry Family Tree allows you to enter everything you know about an individual or a marriage in the form of text notes; you can enter up to 60KB of information for each person or marriage. You might enter biographical information such as anecdotes, stories, journal entries, and quotes by the individual. You should also use the notes to record all the facts contained in all the sources you have for the person—for example, passenger lists, census reports, deeds, city directory entries, wills, obituaries, etc.

You don't have to enter the sources of your information in the notes because sources are entered separately as source records. (Refer to chapter 7, Working with Sources and Source Citations, to learn how to define source records.)

In this chapter

• Creating notes for an individual
• Editing notes for an individual
• Working with note tags

Creating notes for an individual

You can group the notes for an individual using any number of predefined *tags* as you enter them. Using tags allows you to instantly view the portions of the notes under a selected tag only—rather than having to scroll through all of the notes looking for the part you want. However, you don't have to use tags. You can enter all of the notes for an individual without assigning tags to them, or you can enter some notes with tags and some without tags.

Five tags exist for the individual by default: Biography, Birth, Christening, Death, and Burial. You can add other tags that you create yourself. (Refer to "Working with note tags," below, to learn how to create tags.)

If you need to enter extended characters (those other than the standard alphanumeric characters used in English), such as those with diacritical marks, the character map provides a number of less commonly used characters that you can insert in the notes. And, if certain information in notes seems sensitive or is too private to be shared with others, you can define it to be "confidential." Then, when exporting data to share with others or when creating reports, you can choose to exclude the notes defined as confidential.

To enter notes for an individual

1. On the **Add Individual** or **Edit Individual** form, click the **Notes** button.

    The **Notes Selector** form will be displayed.

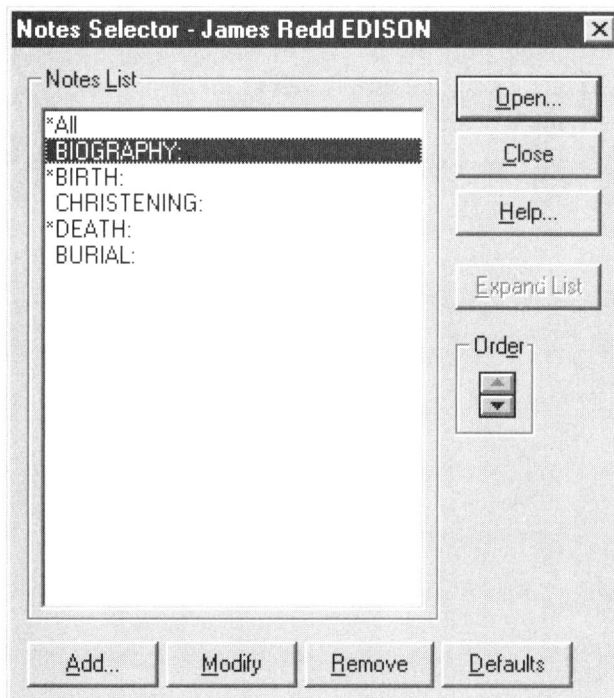

Note: The tags and the notes entered with them will appear in the individual's notes in the order in which they are arranged on the Notes List. If you want to rearrange the order of the tags, highlight the tag in the list and then click the up or down arrows under **Order**.

2. Do one of the following:

   • If you don't want to use tags to group the notes you are entering, highlight *All* in the **Notes List** and then click the **Open** button.

   • If you want to use a tag, highlight the tag that applies to the information you want to enter and then click the **Open** button.

3. A **Notes** form similar to the one shown below will be displayed. (If you selected a tag in the Notes List, the Notes form title displays the name of that tag.) The Notes form allows you to enter text regarding the tag you selected (or any topic if you are not using a tag).

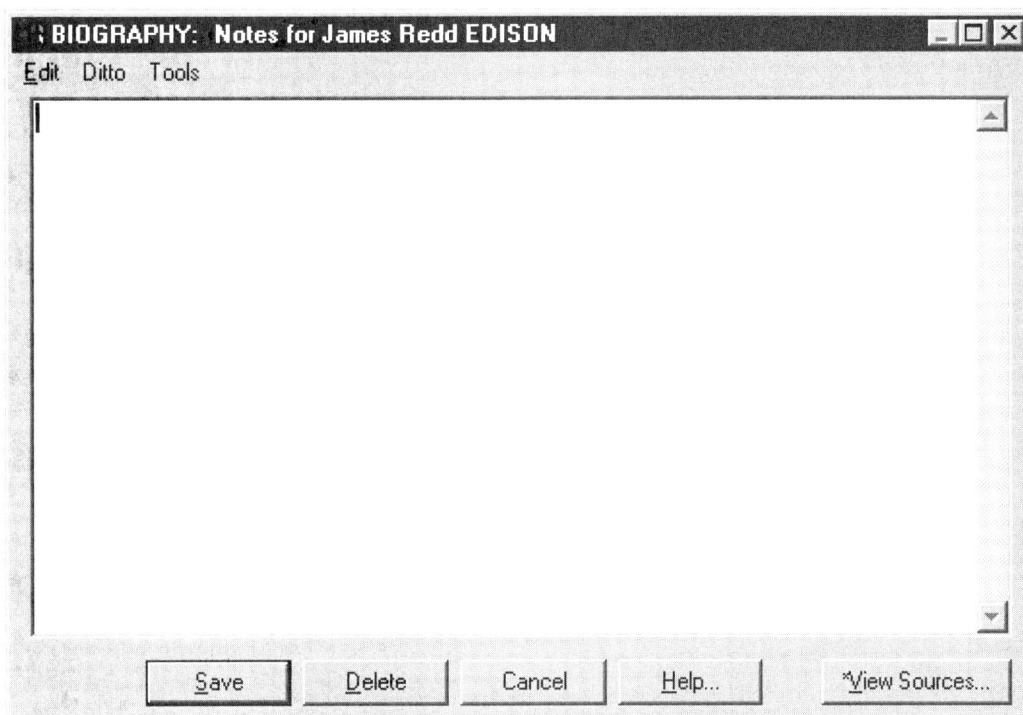

4. Enter the notes text.

5. Click the **Save** button to save the Notes and return to the previous form.

Using menu commands

The **Edit, Ditto**, and **Tools** menus on the Notes form provide a number of tools to help you enter and edit notes text. Refer to the table below to learn about the menu commands.

Edit menu

Menu command	Description
Undo	Undo the previous action. For example, if you inadvertently delete text, you can select the Undo command to restore it.

Menu command	Description
Cut	Delete the highlighted text and place it on the clipboard.
Copy	Copy the highlighted text to the clipboard.
Paste	Paste cut or copied text from the clipboard.
Delete	Delete the highlighted text.

Ditto menu

Menu command	Description
Ditto Primary	Pastes the notes from the primary individual into the current notes.
Ditto Last Record	Pastes the notes from the last record you saved (individual or marriage) into the current notes.
Ditto Father	Pastes the notes from the current individual's father into the individual's notes.
Ditto Mother	Pastes the notes from the current individual's mother into the individual's notes.
Ditto Older Sibling	Pastes the notes from the current individual's next older sibling into the individual's notes. (Both individuals must have birth dates.)

Tools menu

Menu command	Description
Character Map	Opens the standard Windows character map, which lets you enter extended characters (those other than the standard alphanumeric characters used in English, including characters with diacritical marks).

To use the character map

1. On the **Tools** menu of the **Notes** form, click **Character Map**.

   The **Character Map** form will be displayed.

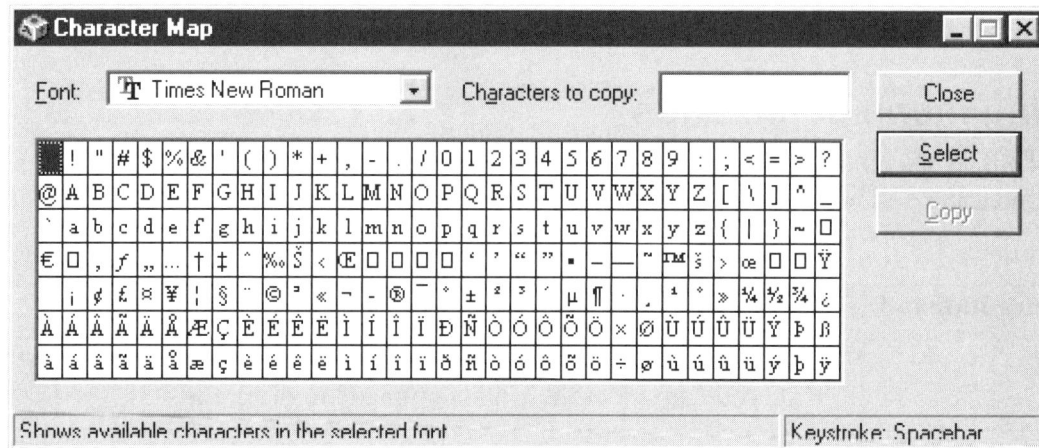

2. Click the character you want to place in the notes; click the **Select** button; and then click the **Copy** button.

3. On the **Notes** form, place the cursor at the point where you want the character to be inserted.

4. On the **Edit** menu of the **Notes** form, click **Paste**.

   The character is pasted into the Notes form.

   Note: Before you select and copy other characters from the Character Map form, clear the previously selected character from the **Characters to copy** box by highlighting it and pressing the DEL key on your keyboard.

5. Click the **Close** button to close the Character Map form.

To make notes confidential

1. Press Enter to create a blank line at the beginning of a note that you want to be confidential.

2. Enter a tilde (~) at the beginning of the first line of confidential note text.

3. Press Enter to create a blank line at the end of the confidential note text.

   Any portion of the note text preceded with a tilde and with a blank line before and after can be excluded from a GEDCOM export or from a report, if you so choose.

To view source citations for the individual

1. On the **Notes** form, click the **View Sources** button.

   Note: If there are source citations for the individual, the View Sources button will contain an asterisk.

   The **View Sources** form will be displayed.

```
View Sources for James Redd EDISON                              [X]

BIRTH:                                                          [▲]

1. James Redd Edison baptism, 3 Aug 1866, Baltimore Episcopal Church, p. 10, Marriott Library at
University of Utah, Salt Lake City, UT.

DEATH:

2. James Redd Edison death certificate, 17 Sep 1912. Photocopy of original death certificate.


                                                               [▼]

   << Previous              [  Close  ]               Next >>
```

The View Sources form displays all of the source citations for the events defined for the individual. Having all the source citations displayed allows you to find the information cited so that you can enter it in the individual's notes.

2. Click the **Close** button to return to the Notes form.

Editing notes for an individual

You can edit the notes for an individual at any time.

To edit notes for an individual

1. On the **Add Individual** or **Edit Individual** form, click the **Notes** button.

   The **Notes Selector** form will be displayed.

2. Do one of the following:

   - If you have used tags with the individual's notes, you can highlight one of the tags in the Notes List to view the notes associated with that tag, or

   - if you haven't used tags or you want to view all of the notes (including all tagged notes), highlight *All* in the Notes List.

3. Click the **Open** button.

   A form containing the notes for the individual will be displayed.

```
┌─────────────────────────────────────────────────────────────────┐
│ DEATH:  Notes for James Redd EDISON              _│□│✕│          │
├─────────────────────────────────────────────────────────────────┤
│ Edit  Ditto  Tools                                                │
│ ┌───────────────────────────────────────────────────────────┬─┐ │
│ │His dying words were Don't sell that scoundrel Frank Baggs one acre│▲│ │
│ │of my land!"                                               │ │ │
│ │                                                           │ │ │
│ │                                                           │ │ │
│ │                                                           │ │ │
│ │                                                           │ │ │
│ │                                                           │ │ │
│ │                                                           │ │ │
│ │                                                           │ │ │
│ │                                                           │ │ │
│ │                                                           │▼│ │
│ └───────────────────────────────────────────────────────────┴─┘ │
│    ┌────────┐ ┌────────┐ ┌────────┐ ┌────────┐ ┌──────────────┐ │
│    │  Save  │ │ Delete │ │ Cancel │ │ Help...│ │*View Sources.│ │
│    └────────┘ └────────┘ └────────┘ └────────┘ └──────────────┘ │
└─────────────────────────────────────────────────────────────────┘
```

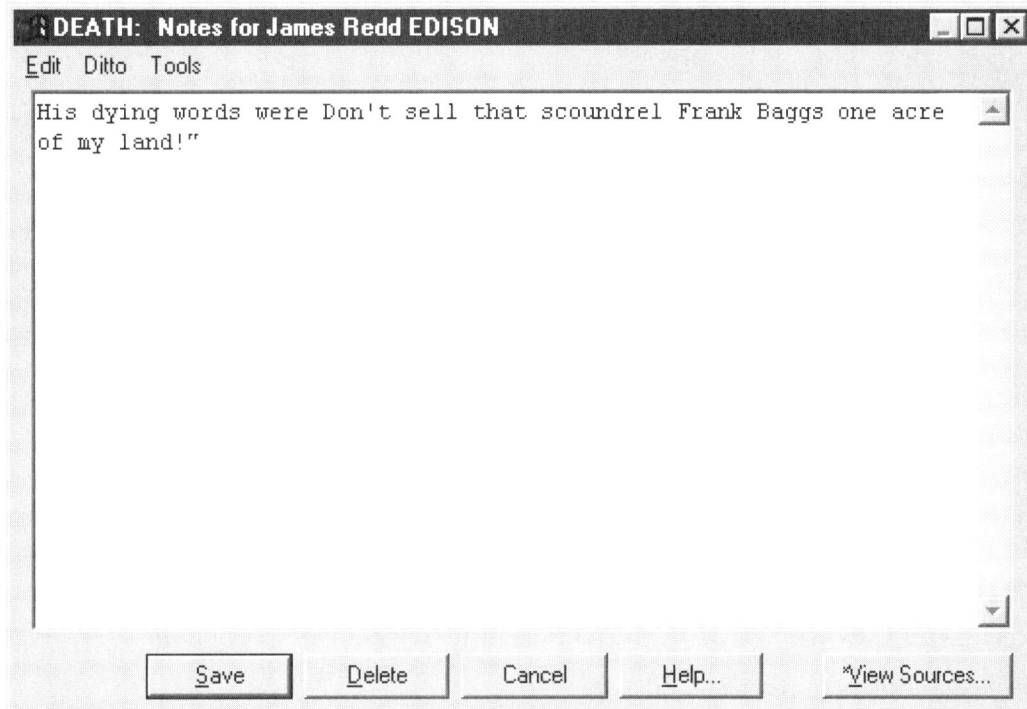

4. Edit the notes as necessary using the keyboard and the Note form menu commands described above.

Working with note tags

You can group the notes for an individual using any number of predefined *tags* as you enter them. You can also create new note tags, modify existing tags, and delete tags.

Creating new tags

You can create new tags that can be used with notes for any individual in the database. You can also add tags that are *individual-specific,* meaning they are unique to the notes for one individual in the database. You might want to do this if the topic represented by the tag is unlikely to be necessary for other individuals in the database. By creating an individual-specific tag, you can view it in the Notes Selector form for the individual and select it to go directly to that part of the individual's notes.

To create a new tag that can be used for any individual in the database

1. On the **Add Individual** or **Edit Individual** form, click the **Notes** button.

    The **Notes Selector** form will be displayed.

2. Click the **Add** button.

    The **Add Note Tag** form will be displayed.

Add Note Tag   ☒

New Tag:

[   ]

[OK   ]   [Cancel]

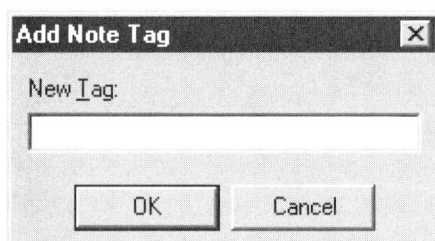

3. Enter the tag in the **New Tag** box. The tag must be a single word; the recommended format is all-uppercase letters followed by a colon. For example, a tag to be used for notes regarding military service might be MILITARY.

4. Click the **OK** button to close the Add Note Tag form and return to the Notes Selector form.

    The new tag is added to the Notes List on the Notes Selector form. You can now select it for use with the notes for any individual in the database.

To create an individual-specific tag

1. On the **Add Individual** or **Edit Individual** form, click the **Notes** button.

    The **Notes Selector** form will be displayed.

2. Highlight *All* in the Notes List and then click the **Open** button.

    A **Notes** form containing the notes for the individual will be displayed.

3. Enter the tag while observing the following conditions:

    - The tag must be preceded by a blank line,

    - the tag must be a single word, and

    - the recommended format is all-uppercase letters followed by a colon.

    You can begin entering the notes immediately afterward. For example, an individual-specific tag and notes regarding military service might begin as follows:

    MILITARY: He was inducted in 1917. . . .

4. Click the **Save** button to save the notes and return to the Notes Selector form.

    The new tag is added to the Notes List. However, it is grayed-out to indicate that it is an individual-specific tag.

    Note: To delete an individual-specific tag, you must open the tagged notes, delete the notes text, and then save the Notes form. The tag will be removed from the Notes List on the Notes Selector form.

Modifying existing tags

You can modify any existing tag that is not individual-specific, changing it to any word you want. The modified form of the tag will be available for any individual in the database; if the tag you modify is already present in other individuals' notes, it will become an individual-specific tag for each of those individuals.

For example, suppose you change the tag CHRISTENING to BLESSING for one individual. The tag BLESSING will now be available for any individual in the database. In the notes for any other individual that had already used the tag CHRISTENING, CHRISTENING will be changed to an individual-specific tag.

To modify an existing tag

1. On the **Add Individual** or **Edit Individual** form, click the **Notes** button.

   The **Notes Selector** form will be displayed.

2. In the Notes List, highlight the tag you want to modify and then click the **Modify** button. (It cannot be an individual-specific tag.)

   The **Modify Note Tag** form will be displayed.

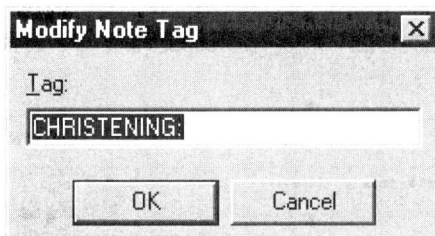

3. Modify the tag as necessary. (The recommended format is all-uppercase letters followed by a colon.)

4. Click the **OK** button to save the modified tag and return to the Notes Selector form.

   The modified tag is added to the Notes List on the Notes Selector form and is available for use with the notes for any individual in the database.

Deleting tags

You can delete existing tags that are not individual-specific. If you do, the tag will no longer be available for any individual in the database. If the tag you delete is already present in other individuals' notes, it will become an individual-specific tag for each of those individuals.

To delete a tag

1. On the **Add Individual** or **Edit Individual** form, click the **Notes** button.

   The **Notes Selector** form will be displayed.

2. In the Notes List, highlight the tag you want to delete and then click the **Remove** button. (An individual-specific tag cannot be deleted.)

   A warning dialog box similar to the one shown below will be displayed.

```
┌─────────────────────────────────────────────────┐
│ Ancestry Family Tree                         [X] │
├─────────────────────────────────────────────────┤
│                                                  │
│  CHRISTENING:                                    │
│                                                  │
│  This will remove the tag from the permanent list.│
│  Do you want to continue?                        │
│                                                  │
│       ┌──────────────┐    ┌──────────────┐       │
│       │     OK       │    │    Cancel    │       │
│       └──────────────┘    └──────────────┘       │
│                                                  │
└─────────────────────────────────────────────────┘
```

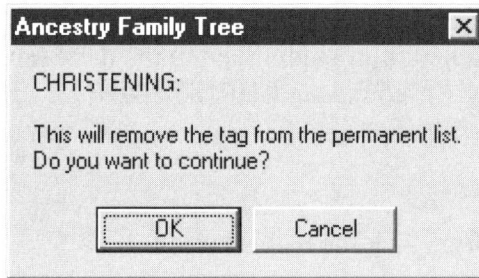

3. Click the **OK** button to delete the tag and return to the Notes Selector list.

CHAPTER 7

Working with Sources and Source Citations

A source is the origin of the information you enter in a family database—a birth certificate or published family history, for example. Thorough researchers cite the sources of their information when entering specific information in their records. In Ancestry Family Tree, you create a record for each source of information that you include in a database. Then, for the individual's name and for each event (birth, marriage, death, burial, and one or more additional events), you can create one or more source citations that refer to a source.

In this chapter

- Entering data for the source
- Editing a source record
- Selecting an existing source
- Creating a source citation
- Editing a source citation
- Deleting a source citation
- Attaching a media item to a source or source citation

Creating a source

Before you can cite a source as the "source" of your information, you must create a record for it in the database. There are two ways to create a new source record:

- Enter all of the information for the source using the Define Source form and save the record, or

- copy an existing source record and use it as the basis for the new source record.

To enter a new source

Do one of the following:

- In the **Tools** menu, click **Edit Source List**.

  The **Edit Source List** form will be displayed.

Click the **Add** button.

The **Define Source** form will be displayed. Refer to "Entering data for the source," below, to learn how to enter data using the Define Source form.

- On the **Add Individual** or **Edit Individual** form or the **Marriage** form, click the source citation button ⬚ˢ adjacent to the name or the event for which you want to create a citation, or

- on the **Additional Event** form (opened from the Additional Individual Information form), click the **Source** button.

A **Source Citation** form similar to the one shown below will be displayed.

Click the **Create** button.

The **Define Source** form will be displayed. Refer to "Entering data for the source," below, to learn how to enter data using the Define Source form.

To copy an existing source record

1. In the **Tools** menu, click **Edit Source List**.

   The **Edit Source List** form will be displayed. It lists all of the source records for the database that is currently open.

2. If you want to view a list of sources of a particular type, highlight the type in the **Sources to View** box. (A source's type is assigned on the Define Source form.)

3. In the **Short Title** list, highlight the source you want to copy and then click the **Duplicate** button.

   The **Define Source** form will be displayed.

4. Refer to "Entering data for the source," below, to learn how to use the Define Source form to modify the existing data and save the record as a new source.

Entering data for the source

The Define Source form lets you enter and save detailed information about a source of information.

To enter data for the source

1. Open the **Define Source** form as described in "Creating a source," above.

```
┌─────────────────────────────────────────────────────────────────────────┐
│ Define Source                                                       [X]   │
│                                                                           │
│  Type: │Unspecified                    ▼│   Qual: │U=Undetermined     ▼│  │
│        Title: ┌─────────────────────┐    ☑ Show on Master Source List     │
│              │                     │    ☐ Title in Italics  ☐ Facts in    │
│  Short Title: ┌─────────────────────┐       (Parentheses)                 │
│              │                     │    Image:                            │
│       Author: ┌─────────────────────┐  ┌─────────────┐  ┌─────────────┐   │
│              │                     │  │             │  │    View     │   │
│              │                     │  │             │  └─────────────┘   │
│  Abbr. Author: ┌─────────────────────┐ │             │  ┌─────────────┐   │
│               │                    │  │             │  │   Attach... │   │
│  Additional Info: ┌──────────────────┐ │             │  └─────────────┘   │
│                  │                 │  │             │  ┌─────────────┐   │
│                  │                 │  └─────────────┘  │   Remove    │   │
│     Publisher/ ┌─────────────────────┐                 └─────────────┘   │
│        Facts: │                     │  ┌─Guidelines──────────────────┐    │
│              │                     │  │ Select a type for this source.│    │
│  Repository: ┌─────────────────────┐  │ If you're not sure, use        │    │
│             │                     │  │ 'Unspecified'. See Help for    │    │
│     Call No: ┌─────────────────────┐  │ more.                          │    │
│             │                     │  │                                │    │
│  Actual Text: ┌─────────────────────────────────────────────┐  [▲]       │
│              │                                             │  [▼]       │
│              │                                             │            │
│    Comments: ┌─────────────────────────────────────────────┐  [▲]       │
│              │                                             │  [▼]       │
│              │                                             │            │
│      Sample  ┌─────────────────────────────────────────────┐  [▲]       │
│    Footnote: │                                             │  [▼]       │
│              └─────────────────────────────────────────────┘            │
│                                                                           │
│          ┌─────────┐      ┌─────────┐      ┌─────────┐                    │
│          │   OK    │      │ Cancel  │      │ Help... │                    │
│          └─────────┘      └─────────┘      └─────────┘                    │
└─────────────────────────────────────────────────────────────────────────┘
```

2. Use the **Type** box to specify the type of source you are referring to. Selecting a source type will allow you to view and select from a list of sources of that type when you want to assign an existing source to another name or event. For example, if you identify a source's type as Birth Registration, you will later be able to cite the same source by selecting it from a list of birth registration sources that you previously defined in the database.

   Click the arrow button to the right of the box and select the source type from the list.

3. The **Qual:** (quality) box allows you to specify the quality ranking of the source—that is, how reliable the source is. If there are multiple sources for one event, quality rankings can help you and others with whom you share your data to decide which sources are the most trustworthy.

   Click the arrow button to the right of the box and select the source's quality ranking from the list.

4. The **Show on Master Source List** box determines whether this source is designated a "master source." A master source might be one that you expect to use repeatedly; or you can use this designation to establish some other grouping of sources—for example, all sources for the state of Alabama. You can then view a list of the master sources on the Select Source form to quickly find one of these sources. (Refer to "Selecting an existing source," below, to learn about the Select Source form.)

Check the box to designate the source as a master source.

5. The Define Source form contains a number of fields that allow you to enter information regarding the source. Refer to the table below to learn about the purpose of each field and then enter the appropriate information in the fields.

Note: As you enter information about a source—title, author, etc.—the **Sample Footnote** box shows you how the footnote for the source will appear on reports.

Field	Description
Title	Enter the full title of the source or document. Because not all sources of information have titles, you will have to enter a description of the source as the title in some cases. The full title entry will appear in primary endnotes the first time the source is cited; subsequent citations of that source will use the short title. • To cause the entire title to be italicized onscreen and on reports, check the **Title in Italics** box. • To italicize only part of the title, type <I> where the italics should begin and </I> where they should end. (Do not check the Title in Italics box.) For example, if citing a title that itself contains a title, you would enter "<I>Subject Index to</I> The Alaskan, <I>1885-1907, a Sitka Newspaper</I>".
Short Title	Enter a short title that is unique to this source (you would not want several instances of "Parish Record" or "Birth Certificate" as short titles); this is the title for the source that will appear in the source list on the Select Source form. The short title may well be the same as the title (unless the title is very long). You should also try to keep the number of entries on the source list as low as possible so that the list will be more manageable. You might find "Utah Birth Certificate" a more efficient entry than "Birth Certificate for . . ." followed by a separate title for each person's birth certificate. The unique citation for each instance of Utah Birth Certificate would then be displayed on the Source Citation form.
Author	If the author is a person, enter the name in this format: first name, middle name, surname; this is the correct format for footnotes. (The surname-first format is for bibliographies.) The author can also be an organization or other entity.
Abbr. Author	Enter the author's surname only (or, if you have more than one author with the same surname, include the given name). This entry will be used in subsequently repeated endnotes for this source on reports.
Additional Info.	Enter such information as the name of a compiler or translator. (This option is available only with Ancestry Family Tree

Field	Description
	databases. Users of .paf files can enter this type of information also but will have to add it to other fields and observe in the Sample Footnote box how it will be formatted. If you enter additional information in the Title field, do not click the Title in Italics box to italicize the contents for the Title field; instead, enclose the title in the marks for italics as described above for the Title field. If you enter additional information in the Publisher/Facts field, type the parentheses for the publishing facts and do not check the Facts in (Parentheses) check box.)
Publisher/Facts	For published sources, enter facts about the publisher in the format Place: Publisher, YYYY—for example, Salt Lake City: Ancestry, 1997. Check the **Facts in (Parentheses)** box to cause Ancestry Family Tree to add parentheses around the publisher/facts information on reports.
Call No.	Enter a repository call number for the source (if there is one).
Actual Text	You can enter actual text from the source if you do not plan to enter actual text when you create source citations that refer to this source. If you will be entering actual text separately for each citation, leave this box blank and enter the actual text on the Source Citation form when you create a source citation.
Comments	Enter any comments regarding the source—for example, "No documentation" or "Only copy known to exist."
Sample Footnote	Displays the footnote for this source as it will appear on reports.

Defining a repository record for the source

Many sources are located in repositories—libraries, government archives, etc. You can create a new record to store details about a repository where the source is located, or you can select an existing repository record.

To create a new repository record and assign it to a source

1. Do one of the following:

   - In the **Tools** menu, click **Edit Repository List**, or

   - on the **Define Source** form, click the **Repository** button.

   The **Select Repository** form will be displayed. It lists all of the repository records for the database that is currently open.

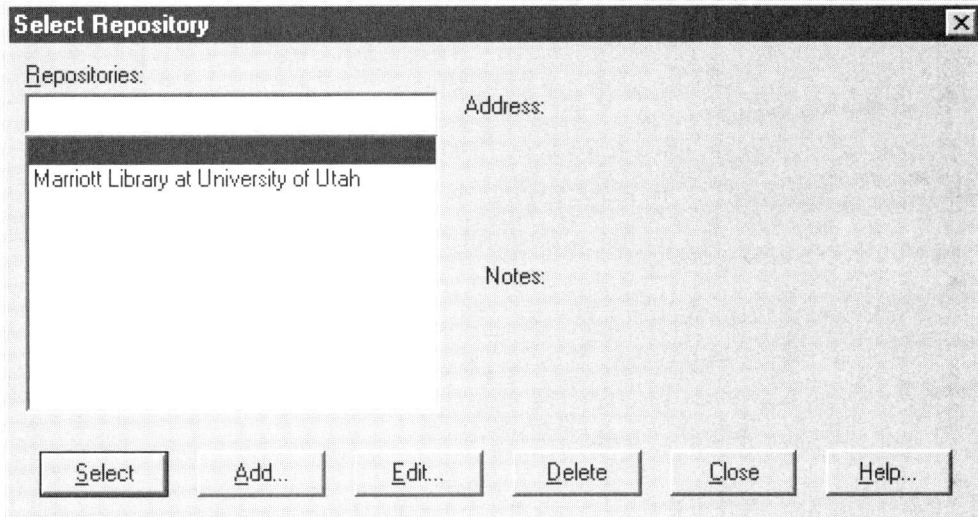

2. Click the **Add** button.

   The **Define Repository** form will be displayed.

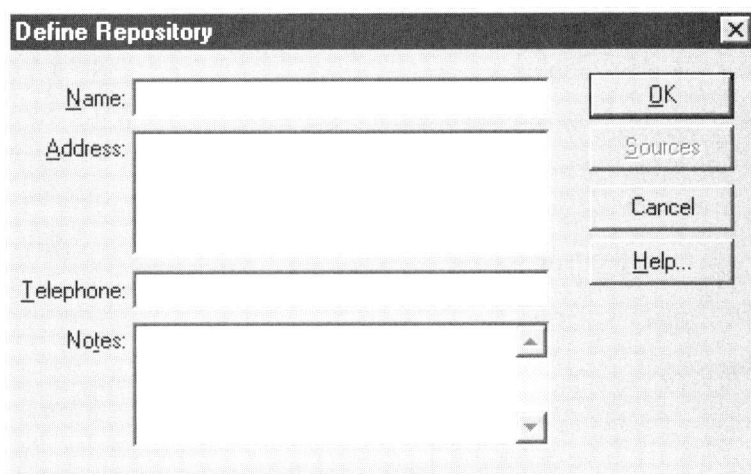

3. In the **Name**, **Address**, and **Telephone** fields, enter the appropriate information for the repository. In the **Notes** field, enter any other information about the repository, such as days and hours of operation, emphasis, etc.

   Note: The **Sources** button allows you to view a list of all the sources in the database to which you have assigned the repository. This list is not available when you are creating a new repository.

4. Click the **OK** button

   The repository record will be saved and the Define Repository form will close.

5. On the **Select Repository** form, highlight the new repository in the **Repositories** list.

6. Click the **Select** button.

   The Select Repository form will close and the name of the repository will be displayed on the Define Source form.

Repository: Marriott Library at University of Utah

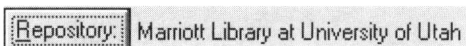

To select an existing repository record

1. On the **Define Source** form, click the **Repository** button.

   The **Select Repository** form will be displayed.

2. On the **Select Repository** form, highlight the repository you want to select in the **Repositories** list.

3. Click the **Select** button.

   The Select Repository form will close and the name of the repository will be displayed on the Define Source form.

To edit an existing repository record

1. Do one of the following:

   - In the **Tools** menu, click **Edit Repository List**, or

   - on the **Define Source** form, click the **Repository** button.

   The **Select Repository** form will be displayed.

2. On the **Select Repository** form, highlight the repository you want to edit in the **Repositories** list.

3. Click the **Edit** button.

   The **Define Repository** form will be displayed.

4. Edit the information in the **Name**, **Address**, **Telephone**, and **Notes** fields as necessary.

5. Click the **OK** button to save the repository record and return to the previous form.

To delete a repository record

1. Do one of the following:

   - In the **Tools** menu, click **Edit Repository List**, or

   - on the **Define Source** form, click the **Repository** button.

   The **Select Repository** form will be displayed.

2. On the **Select Repository** form, highlight the repository you want to delete in the **Repositories** list.

3. Click the **Delete** button.

   A confirmation form similar to the one shown below will be displayed.

```
Ancestry Family Tree                                                    [X]

  (?)   You are about to remove Marriott Library at University of Utah as repository. Any references to this repository will be
        removed. Are you sure?

                            [  Yes  ]        [  No  ]
```

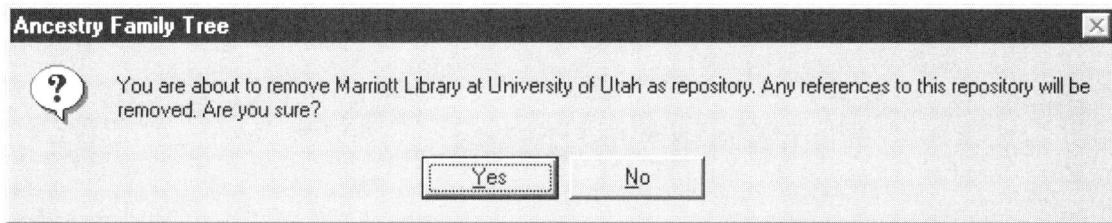

4. Click the **Yes** button to delete the repository record from the database (or click the **No** button to cancel the deletion).

Attaching a media item to the source

You can attach an image file, a sound file, or a video file to the source—for example, a photo image of the title page.

To attach a media item to the source

1. On the **Define Source** form, click the **Attach** button.

   The **Add Multimedia Object** form will be displayed.

2. Refer to "Attaching a media item to a source or source citation," below, to learn how to attach a media file to the source.

Saving the source

After you have created and saved a source record, you can create a citation that refers to that source.

To save the source

On the **Define Source** form, click the **OK** button.

The new source record is saved and the Source Citation form will be displayed. Refer to "Creating a source citation," below, to learn how to create a source citation.

Editing a source record

You can edit the contents of an existing source record at any time. You can also copy an existing source record and use it as the basis of a new source record, or you can delete a source record from the database.

To edit the contents of a source record

1. In the **Tools** menu, click **Edit Source List**.

   The **Edit Source List** form will be displayed. It lists all of the source records for the database that is currently open.

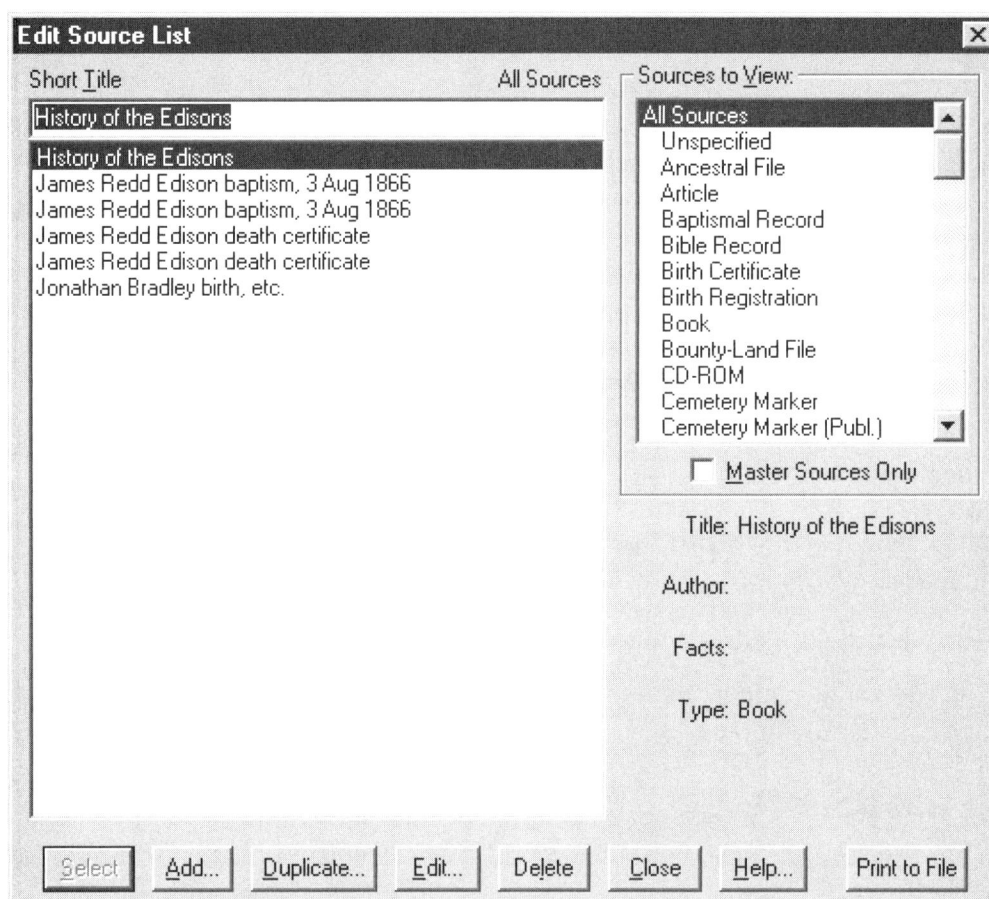

2. If you want to view a list of sources of a particular type, highlight the type in the **Sources to View** box. (A source's type is assigned on the Define Source form.)

3. In the **Short Title** list, highlight the source record that you want to edit and then click the **Edit** button.

   The **Define Source** form will be displayed.

4. Refer to the steps in "Creating a source," above, to learn how to edit the record using the Define Source form.

To copy a source record

1. On the **Edit Source List** form, highlight the source you want to copy and then click the **Duplicate** button.

   The **Define Source** form will be displayed.

2. Edit the information as needed for the new source record and then click the **OK** button.

   The new source record is saved and added to the list of sources on the Edit Source List form.

To delete a source record

1. On the **Edit Source List** form, highlight the source you want to delete and then click the **Delete** button.

   A confirmation form similar to the one shown below will be displayed.

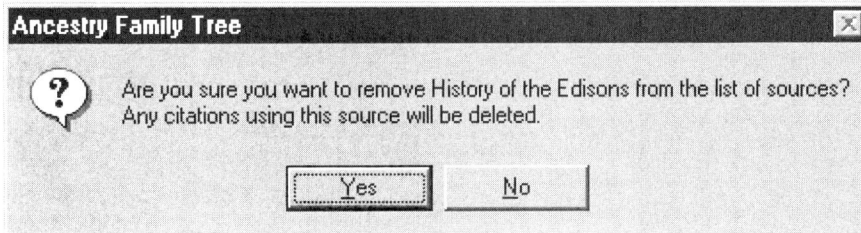

   Ancestry Family Tree

   ? Are you sure you want to remove History of the Edisons from the list of sources? Any citations using this source will be deleted.

   [Yes]   [No]

2. Click the **Yes** button to delete the source record from the database (or click the **No** button to cancel the deletion).

Selecting an existing source

If a record for the source you want to cite already exists in Ancestry Family Tree, you can cite it as the source of information for names and events.

To select an existing source

1. On the **Add Individual** or **Edit Individual** form, click the source citation button [S] adjacent to the name or the event for which you want to create a citation.

   A **Source Citation** form similar to the one shown below will be displayed.

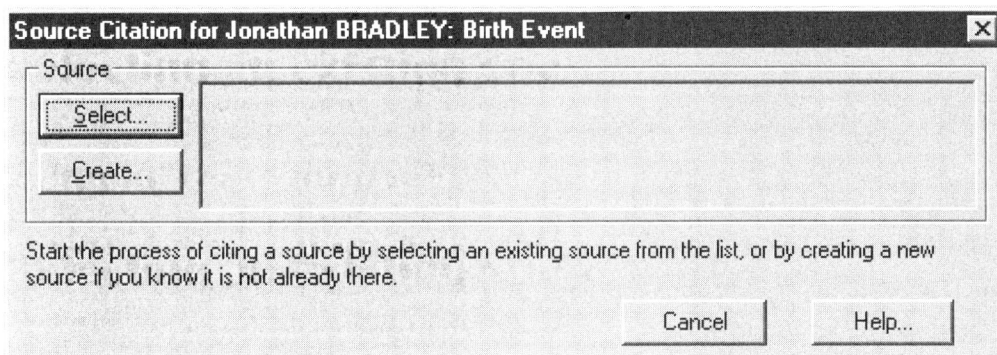

   Source Citation for Jonathan BRADLEY: Birth Event

   Source

   [Select...]

   [Create...]

   Start the process of citing a source by selecting an existing source from the list, or by creating a new source if you know it is not already there.

   [Cancel]   [Help...]

2. Click the **Select** button.

   The **Select Source** form will be displayed.

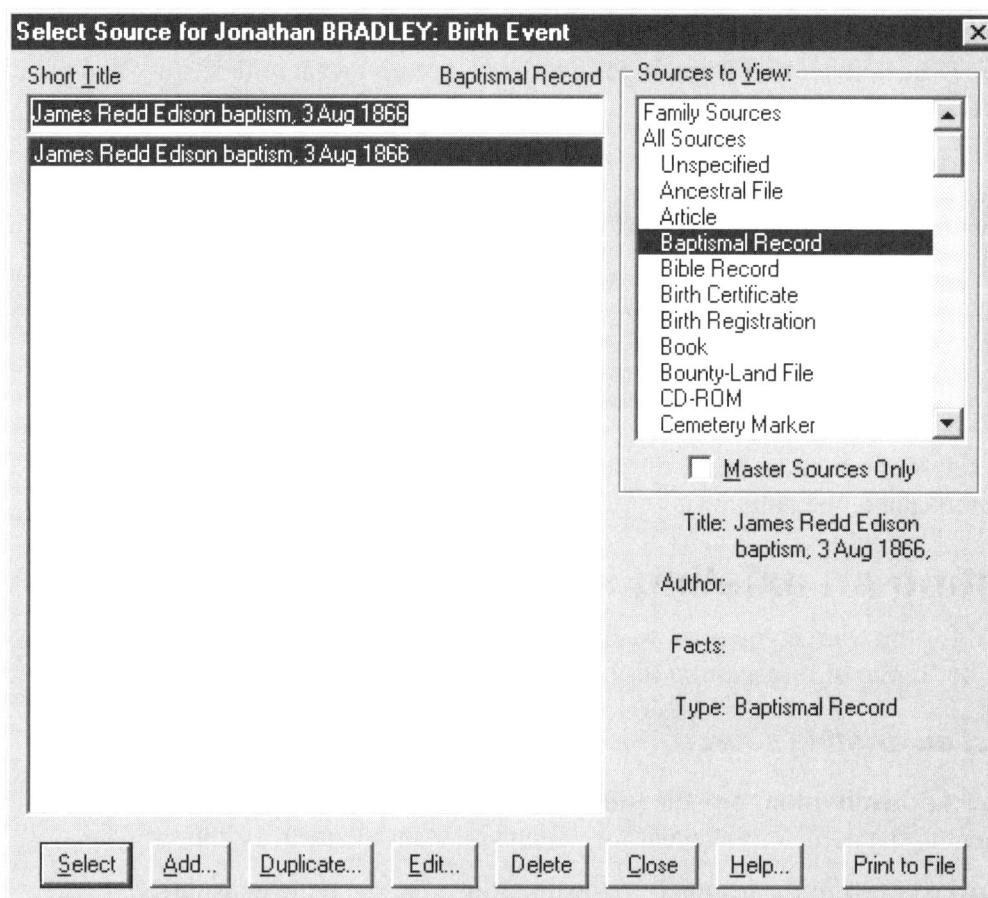

3. The **Sources to View** list contains all the source types from which you can select.

   In the Sources to View list, highlight the type of source from which you want to select a source.

   Note: To view only the sources defined as "master" sources, check the **Master Sources Only** box. Refer to "Creating a source," above, to learn how to define sources and designate them as master sources.

4. The **Short Title** list contains all the sources of the type you selected in the Sources to View list. (Refer to "Creating a source," above, to learn how to define sources and assign types to them.) For example, if you selected Baptismal Record in the Sources to View list, all sources in your database that were assigned a type of Baptismal Record will be displayed in the Short Title list.

   Highlight the source you want to cite.

5. Click the **Select** button to select the source.

   - If there are not yet any citations for the source, the **Source Citation** form will be displayed. Proceed to "Creating source citations," below, to learn how to create a source citation.

   - If there are existing citations for the source, the **Select Citation** form will be displayed.

This form lets you select an existing citation for the source or create a new citation for the source.

Do one of the following:

- To select an existing citation, highlight the citation in the **Existing Citations** list and then click the **Select from List** button.

  The **Source Citation** form for the individual will be displayed; it contains the citation you selected.

- To create a new citation for the source, click the **Create New Citation** button.

  The **Source Citation** form for the individual will be displayed. You can now enter information for this citation. Refer to "Creating source citations," below, to learn how to create a new source citation.

Creating a source citation

A source citation identifies the source of information you enter. You define sources using the Define Source form (refer to "Creating a source," above, to learn how to define a source). Then you create citations that refer to those sources to identify the sources of data you enter for an individual.

To create a source citation

1. Create a new source record as described above under "Creating a source," or select an existing source record as defined above under "Selecting an existing source."

   If you elect to create a new source at the end of the source creation or selection process, the **Source Citation** form will be displayed.

```
┌─────────────────────────────────────────────────────────────────────────┐
│ Source Citation for James Redd EDISON: Alt. Birth Event            [X]   │
│ ┌─ Source ─────────────────────────────────────────────────────────────┐ │
│ │  ┌──────────┐   ┌─────────────────────────────────────────────────┐  │ │
│ │  │ Replace..│   │ James Redd Edison baptism, 3 Aug 1866, Baltimore│  │ │
│ │  └──────────┘   │ Episcopal Church, Marriott Library at University │  │ │
│ │  ┌──────────┐   │ of Utah, Salt Lake City, UT.                    │  │ │
│ │  │  Edit... │   │                                                 │  │ │
│ │  └──────────┘   └─────────────────────────────────────────────────┘  │ │
│ └──────────────────────────────────────────────────────────────────────┘ │
│  Enter a page number, volume and page #, film #, or other specific        │
│  reference to record where, in the source, information on this event      │
│  can be found                                                             │
│ ┌─ Citation Detail ───────────────────────────────────┐ ┌─Apply to─┐     │
│ │ Vol./Page/Film #: [_____]  Entry Date: [____] │ │ ○ Date   │     │
│ │ Quality: [U=Undetermined        ▼] Reference: [____] │ │ ○ Place  │     │
│ │ Actual Text:                          Image:        │ │ ○ Both   │     │
│ │ ┌──────────────────────────┐▲ ┌──────────┐          │ │ ⦿ Event  │     │
│ │ │                          │  │          │          │ │          │     │
│ │ │                          │▼ │          │  ┌──────┐ │ │          │     │
│ │ Comments:                     │          │  │ View │ │ │          │     │
│ │ ┌──────────────────────────┐▲ │          │  └──────┘ │ │          │     │
│ │ │                          │  │          │  ┌──────┐ │ │          │     │
│ │ │                          │▼ │          │  │Attach│ │ │          │     │
│ │ └──────────────────────────┘  └──────────┘  └──────┘ │ │          │     │
│ │                                              ┌──────┐ │ │          │     │
│ │                                              │Remove│ │ │          │     │
│ └──────────────────────────────────────────── └──────┘ ┘ └──────────┘     │
│  [<< Previous]  [Attach to Other Events...]  [Next >>]       1 of 1       │
│  [  OK  ]   [ Add New ]   [ Delete ]   [ Cancel ]   [ Help... ]          │
└─────────────────────────────────────────────────────────────────────────┘
```

Note: At this point you can choose to edit the source you have selected—title, author, etc. Click the **Edit** button to edit the source.

The **Define Source** form will be displayed. Refer to the steps in "Creating a source," above, to learn how to edit a source.

Note: You can also choose to replace the source that this citation will refer to—that is, use a different source than the one represented in the current Source Citation form. Click the **Replace** button to replace the source.

The form shown below will be displayed:

```
┌──────────────────────────────────────┐
│ Ancestry Family Tree          [X]    │
│                                      │
│  ┌─┐   You are about to replace the  │
│  │?│   Source that this Citation     │
│  └─┘   refers to!                    │
│        (Use 'New' to create a new    │
│         Citation.)                   │
│                                      │
│        Continue?                     │
│                                      │
│   ┌────────┐      ┌────────┐         │
│   │  Yes   │      │   No   │         │
│   └────────┘      └────────┘         │
└──────────────────────────────────────┘
```

Click the **Yes** button to open the **Select Source** form, which allows you to select a different source. Refer to steps 3–5 in "Selecting an existing source," above, to learn how to select a source.

2. The Source Citation form contains a number of fields that allow you to enter information regarding the source citation. Refer to the table below to learn about the purpose of each field and then enter the appropriate information in the fields.

Field	Description
Vol./Page/Film #	Enter the volume, page, or microfilm number as applicable. Be sure to indicate which you are referring to as you enter the numbers—for example, page 45, or vol. 3, p. 7 (or use the format 3:7).
Entry Date	Enter the date on which the record was created (not the date on which you are entering it in your database). This date is often unknown.
Quality	Specify the quality ranking of the evidence for this citation—that is, how reliable the evidence is. Click the arrow button to the right of the box and select the source's quality ranking from the list.
Apply to	If you are creating a citation for an event, click an option button to indicate whether the citation will be applied to the **Date** or the **Place** associated with the event, **Both** the date and the place, or to the **Event** itself (if no date or place is known for the event). (These option buttons are not available if you are creating a citation for a name.) When this event is footnoted on a family group record, the footnote number will be attached to the date or place or both, or to the event, accordingly.
Reference	If you have a numbering system for your paper files, enter the number that indicates where in your paper files this document is located.
Actual Text	Type text from the source that supports the name or event you are documenting.
Comments	Enter any comments regarding the citation.

To view other source citations for the name or event

If there are multiple source citations for a particular name or event, the **Previous** and **Next** buttons will be available on the Source Citation form. Note that the number of the current citation and the total number of citations for the name or event are displayed in the lower right-hand corner of the Source Citation form (for example, "2 of 3").

Click the **Previous** or **Next** button to view the preceding or subsequent source citation for the name or event.

To create additional source citations for a name or event

1. On the **Source Citation** form, click the **Add New** button.

    A **Source Citation** form similar to the one shown below will be displayed.

Source Citation for James Redd EDISON: Alt. Birth Event	☒

Source

[Select...]　[Create...]

Start the process of citing a source by selecting an existing source from the list, or by creating a new source if you know it is not already there.

Citation Detail

Vol./Page/Film #: [＿＿＿＿＿]　Entry Date: [＿＿＿]

Quality: [U=Undetermined ▼]　Reference: [＿＿＿]

Apply to
- ○ Date
- ○ Place
- ○ Both
- ◉ Event

Actual Text: [＿＿＿＿＿]　Image: [＿＿＿＿]

[View]　[Attach]

Comments: [＿＿＿＿＿]

[Remove]

[<< Previous]　[Attach to Other Events...]　[Next >>]　2 of 2

[OK]　[Add New]　[Delete]　[Cancel]　[Help...]

2. You must create a new source or select an existing source before you can create an additional source citation. To learn how to create a new source or select an existing source, refer to "Creating a source" or "Selecting an existing source," above.

To attach the source citation to other events

1. On the **Source Citation** form, click the **Attach to Other Events** button.

    The **Citation Links** form will be displayed. This form allows you to apply the current source citation to other events for the current individual or for other individuals in the database.

Citation Links

Source Citation:

James Redd Edison baptism, 3 Aug 1866, Baltimore Episcopal Church, p. 19, Marriott Library at University of Utah, Salt Lake City, UT.

Events Using This Citation

I/M	Record #	Name	Event
I	1	James Redd EDISON	

Remove

Attach Citation to New Event

Record: [Search...] Ind-7 Jonathan BRADLEY

Event:
- Record
- Birth

Apply to
- ○ Date
- ○ Place
- ○ Both
- ● Event

[Attach]

[Close] [Help...]

2. Under **Attach Citation to New Event**, click the **Search** button.

   The **Find Individual** form will be displayed. This form allows you to search for an individual who has an event to which you want to attach the citation, or for a marriage to which you want to attach the citation.

Find Individual

Select by Record Number

RIN: [7]   Valid Range: 1 to 18

● Individual RIN   ○ Marriage RIN

[Browse List...] [Descendancy List...]

[OK] [Cancel] [Help...]

3. Do one of the following:

   - If you know the RIN of the individual you want, click the **Individual RIN** option button; or, if you know the MRIN of the marriage you want, click the Marriage RIN option button; then type the number in the box above. (The box will be labeled **RIN** or **MRIN** accordingly.)

- To search for an individual in the database, click the **Individual RIN** option button; or, to search for a marriage in the database, click the **Marriage RIN** option button; then click the **Browse List** button. Refer to chapter 9, Searching the Database, to learn how to search for an individual or marriage.

- To search a descendancy list for the individual whose record you are defining or editing, click the **Individual RIN** option button, then click the **Descendancy List** button. Refer to "Viewing the descendants of an individual" in chapter 4, Working with Individuals in a Database, to learn how to use the descendancy list.

4. After you have identified the individual, click the **OK** button to close the Find form and add the individual or marriage and a list of associated events to the Citation Links form.

5. The **Event** box on the **Citation Links** form contains a list of events for the selected individual or marriage.

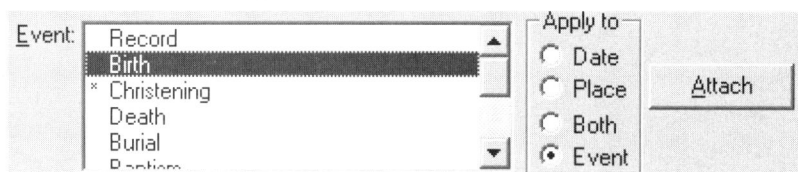

Highlight the event to which you want to attach the source citation.

6. Under **Apply to**, click an option button to indicate whether the citation will be applied to the **Date** or the **Place** associated with the event, **Both** the date and the place, or to the **Event** itself (if no date or place are known for the event). When this event is footnoted on a family group record, the footnote number will be attached to the date or place or both, or to the event, accordingly.

   Note: If you selected Record or Marriage Record in the Event box, you cannot select an event under Apply to; the citation will be attached to the individual record or marriage record.

7. Click the **Attach** button to attach the citation to the event.

8. To attach the source citation to additional events, repeat steps 2–7 above for each additional event.

9. Click the **Close** button to return to the Source Citation form.

To attach a media item to the source citation

1. On the **Source Citation** form, click the **Attach** button.

   The **Add Multimedia Object** form will be displayed.

2. Refer to "Attaching a media item to a source or source citation," below, to learn how to attach a media item to the source citation.

Note: If a media item is already attached to the source citation, you can view a photo image or video clip item or play an audio clip item by clicking the **View** button on the Source Citation form; edit the item by clicking the **Edit** button (refer to "Modifying a media item" in chapter 8, Working with Media Collections, to learn how to edit the file);

or remove the item from the source or source citation by clicking the **Remove** button (the media file itself will not be removed from your computer).

To save the source citation

On the **Source Citation** form, click the **OK** button to save the source citation and return to the previous form.

Editing a source citation

You can edit the contents of an existing source citation at any time.

To edit a source citation

1. Do one of the following:

   - On the **Edit Individual** form or the **Marriage** form, click the source citation button ˣS adjacent to the name or the event for which there is a citation you want to edit (names or events for which source citations already exist are denoted by an asterisk on the source citation button), or

   - on the **Additional Event** form (opened from the Additional Individual Information form), click the **Source** button (additional events for which source citations already exist are denoted by an asterisk on the Source button).

   The **Source Citation** form will be displayed.

2. Refer to the steps in "Creating source citations," above, to learn how to edit the citation using the Source Citation form.

Deleting a source citation

You can delete a source citation that is no longer applicable to an individual.

To delete a source citation

1. Do one of the following:

   - On the **Edit Individual** form or the **Marriage** form, click the source citation button ˣS adjacent to the name or the event for which there is a citation you want to delete (names or events for which source citations already exist are denoted by an asterisk on the source citation button), or

   - on the **Additional Event** form (opened from the Additional Individual Information form), click the **Source** button (additional events for which source citations already exist are denoted by an asterisk on the Source button).

   The **Source Citation** form will be displayed.

2. On the Source Citation form, click the **Delete** button.

   A confirmation form similar to the one shown below will be displayed.

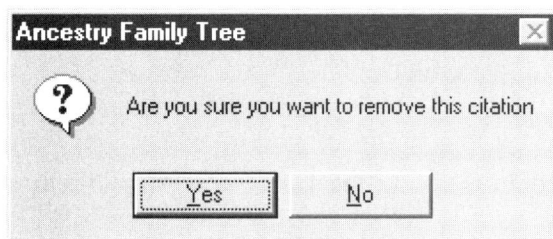

3. Click the **Yes** button to delete the source citation (or click the **No** button to cancel the deletion).

Attaching a media item to a source or source citation

You can attach a media item to a source or source citation. The media item can be a photo image (for example, a bitmap file containing the title page of a published family history), a sound clip, or a video clip (for example, an audio or video recording of an interview) with an accompanying text caption and description.

To attach a media item to the source or source citation

1. On the **Define Source** form or the **Source Citation** form, click the **Attach** button.

   The **Add Multimedia Object** form will be displayed.

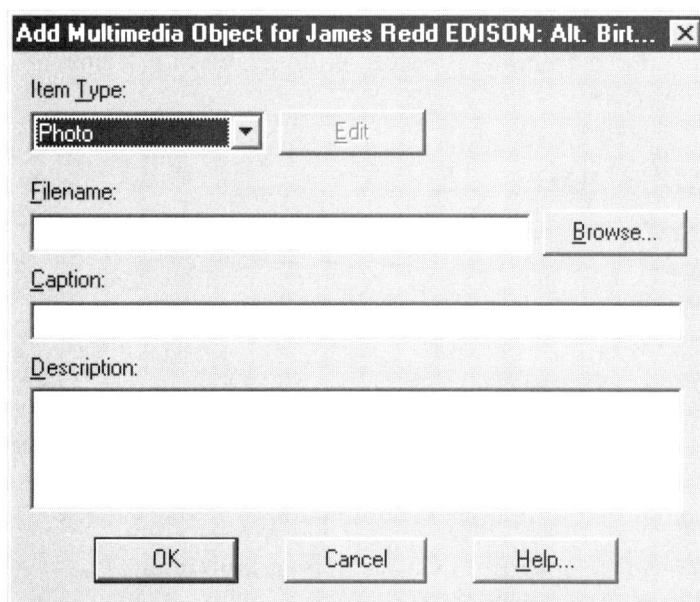

2. Use the **Item Type** box to specify the type of media item you are attaching. The options are *Photo, Sound Clip,* and *Video Clip*.

   Click the arrow button to the right of the box and select the item type from the list.

3. The Add Multimedia Object form contains several fields that allow you to enter information regarding the media file. Refer to the table below to learn about the purpose of each field and then enter the appropriate information in the fields.

Field	Description
Filename	Do one of the following: • Enter the path and file name of the media file you want to attach, or • click the **Browse** button. The Open File for form will be displayed. Refer to "To search for a media item" in chapter 8, Working with Media Collections, to learn how to search for a media file using the Open File for form.
Caption	Enter a brief caption describing the file's contents (optional).
Description	Enter a description of the file's contents (optional).

4. Click the **OK** button to attach the multimedia object to the source or source citation.

CHAPTER 8

Working with Media Collections

A media collection is a collection of electronic media relating to an individual. You can create a media collection for every individual in a family database. A media collection can include three types of electronic media files:

- Photo images (for example, a bitmap file containing a portrait of the individual),
- video clips (for example, a video recording of an interview), and
- sound clips (for example, an audio recording of a recital).

Each file in a media collection is referred to as a media item. Each media item can have an accompanying text caption and description. You can arrange the photo images into "slide shows" and "scrapbooks," and you can attach an audio clip to each photo image.

In this chapter

- Creating a new media collection
- Viewing a photo or video clip
- Viewing the slide show and scrapbook

Creating a new media collection

1. In the **Pedigree** view, **Family** view, or **Name List** view, highlight the individual for whom you want to create a new media collection.

2. Do one of the following:

   - On the button bar, click the multimedia button, 🏛
   - in the **Data** menu, click **Edit Media Collection**, or
   - right-click and select **Media** from the pop-up menu.

   The **Media Collection** form will be displayed.

The Media Collection form displays a list of items in the media collection and lets you arrange them into slide shows and scrapbooks.

To add a media item to the collection

1. Click the **Add** button.

   The **Add Multimedia Object** form will be displayed.

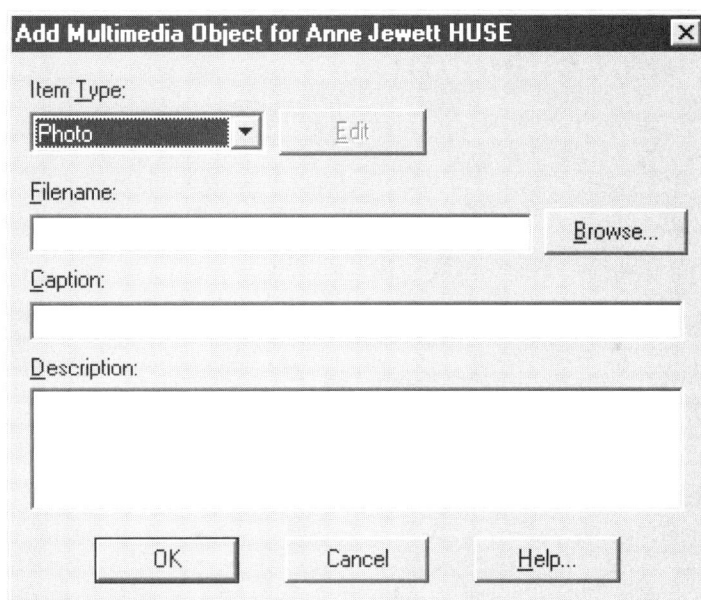

2. Use the **Item Type** box to specify the type of media item you are attaching. The options are *Photo, Sound Clip,* and *Video Clip*.

   Click the arrow button to the right of the box and select the item type from the list.

3. The Add Multimedia Object form contains a number of fields that allow you to enter information regarding the media item. Refer to the table below to learn about the purpose of each field and then enter the appropriate information in the fields.

Field	Description
Filename	Do one of the following: • Type the path and file name of the media file you want to attach, or • click the **Browse** button. The Open File for form will be displayed. (Refer to "To search for a media item," below, to learn how to find a media item using the Open File form.)
Caption	Enter a brief caption describing the item's contents (optional). The caption will appear with a photo image item in a slide show.
Description	Enter a description of the item's contents (optional). The description will appear with a photo image item in a slide show.

4. Click the **OK** button to close the Add Multimedia Object form and add the media item to the collection.

5. Repeat steps 1–4 above to add additional media items to the media collection.

To search for a media item

1. On the **Add Multimedia Object** form, click the **Browse** button.

An **Open File** form similar to the one shown below will be displayed.

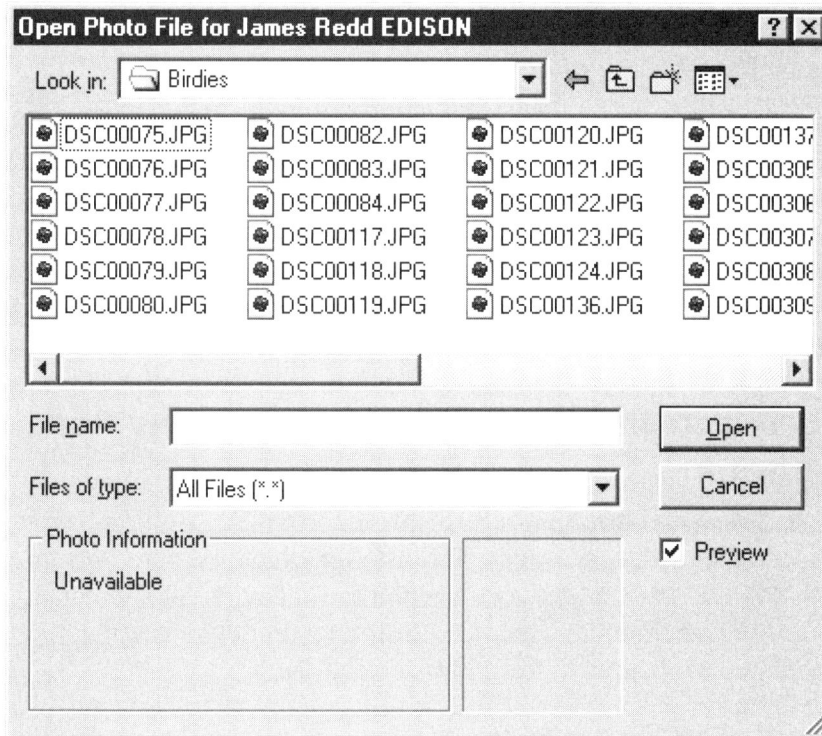

2. Use the controls described below to locate the disk drive or folder containing the file you want.

- Click the drop-down button to the right of the **Look In** box to view the contents of the drives and folders on your computer.

- Click the Up One Level button to view the contents of the folder one level above the folder you are currently viewing.

3. When you locate the file you want to include as a media item, do one of the following to select the file and return to the Add Multimedia Object form:

- Double-click the file, or

- highlight the file and then click the **Open** button.

Hint: If the **Preview** box is checked, you can preview a photo image on the Open File form by highlighting the file name.

To select an image item that will be used in reports

1. In the **Media Item** list on the **Media Collection** form, highlight the image item that you want to be displayed on reports for the individual.

2. Click the **Make Default** button.

An asterisk will appear with the item to indicate that it is the default photo.

- To remove the default status from a photo, highlight the photo in the Media Item list and then click the **Clear Default** button.

To select an audio clip that will be played during the slide show

1. In the Media Item list, highlight the audio clip that you want to be played during the slide show for the individual.

2. Click the **Make Default** button.

   An asterisk will appear with the item to indicate that it is the default audio clip.

   - To remove the default status from an audio clip, highlight the audio clip in the Media Item list and then click the **Clear Default** button.

Arranging the order in which photos appear in the slide show and scrapbook

The photo image items in a media collection can be displayed in a slide show and a scrapbook that are unique to the media collection. The order in which the items appear is determined by the Media Item list on the Media Collection form. (Individual photos in the media item list can be omitted from the slide show or the scrapbook. Refer to "Editing a photo in a media item," below, to learn how to omit them.)

To arrange the order of photo image items

1. In the **Media Item** list on the **Media Collection** form, highlight a media item you want to reposition.

2. Under **Order**, click the up or down arrows to move the item up or down one position in the list with each click.

3. Reposition the remaining media items until they are listed in the order in which you want them to be displayed in the slide show and scrapbook.

Modifying a media item

You can edit the caption and description for an existing media item or even replace the file component (photo image or video or audio clip) of the media item with another one.

To modify a media item

1. On the **Media Collection** form, highlight the item in the **Media Item** list.

Media Item:	Caption:
* Photo	Gerald and Beverly
Photo	Carrie, Laurie, Alyssa, Gail
Video Clip	Horse
* Sound Clip	Adding desktop themes
Video Clip	Bird
Photo	Scrubbie

2. Click the **Modify** button.

   The **Modify Multimedia Item** form will be displayed.

3. Use the controls on this form to modify the multimedia item. (Refer to step 3 in "To add a media item to the collection" to learn how to use the Multimedia Item form.)

Editing a photo in a media item

You can edit various attributes of a photo in a media item. For example, you can crop the image, rotate it, etc.

- On the **Modify Multimedia Item** form, click the **Edit** button.

  The **Edit Photo** form will be displayed.

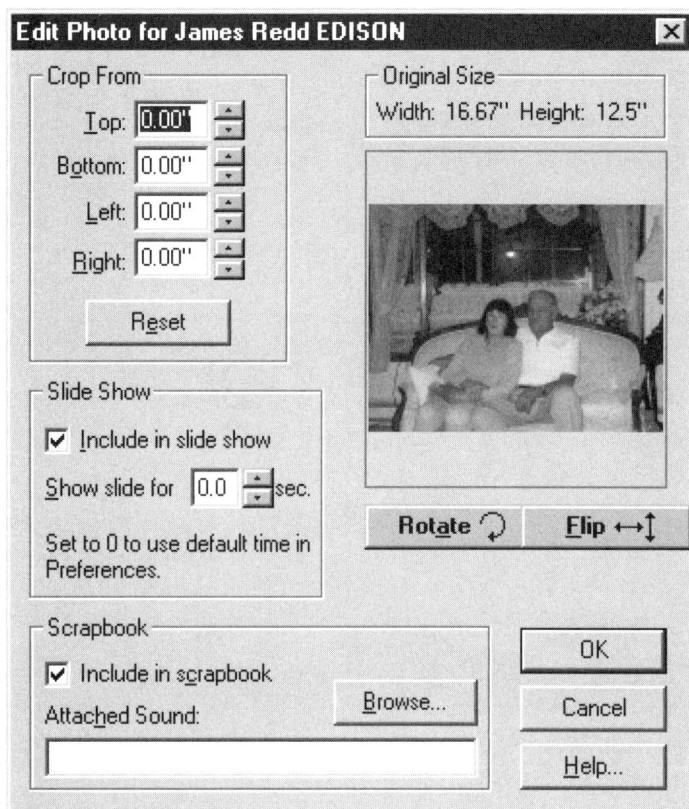

To crop the photo

1. Under **Crop From**, do one of the following:

   - In the **Top**, **Bottom**, **Left**, and **Right** boxes, enter the amount you want to crop the corresponding portion of the photo (in inches), or

   - click the up or down arrows to the right of the **Top**, **Bottom**, **Left**, and **Right** boxes to increase or decrease the amount (in inches) you want to crop the corresponding portion of the photo.

2. If you want to set the amounts entered in the **Top**, **Bottom**, **Left**, and **Right** boxes back to zero, click the **Reset** button.

To specify slide show preferences for the photo

1. If you want the photo to be included in the media collection slide show, the **Include in Slide Show** box must be checked.

   If you do not want the photo to be included in the slide show, be sure the Include in Slide Show box is not checked.

2. If you want the photo to appear in the slide show for an amount of time that is different from the default display time defined in Ancestry Family Tree's overall preferences (refer to chapter 2, "Installation and setup, to learn how to define preferences), the **Show slide for** box allows you to specify the display time (in seconds). (If the amount in the box is 0, the default display time will be used for the photo.) For example, if the default slide show display time is five seconds but you

want a particular photo to be displayed longer than the others in the media collection, you could use this box to specify a display time of ten seconds.

Enter the amount of slide show display time (in seconds) in the box.

To specify scrapbook preferences for the photo

1. If you want the photo to be included in the media collection scrapbook, the **Include in Scrapbook** box must be checked.

   If you do not want the photo to be included in the scrapbook, be sure the Include in Scrapbook box is not checked.

2. To attach an audio file to the photo (or replace the current audio file with a different one), do one of the following:

   - Type the path and file name of the audio file you want to attach, or

   - click the **Browse** button to search for an audio file.

     The **Open** form will be displayed.

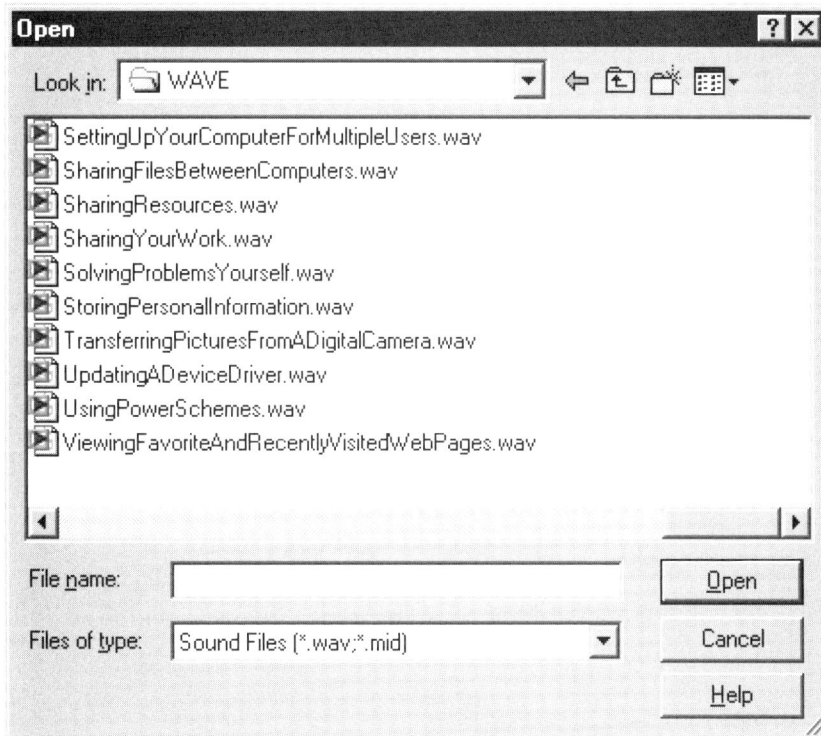

3. Use the controls described below to locate the disk drive or folder containing the audio file you want.

   - Click the drop-down button to the right of the **Look In** box to view the contents of the drives and folders on your computer.

   - Click the Up One Level button to view the contents of the folder one level above the folder you are currently viewing.

4. When you locate the audio file you want to attach to the photo, do one of the following to select the file and return to the Edit Photo form:

   - Double-click the file, or

   - highlight the file and then click the **Open** button.

   You will be able to play the audio clip by clicking an icon on the photo image when you view the scrapbook.

To change the orientation of the photo

1. The **Rotate** button allows you to rotate the photo clockwise in increments of 90 degrees.

   Click the Rotate button to rotate the photo clockwise until it is in the position you want.

2. To reverse the image or turn it upside down, click the **Flip** button.

   The **Flip Image** form will be displayed.

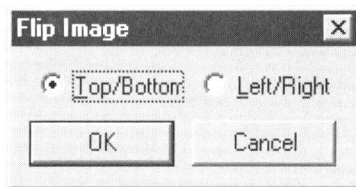

3. To turn the image upside down, click the **Top/Bottom** option; or, to reverse the image horizontally, click the **Left/Right** option and then click the **OK** button.

   The Flip Image form will close and the photo image will be displayed on the Edit Photo form in the orientation you selected.

To save the edited photo

On the **Edit Photo** form, click the **OK** button to close the form and return to the Modify Multimedia Item form.

Removing an item from a media collection

You can remove an item from a media collection. (The photo image or video or audio file component of the media item will not be deleted from your computer.)

To remove an item from a media collection

1. On the **Media Collection** form, highlight the item in the **Media Item** list.

2. Click the **Remove** button.

   The warning dialog box shown below will be displayed.

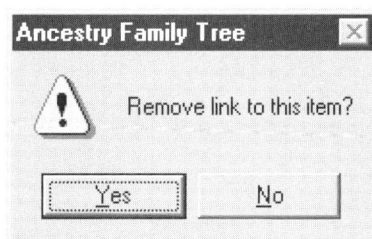

3. Click the **Yes** button to remove the item from the media collection (or click the **No** button to cancel the removal).

Viewing a photo or video clip

You can view a specific photo or video clip in a media collection.

To view a photo or video clip

1. On the **Media Collection** form, highlight the photo image or video clip you want to view in the **Media Item** list.

2. Click the **Show** or **Play** button. (The button will be labeled Show or Play depending on your selection of a photo image or a video clip.)

   The photo image or video clip will be displayed.

   Note: On the Multimedia page of the Preferences form, you can make selections that determine whether the video player installed with Ancestry Family Tree will be used or a different video player installed on your computer will be used.

Viewing the slide show or scrapbook

The photo image items in an individual's media collection can be displayed in a slide show and a scrapbook that are unique to that media collection. The order in which the photo images appear is determined by the Media Item list on the Media Collection form. (Individual photo images in the media item list can be omitted from the slide show or the scrapbook. Refer to "Editing a photo in a media item," above, to learn how to omit them.)

To select an individual for viewing

1. In the **Pedigree** view, **Family** view, or **Name List** view, highlight the individual for whom you want to view the slide show or scrapbook.

2. Do one of the following:

   - On the button bar, click the multimedia button,
   - in the **Data** menu, click **Edit Media Collection**, or
   - right-click and select **Media** from the pop-up menu.

   The **Media Collection** form will be displayed.

To view the slide show

1. On the **Media Collection** form, click the **Slide Show** button.

   Each photo image selected to be in the slide show will be displayed in turn. If you specified an audio clip to be played with the slide show, you will hear it as well. (Refer to "To select an audio clip that will be played during the slide show," above, to learn how to select an audio clip.)

2. The slide show will continue until the last photo will be displayed. To end the slide show before it is finished, press the ESC button on your keyboard.

To view the scrapbook

1. On the **Media Collection** form, click the **Scrapbook** button.

   The Scrapbook window will be displayed.

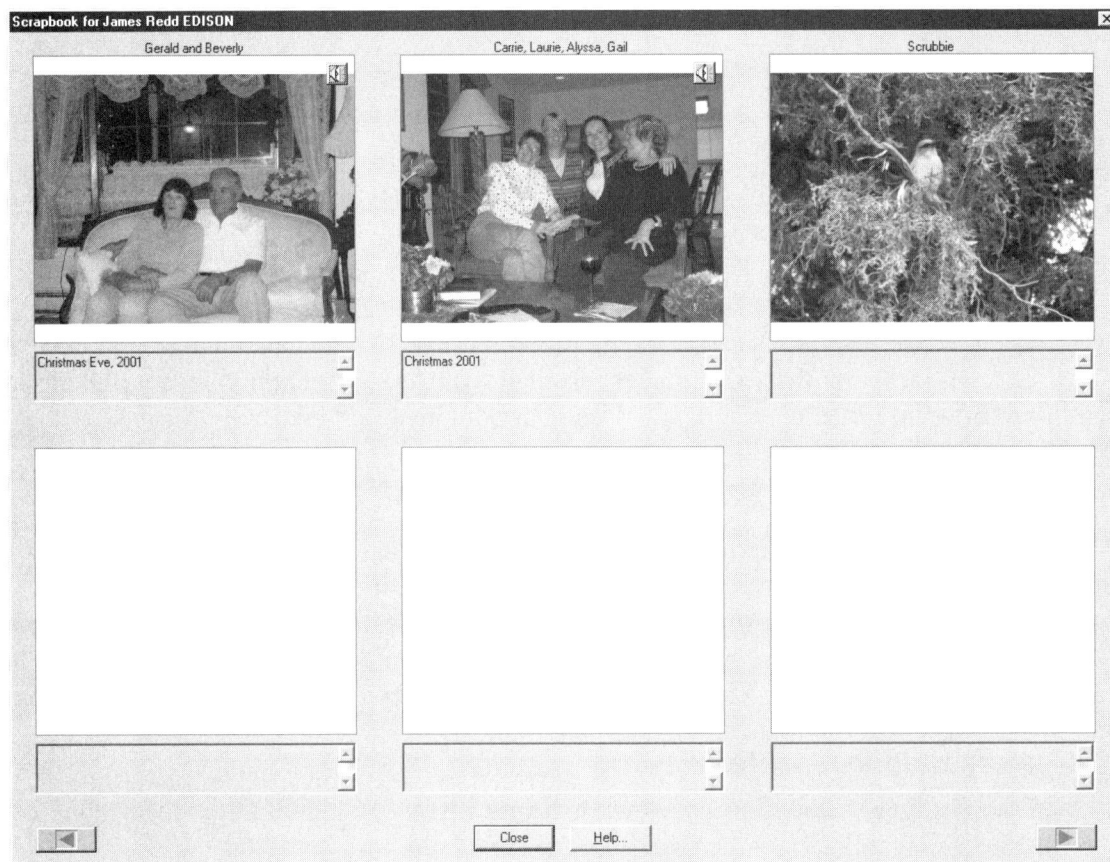

Each photo image selected to be in the scrapbook will be displayed in the window. The description entered for each photo appears below it. (You can use the scroll bar to the right of the text box to view portions of a description that are not visible.)

- Photos that have audio clips attached contain the Sound button in the upper-right corner. (Refer to "To specify scrapbook preferences for the photo," above, to learn how to attach an audio clip to a photo in the media collection.)

  Click the Sound button to play the audio clip attached to a photo.

- If there are more photos in the scrapbook than can fit on the form, you can use the arrow buttons in the lower corners to view the next or previous group of photos.

  Click one of the buttons to display the next or previous group of photos.

2. Click the **Close** button to close the scrapbook.

CHAPTER 9

Searching the Database

A wonderful attribute of an Ancestry Family Tree family database is that it is eminently searchable. Your search can be as simple as a name search or a more complex one using relationships and the contents of database fields to find one or a group of individuals. You can search the entire database, for a descendant of a selected individual, or for a marriage.

In this chapter

• Searching the entire database
• Searching for a descendent of a selected individual
• Searching for a marriage

Searching the entire database

You can start your search with the broadest possible field of candidates: the entire database.

1. Do one of the following:

   - On the **Citation Links** form, click the **Search** button,

   - on the **Relationship Examiner** form, click the **Search** button,

   - on the **Add Parents** form, click the **Find Father** or **Find Mother** button, or

   - click the Search button 🔍 on the button bar.

     The **Find Individual** form will be displayed.

     ```
     ┌─────────────────────────────────────────┐
     │ Find Individual                       [X]│
     │ ┌─Select by Record Number──────────────┐ │
     │ │  RIN: [7]     Valid Range: 1 to 18   │ │
     │ │  (•) Individual RIN   ( ) Marriage RIN│ │
     │ │                                       │ │
     │ │   [ Browse List... ] [ Descendancy List... ] │ │
     │ └───────────────────────────────────────┘ │
     │     [   OK   ]  [ Cancel ]  [ Help... ]   │
     └─────────────────────────────────────────┘
     ```

     On the Find Individual form, click the **Individual RIN** option button, then click the **Browse List** button.

   - Click the Browse List button 🗇 on the button bar, or

   - on the **Tools** menu, click **Browse List**.

   The **Search for Individual** form will be displayed. This form allows you to search a list of all the individuals in the database. You can also use search filters to narrow your search for an individual by relationship or by information that exists for that individual. Note that when you highlight an individual on the list, vital information for that individual will be displayed on the right side of the form.

2. Use the option buttons under **Sort** to determine how individuals are listed. Click **RIN** to list individuals in order by RIN, or click **Alpha** to list individuals alphabetically.

3. Use the scroll bar at the right of the list to locate the individual you are searching for and then highlight the individual.

4. Click the **OK** button to select the individual and return to the previous form.

Searching for individuals using filters

You might want to find individuals in a database based on their meeting certain criteria—such as whom they are related to or when and where they were born. Because a family database might contain hundreds of individuals, searching a single list of all those individuals one person at a time to determine whether each person meets those criteria could be a difficult task. Therefore, Ancestry Family tree lets you use *search filters* that can help you find one or more individuals who meet your criteria.

To search for individuals using filters

On the **Search for Individual** form, click the **Advanced >>** button.

The Search for Individual form expands to include a group of filter controls.

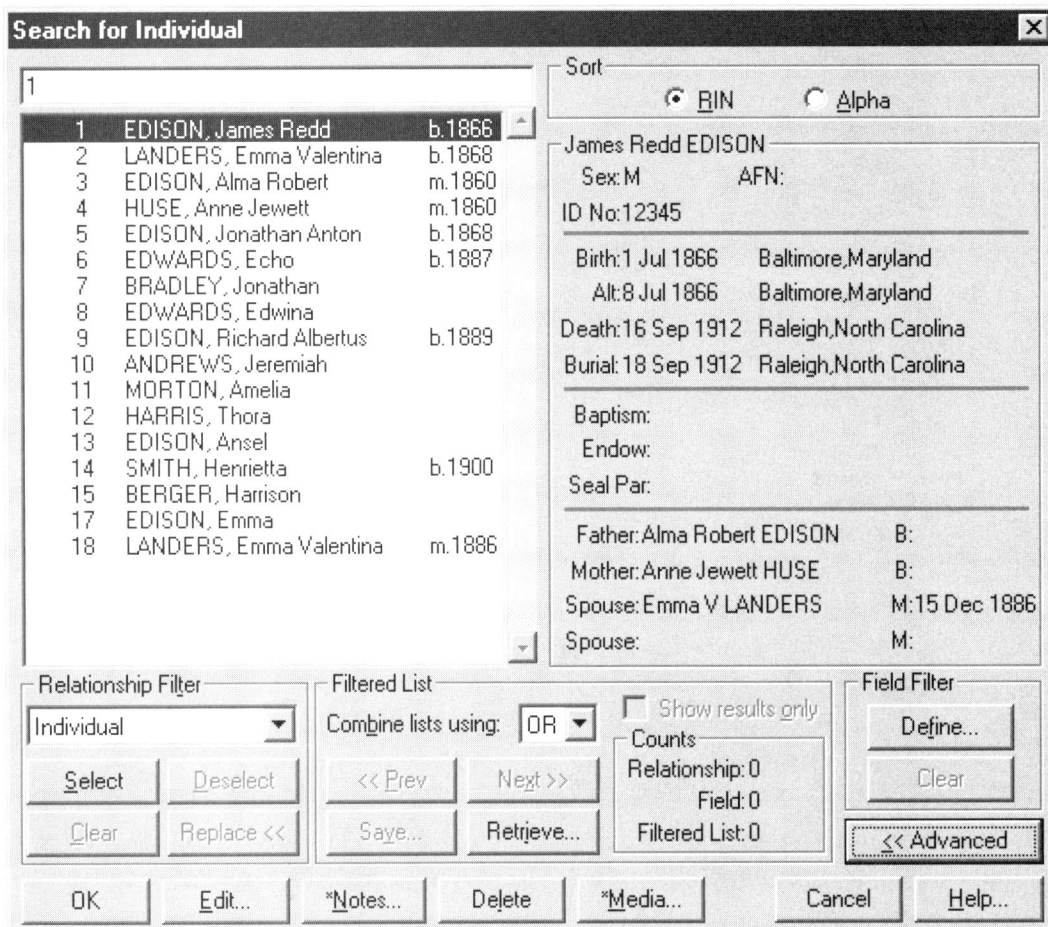

You can use two types of filters to narrow your search for individuals. The *relationship filter* allows you to limit the search to a group of individuals based on their relationship to a selected individual (for example, all descendants of the selected individual). A *field filter* allows you to limit the search to a group of individuals based on information that exists in the database for the individuals (for example, year of birth). Finally, you can combine the contents of the two filtered lists to further limit your search.

Searching for individuals using the relationship filter

The relationship filter allows you to limit the search to a group of individuals based on their relationship to a selected individual (for example, all ancestors of the selected individual).

To search for individuals using the relationship filter

1. In the list of individuals, highlight the individual whose relatives you want to search for.

2. Under **Relationship Filter**, the drop-down list allows you to select the type of relationship you want to use as a filter. The options are:

Option	Description
Individual	Selects only the highlighted individual.

Option	Description
Couple	Selects the highlighted individual and spouse(s). If there is more than one spouse, you can choose whether to include all spouses or to select one spouse.
Family	Selects the highlighted individual, spouse(s), and all children of the individual. If there is more than one spouse, you can choose whether to include all spouses or to select one spouse.
All	Selects all individuals in the list.
All Related	Selects every person in the list who is related to the highlighted individual (usually everyone in the list).
Ancestors	Selects the highlighted individual and ancestors of the individual. **Note:** If you use this option, the **Ancestors** form will be displayed when you click the **Select** button. The **Ancestors** form allows you to specify the number of generations of ancestors that will be selected, the number of generations of descendants of each ancestor that will be selected, and whether to include spouses.
All Ancestral Related	Selects the highlighted individual and everyone related to the individual's ancestors (not including the selected individual's spouse[s], ancestors of the spouse[s], or children of the individual). Essentially, this option will select an entire branch of the family tree.
Descendants	Selects the highlighted individual and descendants of the individual. **Note:** If you use this option, the Descendents form will be displayed when you click the **Select** button. The Descendents form allows you to specify the number of generations of descendents that will be selected and whether to include spouses.
All Descendant Related	Selects the highlighted individual, all descendants of the individual, and all persons related to any of the descendants. Therefore, the spouse(s) of descendants and all siblings, ancestors, etc., of these spouses will be selected. Essentially, this option will select an entire branch of the family tree.

Click the arrow button to the right of the list box and select the type of relationship to use as a filter.

3. Click the **Select** button to narrow the group of individuals based on the relationship filter.

Each individual in the filtered group is marked with a >> symbol in the list of individuals.

Note: To cause only the individuals in the filtered group to be displayed in the list of individuals, check the **Show results only** box.

To remove individuals from the filtered group in the list,

1. Highlight an individual in the list.

2. The type of relationship selected under **Relationship Filter** will determine which individual(s) are removed from the list. For example, if you select the Individual option, only the highlighted individual will be removed (or "deselected") from the filtered group; if you select the Couple option, the highlighted individual and his or her spouse(s) will be removed.

   Click the drop-down button to the right of the list box and select the type of relationship that will determine which individual(s) are removed from the filtered group.

3. Click the **Deselect** button.

   The "deselected" individuals are removed from the filtered group.

To remove the filtered group from the list,

Click the **Clear** button.

The filtered individual markers (>>) are removed and the entire list of individuals will be displayed.

Searching for individuals using a field filter

You can create and save filters that limit the search to one individual or a group of individuals based on information that exists in the database. Specifying one or more fields as *search criteria*—such as the birth date field, for example—in a field filter allows Ancestry Family Tree to search the contents of that field for every individual in a database and find the individuals who meet your search conditions. For example, you could create a field filter that will select every individual who was born in 1924. You can also use various combinations of database fields to create more complex field filters that narrow the search based on more specific information. You could search for all individuals who were born in 1919 in Canton, Ohio, for example, or all individuals having a particular surname who were born between 1905 and 1915.

To select a field to use as a search criterion

1. Under **Field Filter** on the **Search for Individual** form, click the **Define** button.

   The **Field Filtering** form will be displayed.

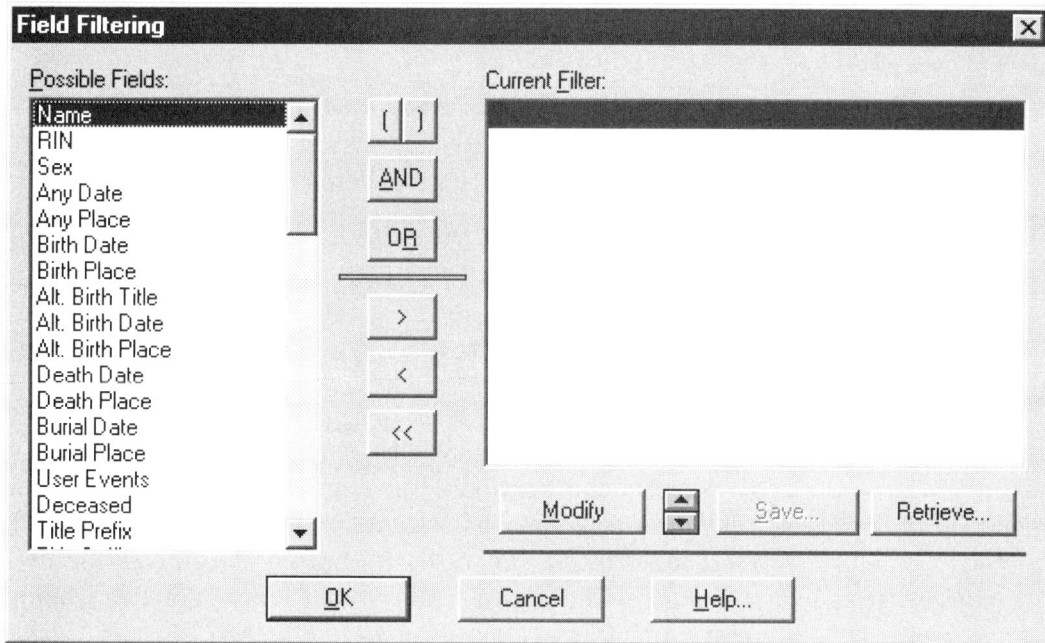

The Field Filtering form allows you to create and save field filters. You create a field filter by selecting one or more fields that you want to use as search criteria from the **Possible Fields** list and placing them in the **Current Filter** list. Each time you place a field in the Current Filter list, you will be prompted to enter appropriate information—for example, a name if you are using the Name field.

2. In the **Possible Fields** list, highlight a database field that will comprise the filter (or part of the filter) and then click the > button to place the field in the **Current Filter** list.

The **Field Filter** form for the database field you selected will be displayed. There are several types of field filter forms that contain various filter options; the information you can enter in them depends on the type of field you select in the Possible Fields list. The field filters described below are representative examples that include most of the filter options you will use.

Name field filter

The name field filter lets you search for individuals based on information contained in the Surname and/or the Given Names fields of the Individual form. (Refer to chapter 4, Working with Individuals in a Database, to learn how to enter information using the Individual form.)

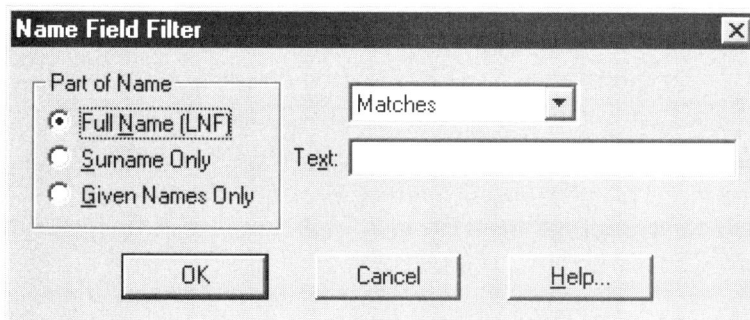

Part of Name Option	Description
Full Name (LNF)	Searches for the full name you enter in the **Text** box. (LNF stands for "last name first;" you must enter the last name first, followed by a comma—as in Thompson, Gregory James.)
Surname Only	Searches only for the surname you enter in the **Text** box.
Given Names Only	Searches only for the given names you enter in the **Text** box.

Filter Option	Description
Matches	Searches for individuals whose names exactly match the name you enter in the **Text** box. For example, to find all individuals who have the surname Jones, you would select Matches and enter Jones in the Text box. This search will find all the individuals who have the surname of Jones. You can enter a wild card either at the start or end of the text, such as "Jo*" to find Jones, Johnson, etc.
Does not match	Searches for individuals whose names do not match the name you enter in the **Text** box. For example, to find all individuals who do not have the given name Mary, you would select Does not match and enter Mary in the Text box. This search will find all the individuals who do not have the given name Mary. You can enter a wild card either at the start or end of the text, such as "Ma*" to select Mary, Marianne, etc.
Contains	Searches for individuals whose names have the characters you enter in the **Text** box. For example, to find every individual who has the letters *ca* in his or her name, you would select Contains and enter "ca" in the Text box. This search will find every individual who has the letters *ca* (in that order) in his or her name.
Does not contain	Searches for individuals whose names do not have the characters you enter in the **Text** box. For example, to find every individual who does not have the letters *ca* in his or her name, you would select Does not contain and type "ca" in the Text box. This search will find every individual who does have the letters *ca* (in that order) in his or her name.
Sounds like	Searches for individuals who have a name that sounds like the one you enter in the **Text** box. Based on the Soundex code, this search is useful for finding individuals with various spellings of a name. For example, to find every individual whose name sounds like *Smith,* you would select Sounds like and enter Smith in the Text box. This search will find every individual who has a name that sounds like *Smith.*

Filter Option	Description
Does not sound like	Searches for individuals who have a name that does not sound like the one you enter in the **Text** box. Based on the Soundex code, this search is useful for finding individuals with various spellings of the name. For example, to find every individual whose name does not sound like *Smith,* you would select Does not sound like and enter Smith in the Text box. This search will find every individual who does not have a name that sounds like *Smith.*
Exists	Searches for individuals who have any name that corresponds to the option you select under **Part of Name**. For example, if you selected the Given names only option, this search would find every individual who has given names.
Does not exist	Searches for individuals who do not have a name that corresponds to the option you select under **Part of Name**. For example, if you selected the Given names only option, this search would find every individual for whom there are no given names.
Is less than	Searches for individuals who have names that alphabetically precede the name you enter in the **Text** box. For example, to find every individual who has a name that would appear alphabetically before *Jones,* you would select Is less than and enter Jones in the Text box. This search will find every individual who has a name that precedes Jones alphabetically.
Is greater than	Searches for individuals who have names that alphabetically follow the name you enter in the **Text** box. For example, to find every individual who has a name that would appear alphabetically after *Jones,* you would select Is greater than and enter Jones in the Text box. This search will find every individual who has a name that follows Jones alphabetically.
Range	Searches for individuals who have names alphabetically between the names you enter in the **From** and **To** boxes. For example, to find every individual who has a name alphabetically between *Adams* and *Buckman*, you would select Range and enter Adams in the From box and Buckman in the To box. This search will choose every individual with a name alphabetically between Adams and Buckman.

Date field filter

Date field filters let you search for individuals based on information contained in date fields—such as marriage date, death date, etc. The example below uses the birth date field. The filter options for other date fields work in the same way.

Birth Date Field Filter [x]

Options

Equals [▼]

Date: [   ]

OK

Cancel

Help...

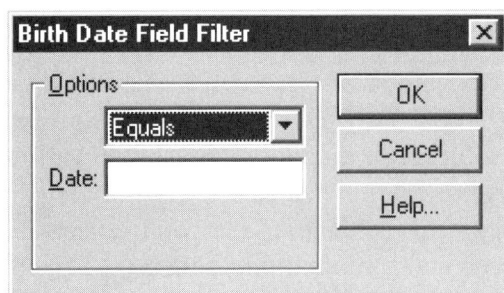

Filter Option	Description
Equals	Searches for dates that exactly match the date you enter in the **Date** box (day, month, and year). For example, to find all individuals who were born on 18 May 1910, you would select Equals and type 18 May 1910 in the Date box. This search will find every individual who has the date 18 May 1910 in the Birth date field.
Does not equal	Searches for dates that do not match the date you enter in the **Date** box (day, month, and year). For example, to find all individuals who were not born on 18 May 1910, you would select Does not equal and type 18 May 1910 in the Date box. This search will find every individual who has a date other than 18 May 1910 in the Birth date field.
Contains	Searches for dates that contain the portion of the date you enter in the **Date** box. For example, to find all individuals who were born in 1910, you would select Contains and enter 1910 in the Date box. This search will find every individual who has 1910 in the Birth date field.
Does not contain	Searches for dates that do not contain the portion of the date you enter in the **Date** box. For example, to find all individuals who were born in years other than 1910, you would select Does not contain and enter 1910 in the Date box. This search will find every individual who has a year other than 1910 in the Birth date field.
Exists	Searches for individuals who have any date in the corresponding date field.
Does not exist	Searches for individuals who do not have any date in the corresponding date field.
Is less than	Searches for a date that precedes the date you enter in the **Date** box. For example, to find all individuals who were born before 1910, you would select Is less than and enter 1910 in the Date box. This search will find every individual for whom there is a date preceding 1910 in the Birth date field.
Is greater than	Searches for a date that follows the date you enter in the **Date** box. For example, to find all individuals who were born after

Filter Option	Description
	1930, you would select Is greater than and enter 1930 in the Date box. This search will find every individual for whom there is a date after 1910 in the Birth date field.
Range	Searches for dates that lie between the dates you enter in the **From** and **To** boxes. For example, to find all individuals who were born between 1910 and 1940, you would select Range and enter 1910 in the From box and 1940 in the To box. This search will find every individual who has a birth date between 1910 and 1940.

Place field filter

Place field filters let you search for individuals based on information contained in place fields—such as death place or burial place. The example below uses the birth place field. The filter options for other place fields work in the same way.

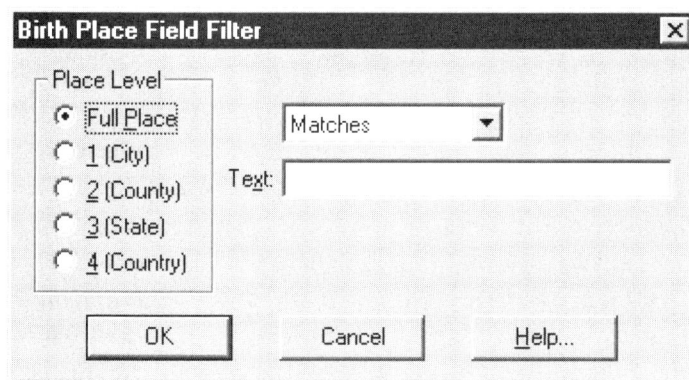

Place Level Option	Description
Full Place	Searches for the full place you enter in the **Text** box. The full place includes City, County, State, Country.
1 (City)	Searches only for the first element of the place field (which you enter in the **Text** box): City. **Note:** When entering place information for an individual in the Add Individual or Edit Individual form, you should enter it from smallest level to largest, separating each level with a comma. For example, if the individual was born in the city of Oakland, in the county of Alameda, in California, you would enter: Oakland, Alameda County, California, USA. This format is necessary to allow searching by place level.
2 (County)	Searches only for the second element of the place field (which you enter in the **Text** box): County.
3 (State)	Searches only for the third element of the place field (which you enter in the **Text** box): State.

Place Level Option	Description
4 (Country)	Searches only for the fourth element of the place field (which you enter in the **Text** box): Country.

Filter Option	Description
Matches	Searches for places that exactly match the place you enter in the **Text** box. You must include commas but omit spaces when entering the place in the Text box. For example, to find all individuals who were born in Ogden, Weber County, Utah, USA, you would select Matches and enter Ogden,Weber County,Utah,USA in the Text box. This search will find all individuals for whom the place of birth was entered as Ogden, Weber County, Utah, USA. You can enter a wild card either at the start or end of the text, such as "Bl*" to select Bloomington, . . . ; Blue Bayou, . . . ; etc., or "*Germany" to select any place name ending in Germany.
Does not match	Searches for places that do not match the place you enter in the **Text** box. (You must include commas but omit spaces when entering the place in the Text box.) For example, to find all individuals who were not born in Ogden, Weber County, Utah, USA, you would select Does not match and enter Ogden,Weber County,Utah,USA in the Text box. This search will find all individuals for whom the place of birth is other than Ogden, Weber County, Utah, USA. Again, you can enter a wild card either at the start or end of the text, such as "Bl*" to select Bloomington, . . . ; Blue Bayou, . . . ; etc., or "*Germany" to select any place name ending in Germany.
Contains	Searches for place fields that contain the place entered in the **Text** box. For example, to find all individuals who were born in Ohio, you would select Contains and enter Ohio in the Text box. This search will find every individual whose birth place field contains Ohio (regardless of city, county, and country).
Does not contain	Searches for place fields that do not contain the place entered in the **Text** box. For example, to find all individuals who were not born in Ohio, you would select Does not contain and enter Ohio in the Text box. This search will find every individual whose birth place field does not contain Ohio (regardless of city, county, and country).
Exists	Searches for place fields that contain any entry in the corresponding place element. For example, to find all individuals who have an entry for the birth city field, you would select 1 (City) under **Place Level** and Exists. If you select Full Place

Filter Option	Description
	under **Place Level**, the search will find all individuals who have any entry in the birth place field.
Does not exist	Searches for place fields that do not contain an entry in the corresponding place element. For example, to find all individuals for whom there is no entry in the birth city field, you would select 1 (City) under **Place Level** and Does not exist. If you select Full Place under **Place Level**, the search will find all individuals who have no entries in the birth place field.
Is less than	Searches for places that alphabetically precede the place you enter in the **Text** box. If you select Full Place Name under **Place Level** you must enter a city, county, state, and country for a proper search. The search will proceed by country, then state, then county, and then city. For example, to find all individuals having a birth place that would appear alphabetically before *Salt Lake City, Salt Lake County, Utah, USA,* you would select Is less than and enter Salt Lake City, Salt Lake County, Utah, USA in the Text box. This search will find all individuals having a birth place that alphabetically precedes the entry Salt Lake City, Salt Lake, Utah, USA.
Is greater than	Searches for places that alphabetically follow the place you enter in the **Text** box. If you select Full Place Name under **Place Level** you must enter a city, county, state, and country for a proper search. The search will proceed by country, then state, then county, and then city. For example, to find all individuals having a birth place that would appear alphabetically following *Salt Lake City, Salt Lake County, Utah, USA,* you would select Is greater than and enter Salt Lake City, Salt Lake, Utah, USA in the Text box. This search will find all individuals having a birth place that alphabetically follows the entry Salt Lake City, Salt Lake County, Utah, USA.
Range	Searches for places that are alphabetically between the places you enter in the **From** and **To** boxes. If you select Full Place Name under **Place Level** you must enter a city, county, state, and country for a proper search. The search will proceed by country, then state, then county, and then city. For example, to find all the individuals who have a birth place in a state that would appear alphabetically between *Ohio* and *Utah*, you would select 3 (State) under Place Level and then Range, and then enter Ohio in the Start box and Utah in the To box. This search will find all individuals having a birth place that is between Ohio and Utah alphabetically.

Title field filter

The title field filters allow you to search for individuals based on information contained in the Title (Prefix) and Title (Suffix) fields. The example below is for the Title (Prefix) field. The search options for the Title (Suffix) field work in the same way. (You enter information in these fields using the **Title (Prefix)** and **Title (Suffix)** boxes on the Individual form. Refer to chapter 4, Working with Individuals in a Database, to learn how to enter information on the Individual form.)

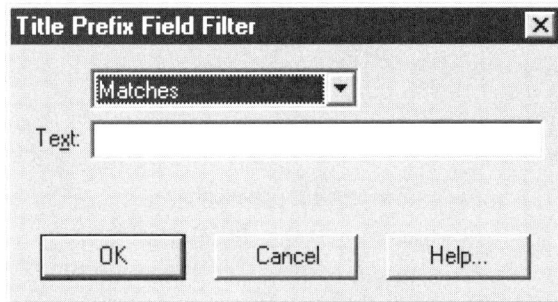

Filter Option	Description
Matches	Searches for individuals whose title exactly matches the title you enter in the **Text** box. For example, to find all individuals who have the title prefix "Doctor," you would select Matches and enter Doctor in the Text box. This search will find all individuals who have the title prefix "Doctor." You can enter a wild card either at the start or end of the text, such as "D*" to select Dr., Doctor, etc.
Does not match	Searches for individuals whose title does not match the title you enter in the **Text** box. For example, to find all individuals who do not have the title prefix "Doctor," you would select Does not match and enter "Doctor" in the Text box. This search will find all individuals who do not have the title prefix Doctor. You can enter a wild card either at the start or end of the text, such as "D*" to select Dr., Doctor, etc.
Contains	Searches for individuals whose title has the characters you enter in the **Text** box. For example, to find every individual who has the letters "gen" in his or her title prefix, you would select Contains and type "gen" in the Text box. This search will find every individual who has the letters "gen" (in that order) in his or her title prefix, such as General, Major General, Maj. Gen., etc.
Does not contain	Searches for individuals whose title does not have the characters you enter in the **Text** box. For example, to find every individual who does not have the letters "gen" in his or her title prefix, you would select Does not contain and type "gen" in the Text box. This search will find every individual who does not have the letters "gen" (in that order) in his or her title prefix.

Filter Option	Description
Exists	Searches for individuals who have any entry in the title field.
Does not exist	Searches for individuals who have no entry in the title field.

ID field filter

The ID field filter allows you to search for individuals based on information in the ID # field. (You enter information in this field using the **ID #** box on the Individual form. Refer to chapter 4, Working with Individuals in a Database, to learn how to enter information on the Individual form.)

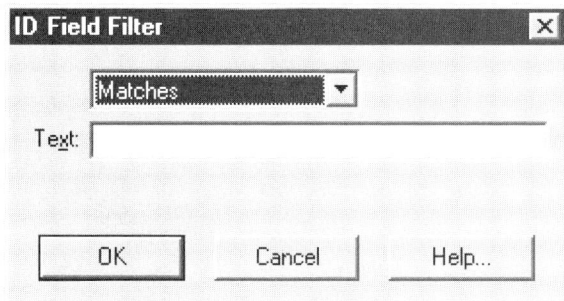

Filter Option	Description
Matches	Searches for the individual whose ID number exactly matches the ID number you enter in the **Text** box.
Does not match	Searches for individuals whose ID number does not match the ID number you enter in the **Text** box.
Contains	Searches for individuals whose ID number contains the characters you enter in the **Text** box.
Does not contain	Searches for individuals whose ID number does not contain the characters you enter in the **Text** box.
Exists	Searches for individuals who have any ID number.
Does not exist	Searches for individuals who do not have an ID number.
Is less than	Searches for individuals whose ID number is less than the ID number you enter in the **Text** box.
Is greater than	Searches for individuals whose ID number is greater than the ID number you enter in the **Text** box.
Range	Searches for individuals whose ID numbers are between the numbers you enter in the **From** and **To** boxes. For example, to find all individuals who have ID numbers between 0300 and 0350, you would select Range and enter 0300 in the From box and 0350 in the To box. This search will find every individual whose ID number is between 0300 and 0350.

Notes field filter

The notes field filter lets you search for individuals based on the information contained in individuals' notes. (You enter information in individuals' notes using the Notes form. Refer to chapter 6, Working with Notes, to learn how to enter notes for an individual.)

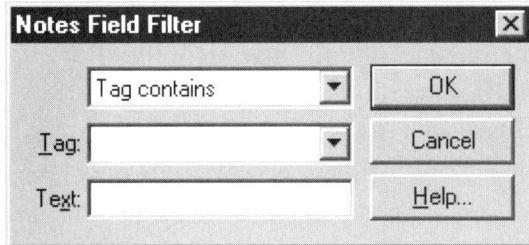

```
Notes Field Filter                    [X]

        Tag contains        [▼]    [   OK   ]

Tag:  [              ] [▼]    [ Cancel ]

Text: [                    ]    [ Help... ]
```

Filter Option	Description
Contains	Searches for individuals whose notes contain the text entered in the **Text** box.
Does not contain	Searches for individuals whose notes do not contain the text entered in the **Text** box.
Exists	Searches for individuals for whom there are notes.
Does not exist	Searches for individuals for whom there are no notes.
Tag contains	Searches for individuals for whom the selected note tag contains the text entered in the **Text** box. You must select a tag in the **Tag** box.
Tag does not contain	Searches for individuals for whom the selected note tag does not contain the text entered in the **Text** box. You must select a tag in the **Tag** box.
Tag exists	Searches for individuals for whom the selected note tag contains any text. You must select a tag in the **Tag** box.
Tag does not exist	Searches for individuals for whom the selected note tag does not contain any text. You must select a tag in the **Tag** box.

Number filter

The number filter lets you search for individuals based on the number of times a particular event occurred—such as number of marriages and number of parents. The example below is for the number of children.

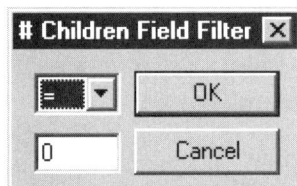

```
# Children Field Filter [X]

[ = ▼]    [    OK    ]

[0   ]    [  Cancel  ]
```

Filter Option	Description
=	Searches for individuals who have the number of children you enter in the box below.

Filter Option	Description
<	Searches for individuals who have fewer than the number of children you enter in the box below.
>	Searches for individuals who have more than the number of children you enter in the box below.

Is/is not filter

The is/is not filter lets you search for individuals based on whether they meet a particular condition—such as whether the individual is deceased. The example below performs searchcs based on whether the individual is at the end of a family line.

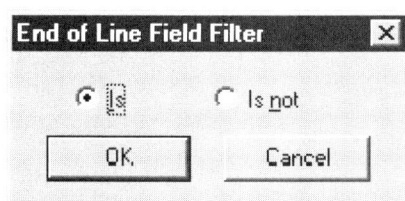

Filter Option	Description
Is	Finds every individual who is at the end of a family line.
Is not	Finds every individual who is not the end of a family line.

3. After you have added a field filter to the **Current Filter** list, you can:

    • Click the **OK** button to close the Field Filtering form and perform the search.

    Each individual in the filtered group is marked with a >> symbol in the list of individuals on the Search for Individual form.

    Note: To cause only the individuals in the filtered group to be displayed in the list of individuals, check the **Show results only** box on the Search for Individual form.

    • Add more fields to the Current Filter list to create additional search criteria.

To use multiple fields as search criteria

1. The parentheses buttons ( ) and the **AND** and **OR** buttons on the **Field Filtering** form allow you to use multiple criteria in field filters.

    • To find individuals who exactly match two or more criteria, you would use the AND button to define the search condition. For example, to find all the individuals who were born in 1910 and have the last name of Jones, you would perform the following steps:

        Under **Possible Fields** select Birth Date, click the > button, select Contains filter option, enter 1910 in the **Date** box, click the **OK** button, click the AND button, under **Possible Fields** select Name, click the > button, under **Part of Name** click Surname Only, select Matches filter option, enter Jones in the **Text** box, click the **OK** button.

The Current Filter box would look like this:

Birth Date Contains 1910

AND

Name (Surname only) Matches Jones

This search would find all individuals who have a birth date in 1910 and have the surname Jones.

- To find all individuals who match any of two or more criteria, you would use the OR button to define the search condition. For example, to find all individuals who were born in 1910 or have the last name Jones, you would perform the following steps:

    Under **Possible Fields** select Birth Date, click the > button, select Contains filter option, enter 1910 in the **Date** box, click the **OK** button, click the **OR** button, under **Possible Fields** select Name, click the > button, under **Part of Name** click Surname Only, select Matches filter option, enter Jones in the Text box, click the **OK** button.

The Current Filter box would look like this:

Birth Date Contains 1910

OR

Name (Surname only) Matches Jones

This search would find all individuals who have a birth date in 1910 or have the last name Jones.

- The parentheses buttons allow you to search for one set of individuals and then further limit the set. For example, if you want to find all individuals who were born in 1910 and have the surname Jones and want to know who among that set of individuals is male, you would perform the following steps:

    Click the (button, under **Possible Fields** select Birth Date, click the > button, select Contains filter option, enter 1910 in the **Date** box, click the **OK** button, click the **AND** button, under **Possible Fields** select Name, click the > button, under **Part of Name** click Surname Only, select Matches filter option, enter Jones in the **Text** box, click the **OK** button, click the **)** button, click the **AND** button, under **Possible Fields** select Sex, click the > button, select Matches and Male filter options, click the **OK** button.

The Current Filter box would look like this:

(

Birth Date Contains 1910

AND

Name (Surname only) Matches Jones

)

AND

Gender Matches Male

This search would find all individuals who have a birth date in 1910, the last name Jones, and are male.

2. On the **Field Filtering** form, click the **OK** button to close the Field Filtering form and perform the search.

Each individual in the filtered group is marked with a >> symbol in the list of individuals on the Search for Individual form.

Note: To cause only the individuals in the filtered group to be displayed in the list of individuals, check the **Show results only** box on the **Search for Individual** form.

To modify a search criterion

1. In the **Current Filter** box on the **Field Filtering** form, highlight the criterion that you want to modify and then click the **Modify** button.

The **Field Filter** form for the selected criterion will be displayed. You can modify the filter options and any entered data.

2. Click the **OK** button to save the modified criterion and close the Field Filter form.

To modify the order of the search criteria

1. In the **Current Filter** box, highlight the criterion that you want to move.

2. Click the move up or move down button to move the criterion up or down in the list.

Saving field filters for future use

You'll probably find some field filters useful enough that you'll want to use them more than once. You can save a field filter so that you can use it repeatedly in the future without having to recreate it each time. You can also copy an existing field filter and then modify it to perform variations on that search.

To save a field filter

1. Create a field filter as described above in "To select a field to use as a search criterion" and "To use multiple fields as search criteria."

2. On the **Field Filtering** form, click the **Save** button.

The **Save Filter** form will be displayed.

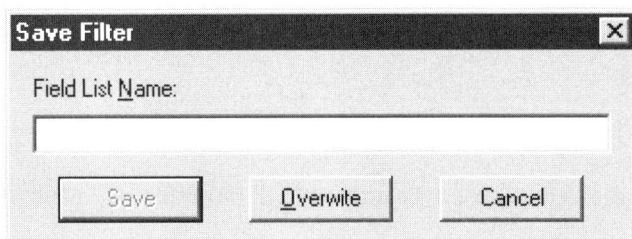

3. In the **Field List Name** box, enter a unique name for the filter and then click the **Save** button.

The filter will be saved and the Save Filter form will close.

To retrieve a saved field filter

1. On the **Field Filtering** form, click the **Retrieve** button.

The **Open Filter** form will be displayed.

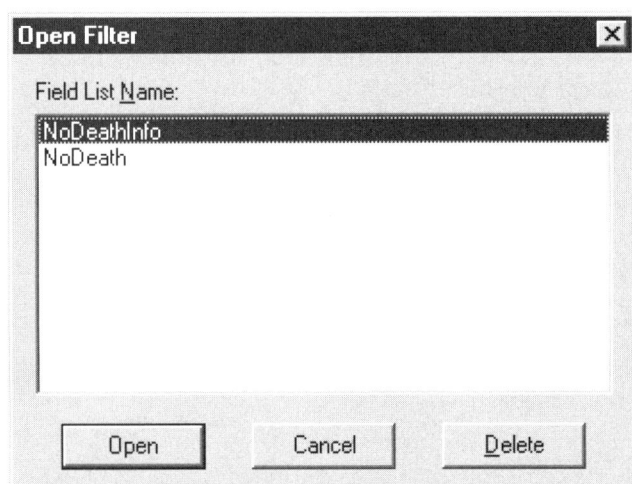

2. Highlight the field filter you want to retrieve and then click the **Open** button.

The Open Filter form will close and the field filter criteria are displayed in the Current Filter box on the Field Filtering form. You can modify the field filter criteria or use the filter to search the database.

To copy an existing field filter

1. Retrieve a saved field filter and modify the search criteria as necessary.

2. On the **Field Filtering** form, click the **Save** button.

The **Save Filter** form will be displayed.

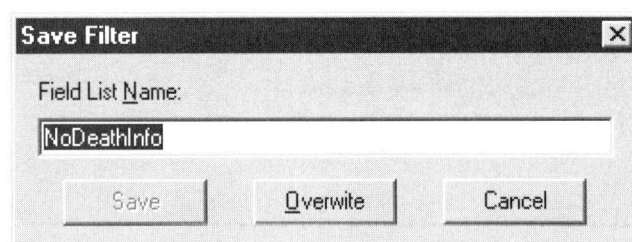

Enter a unique name for the filter in place of the existing name and then click the **Save** button.

The filter will be saved as a new filter and the Save Filter form will close. (The original filter will still exist.)

Combining the results of a relationship filter search and a field filter search

After you have performed a relationship filter search and a field filter search, you can combine the contents of the searches to further limit your search.

To combine the results of a relationship filter and field filter search

On the **Search for Individual** form, click the arrow button to the right of the **Combine lists using** box and select one of the options described below from the list.

Combine lists using: |OR ▼|

Option	Description
AND	The active list will contain only those individuals who are selected in *both* lists. There may be 50 people selected in the relationship filter list and 100 selected in the field filter list, but if none of these people are selected in both lists, then the active list will contain no individuals. However, if all 50 people selected in the relationship filter list are also selected in the field filter list of 100, those 50 people will be selected in the active list.
OR	The active list will contain all individuals who are selected in *either* list. For example, suppose the relationship filter has selected 100 ancestors of Will Johnson and the field filter has selected 50 people in your database with the last name of Johnson. Of these, 15 are in both lists (counted twice). The active list will contain 135 selected individuals: all 100 ancestors of Will Johnson, along with the other 35 people with the last name of Johnson who are not his ancestors.
	In other words, the combined list will select either all people who are ancestors of Will Johnson *or* who have the last name of Johnson.
NOT	The active list will contain only those individuals who are selected in the relationship filter list but are *not* in the field filter list. Using the above example, the active list would contain 85 selected individuals: Will Johnson's 100 ancestors minus the 15 who have the last name of Johnson.
	In other words, the combined list will select all people who are ancestors of Will Johnson who do *not* have the last name of Johnson.

The **Counts** display on the **Search for Individual** form will contain summarized results of the combined search.

┌ Counts ───────────┐
│ Relationship: 4 │
│ Field: 14 │
│ Filtered List: 15 │
└──────────────────┘

Count	Description
Relationship	Indicates the number of individuals who were selected by the relationship filter.
Field	Indicates the number of individuals who were selected by the field filter.
Filtered list	Indicates the number of individuals who were selected by the combined filters.

Saving filtered lists for future use

If you want to work with a filtered list of individuals again, you can save it and then retrieve it whenever you want to. You can save a filtered list that is based only on a relationship filter, a filtered list that is based only on a field filter, or a filtered list that contains the results of a combined search.

To save a filtered list

1. Perform a search using one or both of the filters described above.

2. On the **Search for Individual** form, click the **Save** button.

   The **Save Filter** form will be displayed.

3. In the **Filter Name** box, enter a unique name for the filter and then click the **Save** button.

   The filter will be saved and the Save Filter form will close.

To retrieve a saved filtered list

1. On the **Search for Individual** form, click the **Retrieve** button.

   The **Open Filter** form will be displayed.

Open Filter

Filter Name:

JewettDescendants
BirthDateExists
FamilyBirthDateExists

[Open] [Cancel] [Delete]

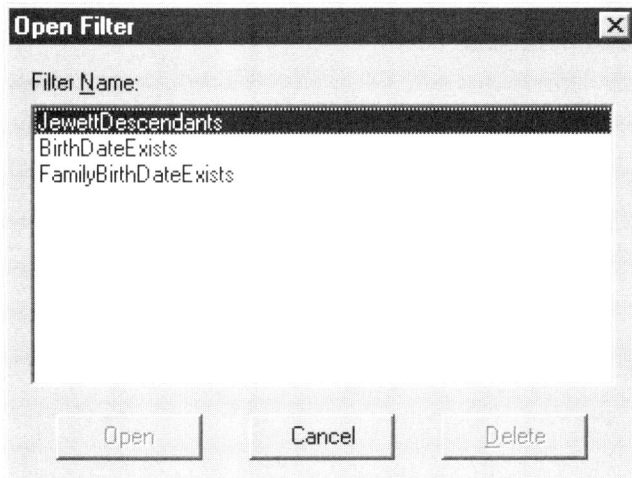

2. Highlight the filtered list you want to retrieve and then click the **Open** button.

The Open Filter form will close and the filtered list will be displayed in the active list on the Search for Individual form.

To copy an existing filtered list

1. Retrieve a saved filtered list and modify it as necessary.

2. On the **Search for Individual** form, click the **Save** button.

The **Save Filter** form will be displayed.

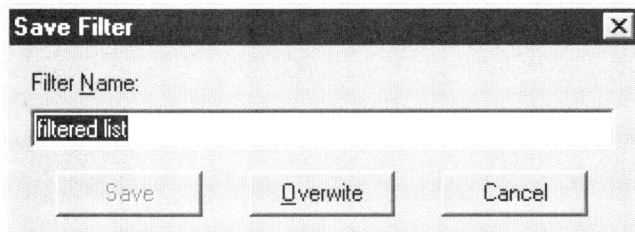

Save Filter

Filter Name:

filtered list

[Save] [Overwrite] [Cancel]

Enter a unique name for the filter in place of the existing name and then click the **Save** button.

The filter will be saved as a new filter and the Save Filter form will close. (The original filter will still exist.)

Searching for a descendant of a selected individual

Instead of searching the entire database, you can easily view a list of all descendants of a selected individual.

To search for a descendant of a selected individual

1. Do one of the following:

- On the **Citation Links** form, click the **Search** button.

   The **Find** form will be displayed.

On the **Find** form, click the **Individual RIN** option button and then click the **Descendancy List** button.

- Click the Descendancy List button 🖳 on the button bar.

- On the **Tools** menu, click **Descendancy List**.

The **Descendancy List** form will be displayed.

The Descendancy List displays the parents, spouse(s), siblings, and children of the individual selected on the previous form.

2. Select a descendant by double-clicking the individual, or highlight the individual and then click the **OK** button. Either of these actions will accept the individual and return to the previous form, making that individual the primary person.

Searching for a marriage

Because marriages, like individuals, exist in Ancestry Family Tree as unique records, you can search for marriages.

To search for a marriage

1. Do one of the following:

   • On the **Citation Links** form, click the **Search** button, or

   • click the Search button 🔍 on the button bar.

   The **Find Individual** form will be displayed.

2. On the **Find Individual** form, click the **Marriage RIN** button and then click the **Browse List** button.

   The **Search for Marriage** form will be displayed.

The **Search for Marriage** form allows you to select a marriage from a list of marriages in the database. The marriages are displayed in numerical order by MRIN.

3. Do one of the following:

- Scroll through the list of marriages until you locate the marriage you are searching for, or

- in the text box above the list of marriages, enter an MRIN to move back or ahead in the list to a group of marriages that might contain the marriage you are searching for.

4. When you locate the marriage you are searching for, double-click the marriage or select the marriage and then click the **OK** button. Either of these actions will accept the marriage and return to the previous form, making the husband the primary person.

CHAPTER 10

Importing and Exporting Files and Merging Records

This chapter describes how to import and export genealogical data as GEDCOM files. Using this common file format, you can share your data with other researchers and receive data from other researchers—even those who use genealogy software other than Ancestry Family Tree.

Importing data into an existing Ancestry Family Tree database often results in duplicate records within the database. This chapter describes how to eliminate duplicate records by merging them.

In this chapter

- Importing and exporting files
- Merging records

Importing and exporting files

You can import data compiled by other researchers and saved in the GEDCOM format. GEDCOM stands for Genealogical Data Communication; it is a data format standard that allows genealogical data created and stored by different genealogy software programs to be shared among their users. Thus, Ancestry Family Tree users can import data created by users of other genealogy software programs if it has been saved in the GEDCOM format. Likewise, Ancestry Family Tree users can share their data with users of other genealogy software by saving and exporting it in the GEDCOM format.

Importing a GEDCOM file

You can import a GEDCOM file into an existing Ancestry Family Tree database or into a new database. During the import process you can define a number of preferences to determine what type of information will be imported for each individual.

Using Ancestry Family Tree, you can import GEDCOM files from several types of sources:

- Directly from other researchers—they may e-mail their GEDCOM files to you or give them to you on a floppy disk.

- From sites on the World Wide Web. Individual family history researchers and organizations often allow you to download family history data in GEDCOM format directly from their Web sites. Ancestry.com, for example, lets you import data from its World Family Tree, a collection of family history data contributed by researchers from all over the world. This option requires Web browser software on your computer and access to the Web through a Web provider.

- An Online Family Tree™ hosted by Ancestry.com on the World Wide Web. Ancestry Family Tree users can export databases to Ancestry.com as Online Family Trees; you can import them if you are given access by the person who created the Online Family Tree. The imported Online Family Tree will be saved as an Ancestry Family Tree file. This option also requires Web browser software on your computer and access to the Web through a Web provider.

To import a GEDCOM file received from another researcher

1. Do one of the following:

   - To import a GEDCOM file into an existing Ancestry Family Tree database, open the database into which you want to import the GEDCOM file and then proceed to the following step, or

   - to import a GEDCOM file into a new database, refer to "Creating a new family database by importing a GEDCOM file" in chapter 3, Working with Family Databases.

2. In the **File** menu, click **Import**.

   The **Import GEDCOM File** form will be displayed.

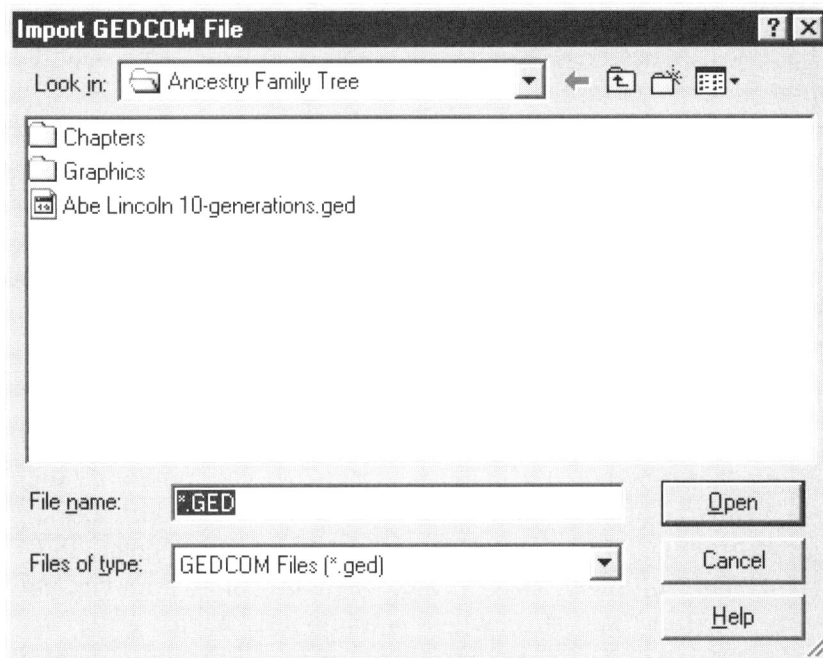

3. Use the controls described below to locate the GEDCOM file you want to import.

- Click the drop-down button to the right of the **Look In** box to view the contents of the disk drives and folders on your computer.

- Click the button to view the contents of the folder one level above the folder you are currently viewing.

4. Highlight the GEDCOM file in the list of files.

5. Click the **Open** button.

   The **GEDCOM Import** form will be displayed.

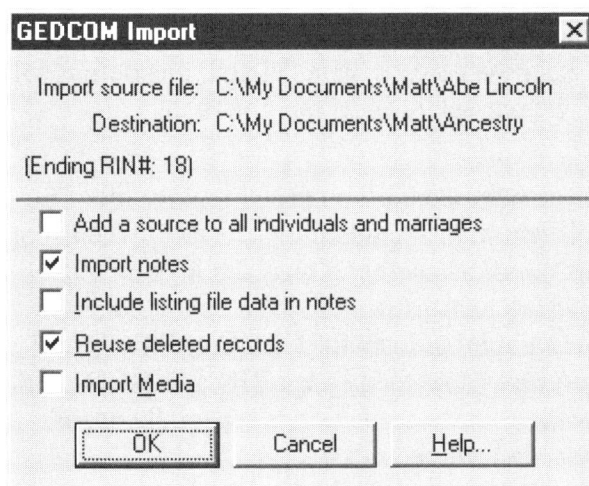

6. The GEDCOM Import form allows you to define import preferences that affect the resulting Ancestry Family Tree database. Refer to the table below to learn about the purpose of each option and then check the appropriate boxes.

Option	Description
Add a source to all individuals and marriages	If you check this box, Ancestry Family Tree will create a new source record and attach a citation to it of every individual record and marriage record that is imported from the GEDCOM file. You will be able to edit this source record during the import process. (Refer to chapter 7, Working with Sources and Source Citations, to learn about sources and source citations.) This option is useful because it allows you to identify the source of every individual and marriage record imported from the GEDCOM file. You might want to indicate the name of the GEDCOM file, where or from whom you got the file, the date on which you imported it, etc.
Import notes	If checked, any notes in the GEDCOM file will be added to the new database.
Include listing file data in notes	Any data in the GEDCOM file that cannot be imported properly into your database will be copied to an exception report called the *listing file*. If you check this box, listing file data will also be added to the notes for each affected individual. This option is recommended because it is much easier to locate the errors and decide how to resolve them when they are noted in the individuals' notes. (Refer to chapter 6, Working with Notes, to learn about notes.)
Reuse deleted records	Check this box to cause any unused RINs and MRINs to be re-used. If any RINs and MRINs in the existing database are unused because those records were deleted, this option will cause them to be re-used for new records as they are imported. Leave this check box blank if you prefer to have all of the imported RINs and MRINs added to the end of the existing database. This option is useful because the RIN or MRIN will indicate which records were in the existing database and which were imported from the GEDCOM file. (Before importing, be sure to note the highest RIN and MRIN in the existing database.) This information is especially useful when merging duplicate records.
Import media	If you check this box, any multimedia objects embedded in the GEDCOM file will be added to your database. (Refer to

Option	Description
	chapter 8, Working with Media Collections, to learn about multimedia objects.)
	If you don't check this box, these objects will be ignored.

7. Click the **OK** button.

   A warning dialog box similar to the one shown below will be displayed.

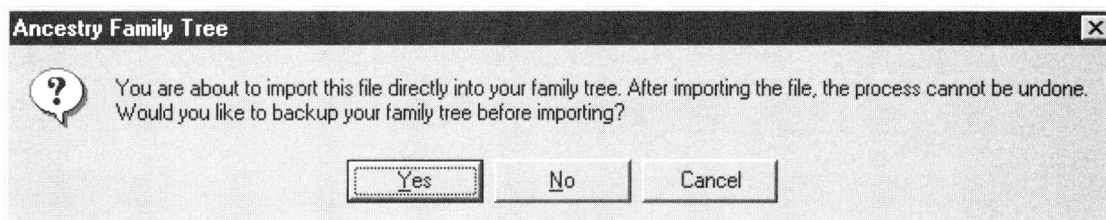

   Ancestry Family Tree

   ? You are about to import this file directly into your family tree. After importing the file, the process cannot be undone. Would you like to backup your family tree before importing?

   [Yes]   [No]   [Cancel]

8. Do one of the following:

   - Click the **Yes** button to back up the existing database. A copy of the existing database will be saved in the same directory as the existing database with the suffix *.tqz. For example, if you are backing up an Ancestry Family Tree database named Edison.aft, the backup file will be saved in the same directory and will be named Edison.tqz. Backing up a database allows you to restore it later in its original form (as it was before you imported data). Refer to chapter 3, Working with Family Databases, to learn how to restore a backup file.

   - Click the **No** button if you don't want to back up the existing database.

   Note: If you checked the **Add a source to all individuals and marriages** box, the Source Citation form will be displayed. Refer to chapter 7, Working with Sources and Source Citations, to learn how to use this form.

   The **GEDCOM Import** confirmation dialog box will be displayed.

   GEDCOM Import

   189 Individuals Imported
   113 Marriages Imported

   [OK]

9. Click the **OK** button to close the form

   The Merge Warning dialog box will be displayed.

Merge Warning

Performing any Merge operation will delete some records and change other records. You should back up your data prior to proceeding.

☐ Don't show this warning in the future

[OK]

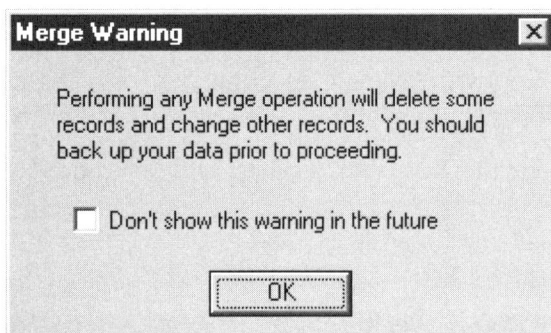

10. Click the **OK** button.

The **Merge Individuals** form will be displayed.

11. If you want to find and merge individual records that might be duplicates, refer to "Merging records," below, to learn how to merge individual records. Otherwise, proceed to the next step. (You don't have to merge duplicate records when importing; you can perform a merge operation to merge duplicate records in a database anytime you choose.)

12. After you have finished merging individual records or if you want to merge individual records at another time, click the **Close** button on the **Merge Individuals** form to close the form and complete the import process.

The **Pedigree** view of the updated database will be displayed.

To import a GEDCOM file from an Online Family Tree

1. Sign on to the World Wide Web through your Web provider.

2. Close all Ancestry Family Tree databases that are currently open.

3. In the File menu, click **Import from Web**.

The **Create New Family File** form will be displayed.

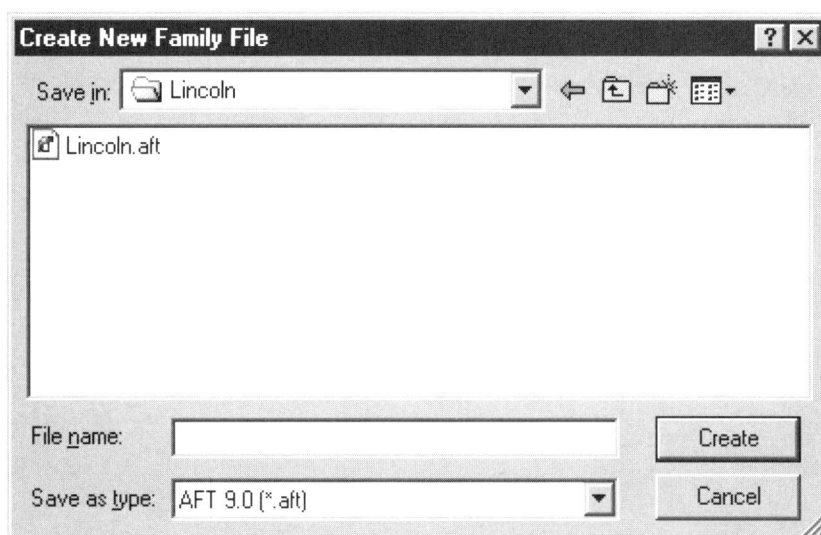

Create New Family File

Save in: ☐ Lincoln

📄 Lincoln.aft

File name: [   ] [Create]

Save as type: AFT 9.0 (*.aft) [Cancel]

4. Use the controls described below to locate the disk drive or directory where you want to save the file.

- Look in: [Hopkins ▼] Click the drop-down button to the right of the **Look In** box to view the contents of the disk drives and folders on your computer.

- Click the [⬆] button to view the contents of the folder one level above the folder you are currently viewing.

- [◻*] Click the New Folder button to create a new sub-folder in the current folder.

5. In the **File Name** box, enter a name for the import file.

   Note: Because the file will be saved as an Ancestry Family Tree database, the file name must end with a *.aft* suffix.

6. Click the **Create** button.

   If you are not currently logged in to Ancestry.com, the **Login** form will be displayed.

7. Do one of the following:

   - If you are a registered user of Ancestry.com, log in.

   - If you are not a registered user, you can register to use Ancestry.com's free services or you can subscribe to access additional resources on Ancestry.com.

After you have logged in or registered, the **Online Family Trees** form will be displayed.

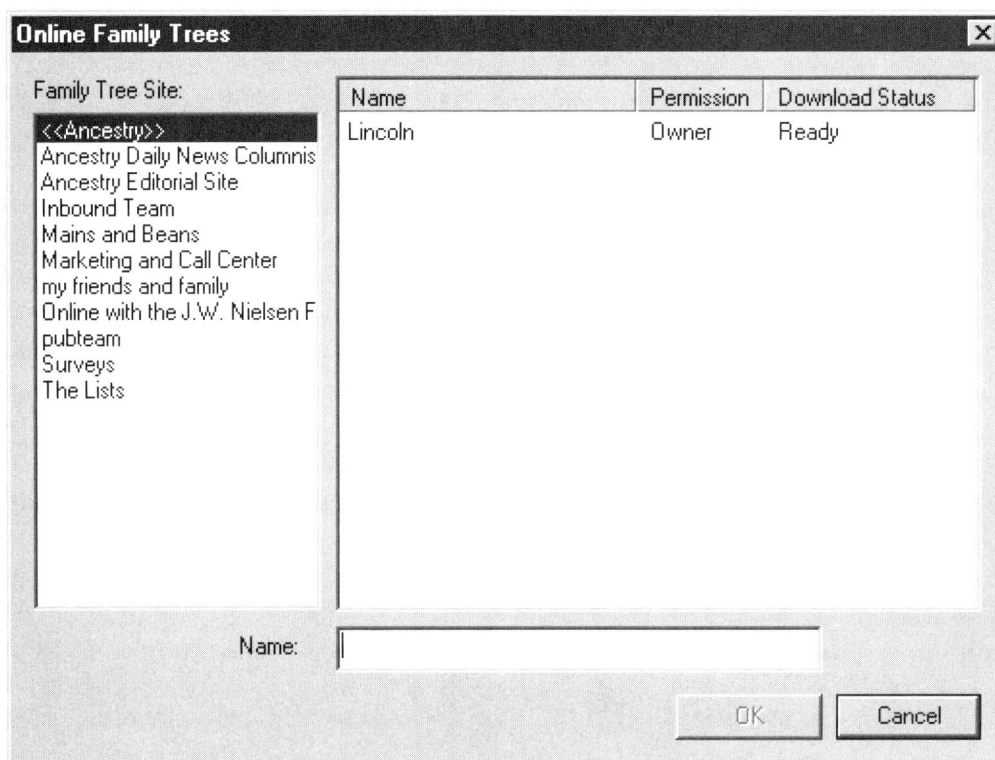

The Online Family Trees to which you have access are listed in the Name/Permission/Download Status list.

8. Highlight the Online Family Tree you want to import and then click the **OK** button.

    The **GEDCOM Import** form will be displayed.

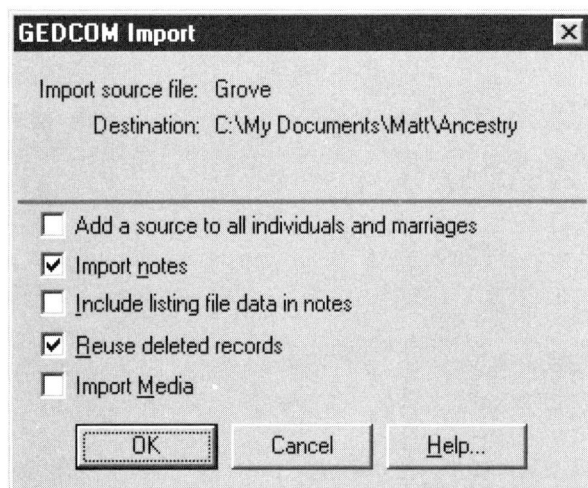

9. Refer to step 6 in "To import a GEDCOM file received from another researcher," above, to learn how to select import preferences that will affect the resulting Ancestry Family Tree database.

10. Click the **OK** button.

The **Percentage Completed** form will be displayed while the import occurs.

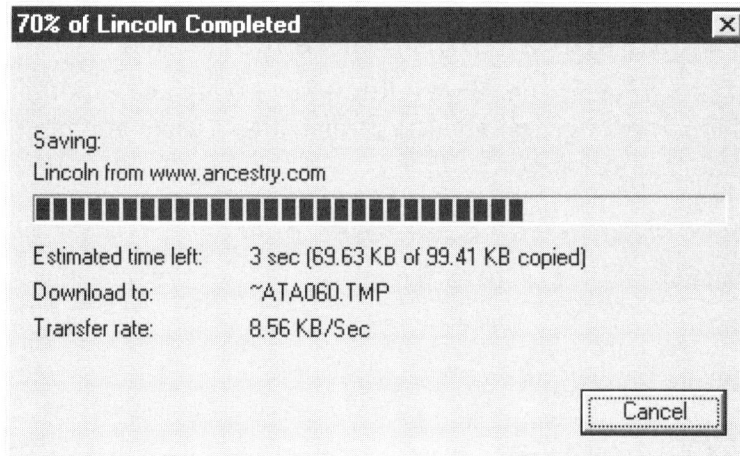

```
┌──────────────────────────────────────────────────────┐
│ 70% of Lincoln Completed                          [X] │
├──────────────────────────────────────────────────────┤
│                                                        │
│                                                        │
│  Saving:                                               │
│  Lincoln from www.ancestry.com                         │
│  ████████████████████████████████                      │
│                                                        │
│  Estimated time left:   3 sec (69.63 KB of 99.41 KB copied) │
│  Download to:           ~ATA060.TMP                    │
│  Transfer rate:         8.56 KB/Sec                    │
│                                                        │
│                                        [  Cancel  ]    │
└──────────────────────────────────────────────────────┘
```

When the import is complete, the **GEDCOM Import** form will be displayed.

```
┌────────────────────────────┐
│ GEDCOM Import        [X]    │
├────────────────────────────┤
│  189 Individuals Imported   │
│  113 Marriages Imported     │
│                             │
│      [     OK     ]         │
└────────────────────────────┘
```

11. Click the **OK** button.

    The GEDCOM file will be saved as an Ancestry Family Tree file and the file will be opened in the Ancestry Family Tree view.

Exporting a GEDCOM file

You can share your data with users of other genealogy software by saving and exporting it in the GEDCOM format. You can export all individuals in a database or select specific individuals to be exported. You can also choose among a number of preferences that determine what type of information is exported for each individual.

You select one of several types of GEDCOM format (depending on how the data you export will be used):

- You can create an export file and share your data with other researchers directly by e-mailing it to them or giving it to them on a floppy disk.

- You can identify and export the records of individuals who are qualified for LDS temple ordinances. For this purpose you create a GEDCOM export file optimized for processing by TempleReady™, a software program that prepares the GEDCOM file for submission to an LDS temple.

- You can choose to export your data to the World Wide Web as an Online Family Tree hosted by Ancestry.com. Then, you and others to whom you grant access can maintain the Online Family Tree online. This option requires Web browser software on your computer and access to the Web through a Web provider.

Exporting a GEDCOM file to share with other researchers

You can share your data with users of other genealogy software by saving and exporting it in the GEDCOM format. This common genealogy data format allows users of other software to import your data into their databases.

To export a GEDCOM file for sharing with other researchers

1. Open the database that contains data you want to export.

2. In the **File** menu, click **Export**.

   The **GEDCOM Export** form will be displayed.

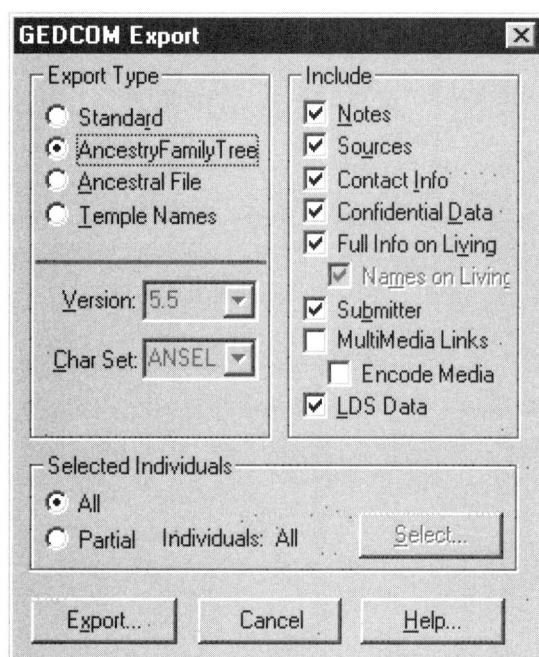

3. Under **Export Type**, select one of the following options based on how the data you are exporting will be used:

Option	Description
Standard	Select if you are exporting data for others who are not using Ancestry Family Tree.
Ancestry Family Tree	Select if you are exporting data for others who are using Ancestry Family Tree. If you aren't sure whether a recipient will use Ancestry Family Tree, you can still select this option. Users of other software might get extra warning messages when importing the data, but Ancestry Family Tree users will get more complete data.
Ancestral File	Select if you are exporting data for submission to the Ancestral File™ database of the LDS church.

Option	Description
Temple Names	Select if you want to prepare names in the database for processing by TempleReady™. (Refer to "Exporting a GEDCOM file for processing by TempleReady," below, to learn how to create a GEDCOM file specifically for TempleReady.)

4. If you selected **Standard** under Export Type, you can specify which version of GEDCOM to use for the exported data.

GEDCOM version	Description
4.0	Select if you are exporting data to be used with Personal Ancestral File 2.x or other pre-1997 genealogy software.
5.5	Select if you are exporting data to be used with Ancestry Family Tree, Ancestral Quest 2.1, or any other post-1997 genealogy software.

Click the arrow button to the right of the **Version** box and select the applicable GEDCOM version.

5. If you selected **Standard** under Export Type, you can specify which character set to use for the exported data. If your database uses extended characters (characters other than the 26 standard characters of the English alphabet), you need to select the appropriate character set.

Character set	Description
ANSEL	Select if you are exporting data to be used with Personal Ancestral File. The ANSEL character set encompasses the ANSI character set used by Windows® programs and accommodates extended characters (including many that use diacritical marks) that are not represented in ANSI.
ANSI	Select if you are exporting data to be used with Windows programs. The ANSI character set is used by Windows programs. It includes the most common diacritical characters.

Click the arrow button to the right of the **Char Set** box and select the applicable character set.

6. Under **Include** you can choose among a number of options that determine what type of information will be exported from each individual record. Refer to the table below to learn about each option, then check or uncheck the boxes to set the options you want.

Option	Description
Notes	This box determines whether all notes in all note fields (including those beginning with *!*) will be included in the exported data. (An exclamation point [!] can be used to mark note paragraphs, allowing them to be excluded from some charts and reports at your discretion. Refer to chapter 6, Working with Notes, for details.) Uncheck the box if you don't want notes to be included.
Sources	This box determines whether sources, source citations, and repositories will be included in the exported data. Uncheck the box if you don't want this information to be included.
Contact Info	This box determines whether the contact information entered for an individual will be included in the exported data. Check the box if you want contact information to be included.
Confidential Data	This box determines whether confidential information will be included in the exported data. (Confidential *notes* are denoted by a tilde [~] at the beginning of the first line of confidential text and a blank line before and after; refer to chapter 6, Working with Notes, for details. *Events* can be marked confidential using the Additional Event form; refer to chapter 4, Working with Individuals in a Database, to learn how to use the Additional Event form.) Uncheck the box if you do not want confidential notes to be included.
Full Info on Living	This box determines whether all information will be included in the exported data for individuals in the database who are still living. (Ancestry Family Tree defines any individual with no entry in the death date field and less than 110 years old as living.) If you choose not to include all information for living individuals,

Option	Description
	only relationship information will be included for them.
	Uncheck the box if you do not want to include all information for living individuals.
Names on Living	If you choose not to include all information for living individuals by unchecking the Full Info on Living box, the **Names on Living** box becomes available. This box determines whether the names of living individuals will be included in the exported data.
	If you choose not to include the names of living individuals, their names will be replaced by the word *Living*.
	Uncheck the box if you do not want to include the names of living individuals.
Submitter	This box determines whether the information entered for the compiler of the database will be included in the exported data. (This information is entered on the Compiler page of the Preferences form. Refer to chapter 2, Installation and Setup, to learn how to define overall Ancestry Family Tree preferences.)
	Uncheck the box if you don't want to include information for the compiler.
MultiMedia Links	This box determines whether multimedia links will be included in the exported data. If there are multimedia objects (photo, video, or audio files) associated with any individual in the exported data, using this option will include the link (the path and name) of each file.
	Note: If you select this option, you will still have to send the multimedia objects separately if you want them to be available to the recipient.
	Check this box if you want to include links to multimedia objects.
Encode Media	This box determines whether multimedia objects associated with individuals in the exported data will be embedded directly in the GEDCOM file. If you select this option, you will not have to send the multimedia objects to the recipient separately.
	Note: Embedding multimedia objects in the exported data will greatly increase the size of the GEDCOM file, possibly making it too large to be e-mailed. In such a case, sending the file on a floppy disk is the best option.
	Also, as of the initial use of this feature in Ancestry Family Tree, no other genealogy software makes use of it. Therefore, you should verify that the recipient of the GEDCOM file can process the multimedia objects; otherwise you will increase the size of the GEDCOM file

Option	Description
	needlessly.
	Check the box if you want multimedia objects to be embedded directly in the GEDCOM file.
LDS Data	This box determines whether LDS data (such as date and place of baptism, endowment, etc.) will be included in the exported data. This box is available only if Use LDS Data is selected on the General page of the Preferences form.
	Uncheck the box if you do not want LDS data to be included.

7. Do one of the following:

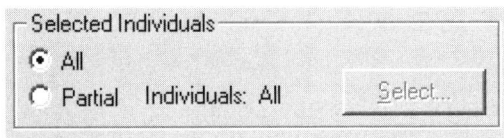

- To export all individuals in the database, ensure that **All** is selected under **Selected Individuals** on the **GEDCOM Export** form and then proceed to the following step, or

- to export one or more selected individuals, click the **Partial** option under **Selected Individuals** and then click the **Select** button.

  The **Select Set of Individuals** form will be displayed. This form lets you select individuals from a list and lets you search for individuals in the database using various search filters. Refer to "Searching for individuals using filters" in chapter 9, Searching the Database, to learn how to use the Select Set of Individuals form to search for and select individuals. (The Select Set of Individuals form is essentially identical to the Search for Individual form described in chapter 9.)

  After you have selected the individual(s) whom you want to include in the exported data, proceed to the following step.

8. Click the **Export** button.

   The **Export GEDCOM File as** form will be displayed.

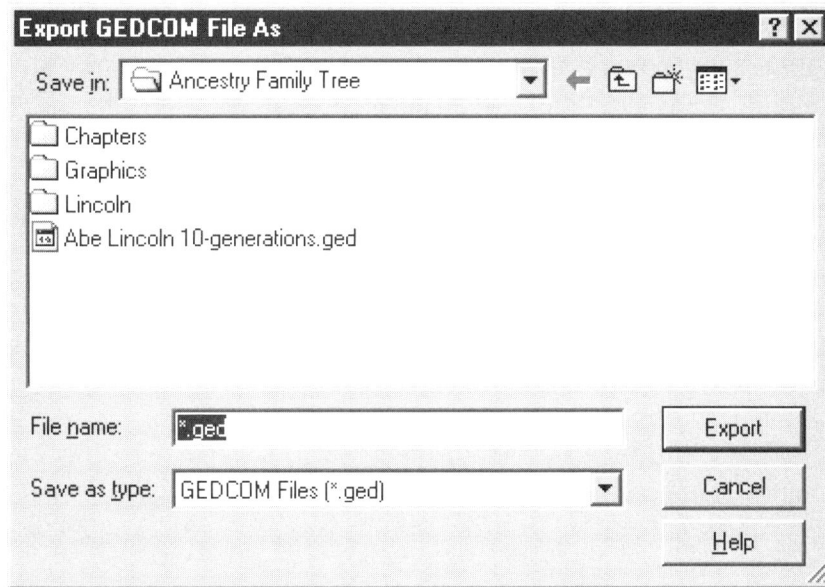

9. Use the controls described below to locate the disk drive or folder where you want to save the GEDCOM file.

    - Click the drop-down button to the right of the **Look In** box to view the contents of the disk drives and folders on your computer.

    - Click the button to view the contents of the folder one level above the folder you are currently viewing.

    - Click the New Folder button to create a new folder in the current directory.

    Note: Data can be submitted to the Ancestral File database or to TempleReady only on floppy disks; therefore, you will need to save a file intended for Ancestral File or TempleReady on a floppy disk now or at some point before submitting it.

10. In the **File Name** box, type a name for the GEDCOM export file.

    Note: The file name must end with a *.ged* suffix.

11. Click the **Export** button.

    The GEDCOM export file will be saved on the disk you specified and the **GEDCOM Export** form will be displayed.

12. Click the **OK** button to close the form and return to the previous Ancestry Family Tree view.

Exporting a GEDCOM file for processing by TempleReady

Ancestry Family Tree allows you to identify and export the records of individuals who are qualified for LDS temple ordinances. You will create a GEDCOM export file optimized for processing by TempleReady™, a software program that prepares the GEDCOM file for submission to the temple. You can select individuals, view their temple ordinance qualification status, and edit their records if necessary before exporting the records to the TempleReady-optimized GEDCOM file.

After you create the GEDCOM file, you must save it on a floppy disk, take it to a local LDS Family History Center, and process it using TempleReady. You will submit the file created by TempleReady to the temple.

To select individuals for submission to TempleReady

1. Open the database that contains data you want to export.

2. In the **File** menu, click **Export**.

   The **GEDCOM Export** form will be displayed.

3. Under **Export Type**, click **Temple Names**.

4. Click the **Select** button.

   The **Select Set of Individuals** form will be displayed. This form lets you select individuals whose names you would like to submit to TempleReady and review their readiness for LDS temple ordinances.

| Select Set of Individuals - Temple Names Preparation | ☒ |

| 1 | |

		Sort
1	EDISON, James Redd	b.1866	☉ BIN ○ Alpha
2	EDISON, Emma Valentina	b.1868
3	EDISON, Alma Robert	m.1860	James Redd EDISON
4	EDISON, Anne Jewett	m.1860	Sex:M AFN:
5	EDISON, Jonathan Anton	b.1868	ID No:12345
6	EDWARDS, Echo	b.1887
7	BRADLEY, Jonathan		Birth:1 Jul 1866 Baltimore,Maryland
8	EDWARDS, Edwina		Alt:8 Jul 1866 Baltimore,Maryland
9	EDISON, Richard Albertus	b.1889	Death:16 Sep 1912 Raleigh,North Carolina
10	ANDREWS, Jeremiah		Burial:18 Sep 1912 Raleigh,North Carolina
11	MORTON, Amelia
12	HARRIS, Thora		Baptism: Qualified
13	EDISON, Ansel		Endow: Qualified
14	SMITH, Henrietta	b.1900	Seal Par: Qualified
15	BERGER, Harrison
17	EDISON, Emma		Father:Alma Robert EDISON B:
18	LANDERS, Emma Valentina	m.1886	Mother:Anne Jewett EDISON B:
			Spouse:Emma V EDISON M:15 Dec 1886
			Spouse: M:

Relationship Filter: Individual

Filtered List — Combine lists using: OR — ☐ Show results only

Counts — Relationship: 0 — Field: 0 — Filtered List: 0

Field Filter — Define... — Clear — Marriages...

Select | Deselect | << Prev | Next >>
Clear | Replace << | Save... | Retrieve...

OK | Edit... | *Notes... | Delete | *Media... | Cancel | Help...

5. Select the individuals whom you would like to submit for temple ordinances. Refer to "Searching for individuals using filters" in chapter 9, Searching the Database, to learn how to use the Select Set of Individuals form to search for and select individuals. (The Select Set of Individuals form is essentially identical to the Search for Individual form described in chapter 9.)

6. Highlight an individual in the list to view the individual's qualification status for LDS baptism, endowment, and sealing to parents ordinances.

    The individual's qualification status will be displayed on the right side of the form.

    | Baptism: Qualified |
    | Endow: Qualified |
    | Seal Par: Qualified |

To edit the records of individuals who are not qualified for ordinances

If the qualification status list shows that an individual is not qualified for one or more of the ordinances, you can click the **Edit** button to open the Edit Individual form and modify the individual's record to qualify him or her for the ordinance. For example, you might need to enter a date of death to ensure that an individual is qualified for all three ordinances. (Refer to "Entering LDS ordinance data" in chapter 4, Working with

Individuals in a Database, to learn how to enter and modify ordinance data using the Edit Individual form.)

To view and edit an individual's qualification for sealing to spouse

1. To view the individual's qualification for the sealing to spouse ordinance, click the **Marriage** button on the **Select Set of Individuals** form.

   The **Seal to Spouse Status** form will be displayed. It shows each marriage record associated with the individual highlighted on the Select Set of Individuals form and the status of the spouses' qualification for sealing.

Temple Names Preparation: Seal to Spouse Status					
Marriages of James Redd EDISON					
MRIN	Spouse	Mar. Date	Marriage Place	Sealing Dt	Sealing Temple/Status
1	Emma V EDISON	15 Dec 1886	R,North Carolina	Qualified	
12	Emma V LANDERS	15 Dec 1886	R,North Carolina	Qualified	

OK   Edit...   Help...

2. You might need to edit a marriage record to qualify the individual for sealing to his or her spouse—for example, by adding a date or place of marriage. To do so, highlight the marriage in the list and click the **Edit** button to open the Marriage form. Refer to "Entering event information for a marriage" in chapter 5, Working with Marriages, to learn how to enter and modify sealing to spouse data using the Marriage form.

3. After you have edited the marriage record and closed the Marriage form, click the **OK** button on the **Seal to Spouse Status** form to close the form and return to the Select Set of Individuals form.

To remove unqualified individuals from the list of individuals to be exported

If any of the individuals selected for export are not qualified for ordinances and you are unable to add the data required for qualification, you can remove them from the list of individuals selected to be exported.

- On the **Select Set of Individuals** form, highlight an individual who is not qualified and click the **Deselect** button.

To export the selected individuals

1. After you have selected all of the individuals whom you want to export for submission to TempleReady, click the **OK** button on the **Select Set of Individuals** form to close the form and return to the GEDCOM Export form.

2. On the **GEDCOM Export** form, click the **Export** button.

   The **Temple Names Submission** form will be displayed.

Temple Names Submission ☒

Press the "Help" button to review special considerations when using the Temple Names Submission option, or continue.

[Continue]   [Cancel]   [Help]

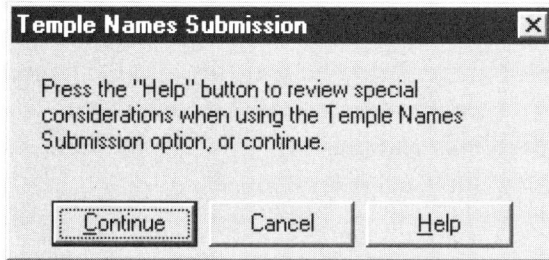

3. Click the **Continue** button to continue with the export process.

    The **Temple Names Submission Options** form will be displayed. This form lets you select some preferences that affect the final content of the GEDCOM export file.

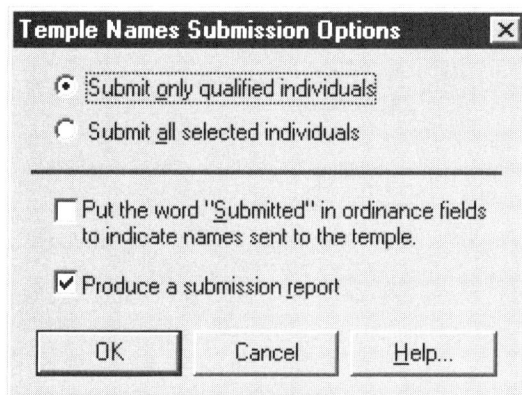

Temple Names Submission Options ☒

◉ Submit only qualified individuals

○ Submit all selected individuals

☐ Put the word "Submitted" in ordinance fields to indicate names sent to the temple.

☑ Produce a submission report

[OK]   [Cancel]   [Help...]

4. Do one of the following:

    - To submit only those selected individuals who are qualified for submission to TempleReady, click **Submit only qualified individuals**. (You might have selected individuals who are not qualified for submission because their records lack necessary data such as event dates and places.)

    - To submit all of the selected individuals (regardless of whether they are qualified for submission), click **Submit all selected individuals**. Use this option if you want TempleReady to estimate missing dates and places or determine itself whether the individuals are qualified for submission.

5. Check or uncheck the boxes described in the table below:

Option	Description
Put the word "Submitted" in ordinance fields . . .	This box determines whether the word *Submitted* will be inserted in the date fields of the ordinances that qualify for submission. If used, this option will help you avoid inadvertently re-submitting records that have already been submitted. Later, when the ordinance is completed, you can enter the date in the field.
	Check the box to cause the word *Submitted* to be inserted in date fields of qualifying ordinances.
Produce a submission report	This box determines whether a submission report will be produced when the export file is created. If used, this option

Option	Description
submission report	will produce a report in the form of a text file with the name of the GEDCOM file and the suffix *.aqr*. The report will indicate which individuals and marriages were submitted, what ordinances they qualified for, etc.
	Uncheck the box if you do not want a submission report to be printed.

6. Click the **OK** button.

    The **Export GEDCOM File as** form will be displayed.

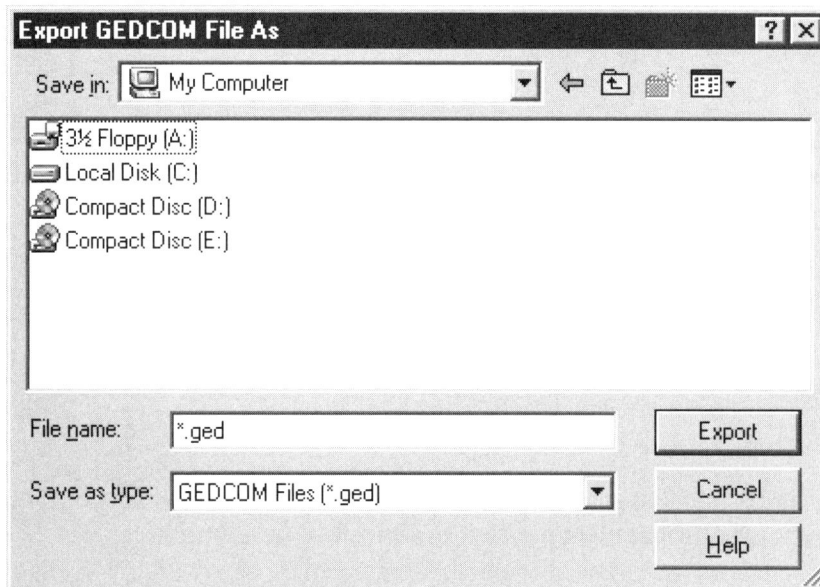

7. Use the controls described below to locate the disk drive or directory where you want to save the GEDCOM file.

    - Click the drop-down button to the right of the **Look In** box to view the contents of the disk drives and folders on your computer.

    - Click the 🔼 button to view the contents of the folder one level above the folder you are currently viewing.

    - 📁 Click the New Folder button to create a new sub-folder in the current folder.

    Note: Data can be submitted to TempleReady only on a floppy disk; therefore, you will need to save a file intended for submission to TempleReady on a floppy disk now or at some point before submitting it.

8. Click the **Export** button.

    The GEDCOM export file will be saved on the disk you specify and the **GEDCOM Export** form will be displayed.

GEDCOM Export ⊠

7 Individuals Exported
3 Marriages Exported

[OK]

9. Click the **OK** button to close the form and return to the previous Ancestry Family Tree view.

Exporting data to Ancestry.com as an Online Family Tree

You can export data to create an Online Family Tree hosted by Ancestry.com. Using this free service, you and others to whom you grant access can all add, edit, or delete information in your Online Family Tree at the same time.

To learn how to use this remarkably fast, convenient service, refer to chapter 13, Publishing Your Data on the World Wide Web.

Merging records

You can import GEDCOM files into existing Ancestry Family Tree databases, as described earlier in this chapter. Importing family data that has already been compiled by others can greatly enhance a database; however, this results in duplicate individual records if one or more individuals in the imported data are already included in the existing database. Therefore, the *merge* feature lets you automatically find individual records that are possible duplicates and merge them into one record if you decide that they are indeed duplicates. For each set of two duplicate records, one will be deleted and one will be kept; you specify what data from each record should be retained in the record that remains.

You can merge records immediately after importing a GEDCOM file (Ancestry Family Tree will prompt you at that time) or any time when working with a database that may have duplicate records. After you begin merging records in a database, you can stop at any time and resume merging records later.

Whenever you use the merge feature, it is wise to do the following two things first:

- Back up the database. Backing up your database before you begin merging allows you to later recover deleted records if a mistake is made. Refer to "Backing up and restoring a database" in chapter 3, Working with Family Databases, to learn how to back up a database.

- Print a Duplicate List report to help identify possible duplicate records. Refer to "Defining a list report" in chapter 11, Creating Reports and Charts, to learn how to create a Duplicate List report.

Merging records manually

You can merge records "manually"—that is, by searching for sets of records that may be for the same individual based on various data contained in those records. You can then merge records that you deem to be duplicates, specifying which records and data contained in them will be retained and which will be deleted.

To open the Merge form

1. Open the database in which you want to search for and merge duplicate records.

2. In the **Tools** menu, select **Merge**.

   The **Merge Warning** dialog box will be displayed.

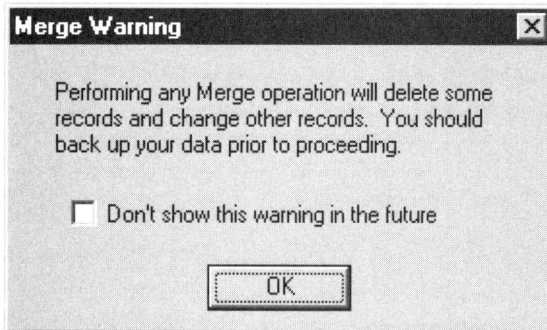

   Merge Warning

   Performing any Merge operation will delete some records and change other records. You should back up your data prior to proceeding.

   ☐ Don't show this warning in the future

   [OK]

3. Click the **OK** button. (If you don't want this warning to appear every time you start the merge feature, check the **Don't show this warning in the future** box.)

   The **Merge Individuals** form will be displayed.

   Merge Individuals

Primary Individual	Search Edit	Duplicate Individual	Search Edit

   Primary Individual: B:, A:, D:, B:, AFN:, Sex:, LMD:, Baptism:, Endowed:, SealPar:, Father:, Mother:

   Duplicate Individual: B:, A:, D:, B:, AFN:, Sex:, LMD:, Baptism:, Endowed:, SealPar:, Father:, Mother:

   MRIN Spouse   Marriage Date

   MRIN Spouse   Marriage Date

   Next Match   Previous Match

   Next Dup   Prev Dup   Select All   Clear All

   Merge   Options...   Switch   Auto Merge   Close   Help

Because you have not yet searched for duplicate records, the form contains no data. After a search, the *primary individual* will appear on the left half of the form and the *duplicate individual* will appear on the right. The primary individual is the individual whose record will be retained after the merge; the record of the duplicate individual will be deleted from the database. The check boxes on the right half of the form let you indicate which data from both records you want to keep and which you want to delete. For example, if the duplicate records have two different dates of birth, you can indicate which date to retain.

Note that there may be more than two duplicate records. There could be three or more individual records for the same person. In such a case, there will be one primary individual and the remainder will be duplicate individuals. You will merge the primary individual with each of the duplicates separately.

You begin the merge process by searching for records that are possible duplicates. The search for duplicate individuals will begin with the database's root person (or "primary individual") by default. You can also begin the search with a specific individual who is not the root person.

When searching for duplicate records, Ancestry Family Tree uses the sound of individuals' given names and surnames and their gender as criteria to determine whether individual records might be duplicates. For example, two males with the names Josia Smith and Josiah Smith would qualify as being possible duplicates. (If one individual is the parent of the other, however, they will not qualify as possible duplicates.) There are also a number of options that you can use to further refine the search for duplicate records.

To define merge options

1. On the **Merge** form, click the **Options** button.

    The **Automatic Match/Manual Merge Options** form will be displayed.

2. This form lets you define some preferences that affect how records are compared and whether they will be considered duplicates. Refer to the table below to learn about each option, then check or uncheck the boxes to select the options you want.

Option	Description
Include Individuals with No Surname?	This box determines whether individuals without surnames will be considered as possible duplicates.
	By default, individual records without surnames will not be considered as possible duplicate records (regardless of other matching information). Check the box to cause individuals without surnames to be considered.
Include Individuals with No Birth Date?	This box determines whether individual records that do not have birth dates will be considered as possible duplicates.
	By default, individuals with no birth dates are considered. Uncheck this box if you don't want individual records that do not have birth dates to be considered as possible duplicates.
Years Between Birthdates	This box lets you specify the maximum number of years between birth dates that will allow individual records to be considered as possible duplicates. For example, if you enter 5, individual records having birth dates 5 years apart or less can be considered as possible duplicate records; individual records having birth dates more than 5 years apart will not be considered as possible duplicate records.
Consider AFNs, IDs	Check the **Consider** box if you want to consider Ancestral File numbers or Ancestry Family Tree ID numbers in the search. Click the **AFNs** or **IDs** option to specify which type of number will be considered.
Consider Middle Names?	This box determines whether names other than the first name in the Given Names field for an individual will be considered when individuals are compared as possible duplicates.
	Middle names are not considered by default. Check the box to cause names other than the first name to be considered.
Consider Parents?	This box determines whether parents will be considered when individuals are compared as possible duplicates. Individuals who have the same name but who have different parents will not be considered duplicates.
	Parents will be considered by default. Uncheck the box if you do not want parents to be considered.
Combine Notes?	This box determines whether notes for a duplicate individual will be added to the notes for the primary individual when they are merged. (The notes for the duplicate individual will be appended to the Notes form below the existing notes for the primary individual.)
	Notes will be combined by default. Uncheck the box if you do not want notes to be combined. (The notes for the duplicate

Option	Description
	individual will be deleted along with the record of the duplicate individual.)
Combine Multimedia Objects?	This box determines whether multimedia objects contained in the media collection for a duplicate individual will be added to the media collection for the primary individual when they are merged.
	Multimedia objects will be combined by default. Uncheck the box if you do not want multimedia objects to be combined. (Multimedia objects for the duplicate individual will be deleted along with the record of the duplicate individual.)

3. Click the **OK** button to close the Automatic Match/Manual Merge Options form and return to the Merge Individuals form.

To search for duplicate records

1. Do one of the following:

   • If you want to begin the search with a specific individual who is not the root person, click the **Search** button on the left half of the **Merge Individuals** form.

   > Primary Individual   Search   Edit

   The **Find Individual** form will be displayed. You can use it to locate the individual with whom the search will begin. Refer to "Searching the entire database" in chapter 9, Searching the Database, to learn how to search for an individual. After you locate the individual you want to begin with, proceed to step 2.

   • To begin the search with the root person, proceed to step 2.

2. Click the **Next Match** button on the **Merge Individuals** form.

   If possible duplicate records are found, the Merge form is populated with data for the first set of duplicate records (the primary individual and first duplicate individual).

3. If there are additional individual records that are possible duplicates of the primary individual (meaning that the search has found three or more records that may all be for the same individual), the **Next Dup** and **Prev Dup** buttons will be available. You can click the **Next Dup** button to proceed to each succeeding duplicate record and click the **Prev Dup** button to move back through previous duplicate records.

4. If there is more than one individual in the database for whom there are possible duplicate records (for example, duplicate records for Martin Smith, duplicate records for Andrew Johnson, etc.), you can click the **Next Match** button to proceed to each succeeding set of duplicate records. You can click the **Previous Match** button to move back through previous sets of duplicate records.

To merge duplicate records

1. Using the data displayed for each record, determine whether the two records are for the same individual.

   Note that you can observe the date and place of the individuals' birth, alternate event, death, and burial (date only), etc., if they exist in the record. (The date and place of LDS baptism, endowment, and sealing to parents will be visible on the form only if the Use LDS Data box on the General page of the Preferences form is checked.) Parents and spouses are shown as well.

If you want to view additional data to help determine whether the individuals are duplicates, click the **Edit** button for the primary or duplicate individual. The **Edit Individual** form will be displayed, allowing you to view (and edit) the individual's notes, sources, multimedia items, etc.

2. Use the boxes under Duplicate Individual to specify which data will be retained in the primary record after merging and which will be deleted along with the duplicate record.

For example, to retain the name from the duplicate record instead of the name from the primary record, you would check the box next to the duplicate individual's name. Otherwise, the name from the primary record would be retained.

Likewise, to retain the birth date from the duplicate record, you would check the box next to the duplicate individual's date of birth. Otherwise, the birth date from the primary record would be retained.

To retain the birthplace from the primary record, you would leave the box next to the duplicate individual's birthplace unchecked.

Note: To retain all of the data from the duplicate record, you can click the **Select All** button to check all of the boxes. To uncheck all of the boxes, you can click the **Clear All** button.

Tip: If you decide that you would prefer to work with the duplicate individual's record as the primary record, click the **Switch** button to cause the duplicate individual to become the primary individual; the former primary individual will become the duplicate individual.

3. Use the list of spouses to specify which spouses from the duplicate record should be retained.

MRIN	Spouse	Marriage Date
28	Bersheba HERRIN	
29	Bathsheba HERRING	9 Jun 1770

MRIN	Spouse	Marriage Date
21	Mary SHIPLEY	
67	Bathsheba HERRING	1770

On the right-hand side of the **Merge Individuals** form, highlight the spouse or spouses that you want to retain in the primary record.

4. Click the **Merge** button to merge the two records.

The record of the duplicate individual is deleted from the database, and the specified data is retained in the record of the primary individual.

5. Do one of the following:

- Refer to the steps under "To search for duplicate records," above, to search for additional duplicate records, or

- if you are finished searching for duplicate records, click the **Close** button to close the Merge Individuals form.

Merging records automatically

You can let Ancestry Family Tree search for and merge records based on Ancestral File number or an ID number. If separate records having identical Ancestral File numbers or ID numbers are found, they can be merged. You can decide whether to merge each set of duplicate records as they are found.

Note: When merging records found to be duplicates based on Ancestral File number or an ID number, you cannot specify which data contained in them will be retained and which will be deleted. The primary record and all associated data will be retained and the duplicate record will be deleted. If no information is present in a primary record field, the equivalent information (if present) from the duplicate record will be retained.

To merge records automatically

1. On the **Merge Individuals** form, click the **Auto Merge** button.

The **Auto Merge on** form will be displayed.

Auto Merge On	☒
⦿ Auto merge on AFN	OK
◯ Auto merge on ID	Cancel

2. Do one of the following:

   - To search for records having identical Ancestral File numbers, click the **Auto merge on AFN** option and then click the **OK** button, or

   - to search for records having identical ID numbers, click the **Auto merge on ID** option and then click the **OK** button.

   Ancestry Family Tree will begin searching for duplicate records.

3. When duplicate records are found, the **Confirm Merge** form will be displayed. (The duplicate records are displayed in the background on the Merge Individuals form.)

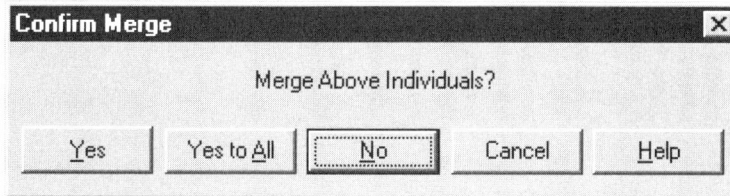

Confirm Merge				☒
		Merge Above Individuals?		
Yes	Yes to All	No	Cancel	Help

   Do one of the following:

   - Click the **Yes** button to merge only the two duplicate records displayed on the Merge Individuals form. The search for duplicate records will then continue until the next duplicates are found; you will again be prompted to confirm whether the merge should take place.

   - Click the **No** button to *not* merge the two duplicate records. The search for duplicate records will then continue until the next duplicates are found; you will again be prompted to confirm whether the merge should take place.

   - To merge all records in the database that have matching Ancestral File or ID numbers (depending upon your selection), click the **Yes to All** button. All records in the database with matching numbers will be merged automatically; you will not be prompted to confirm each merge. *Use this option with caution.*

4. On the **Merge Individuals** form, click the **Close** button to close the form and return to the Ancestry Family Tree view.

CHAPTER 11

Creating Reports and Charts

Software programs like Ancestry Family Tree are wonderful for compiling, sorting, and saving information quickly and conveniently. But you don't necessarily want to be tied to your computer monitor when viewing the information in a database; sometimes you want it on paper. This chapter describes how to create charts and reports that you can print. Nine different types of charts and reports are available to you in Ancestry Family Tree. They are:
- Individual summary
- Scrapbook
- Custom report
- Lists (you can print various types of lists, such as a list of all unlinked individuals, all end-of-line individuals, and others)
- Pedigree chart
- Family group record
- Ancestors of an individual
- Descendents of an individual
- Book summary (Ahnentafel or Modified Register report)

Some reports present information mainly about a specific individual, while others include information about selected groups of people.

For each type of report, you can define a number of preferences to customize its content. You can also define general preferences that apply to all or some of the reports. Finally, you can print the report or save it as a text file.

In this chapter

- Defining preferences for specific report types
- Defining general report preferences
- Printing a chart or report

Defining preferences for specific report types

For each type of report, you can select from a number of options to customize the content of the report. These options include what information is in the report and what is excluded, how the information is arranged, etc.

Defining an individual summary report

The individual summary report comprises a summary of the information contained in the database for a specific individual.

To start an individual summary report

1. Open the database containing an individual for whom you want to create the report.

2. Do one of the following:

   • In the **File** menu, click **Print Reports**, or

   • click the Print Reports button. 🖨

   The **Reports and Charts** form will be displayed.

3. Click the **Individual Summary** tab at the top of the form.

To select an individual for the individual summary report

1. By default, the subject of the report is the individual currently selected in the Ancestry Family Tree view. You can select a different person to be the subject of the report by doing one of the following:

   - To search the database for an individual who will be the subject of the report, click the **Search** button and then proceed to step 2, or

   - to view a list of all individuals in the database from which you can select, click the **Use List** box and then proceed to step 3.

2. The **Find Individual** form will be displayed.

   Refer to "Searching the entire database" in chapter 9, Searching the Database, to learn how to use the Find Individual form.

3. The **Select Set of Individuals** form will be displayed.

   An Individual Summary report will be created for each individual you select. Refer to "Searching for an individual using filters" in chapter 9, Searching the Database, to learn how to select individuals using the Select Set of Individuals form.

To define the content of the individual summary report

The Individual Summary page contains a number of check boxes that affect the content of the Individual Summary report. Refer to the table below to learn about the purpose of each and then check or uncheck the appropriate boxes.

Note: As you select various options to define the report's content, it is very useful to use the **Preview** button to view the report as it will appear when printed. You will be able to see as you go along how the options you select (or do not select) affect the appearance of the report.

Field	Description
Sources	If checked, sources cited for the individual will appear.
Titles Only	If checked, only the titles of the cited sources will appear. (Available only if Sources is checked.)
Actual Text	If checked, actual text entered for the source citation will appear. (Available only if Sources is checked.)
Comments	If checked, comments entered for the source citation will appear. (Available only if Sources is checked.)
General Notes	If checked, all notes that are not preceded by an exclamation mark (!) will appear.
Marked Notes (!)	If checked, note paragraphs that are preceded by an exclamation mark will appear (in addition to notes that are not marked).
Include Photo	If checked, the default photo image in the media collection for the individual (if there is one) will appear. Refer to "Defining options for photo images," below, to learn how to customize the photo

Field	Description
	image size and placement on the report.
Suppress RINs	If checked, the individual's RIN will not appear on the report.
Suppress MRINs	If checked, MRINs for the individual's marriage(s) will not appear on the report.
Display Relationship Codes	If checked, codes indicating adopted {A}, guardian {G}, and sealed {S} parent-child relationships will appear where applicable. (The "sealed" parent-child relationship results from an LDS sealing ordinance.)
Display Multiple Parents	If checked, individuals having multiple parents (more than one father or more than one mother) will be marked with {+}.
Conf. Notes (~) and Events	If checked, confidential notes will appear (these are note paragraphs preceded by a tilde [~]). Confidential events will also appear (events designated as confidential using the Additional Events form; refer to "Entering additional information for an individual" in chapter 4, Working with Individuals in a Database, to learn how to use the Additional Events form).
Display Contact Info	If checked, contact information entered for an individual will appear. (Contact information is entered in the Contact Information form via the Address button on the Edit Individual form.)

To print the individual summary report

You can now print the report as it is by clicking the **Print** button. However, you can define a number of general report preferences and print options that will further affect the appearance of the printed report. Refer to "Defining general report preferences" and "Printing a report," below, to finish preparing the report for printing.

Defining a scrapbook

A scrapbook comprises printed photo images from the "scrapbook" in an individual's media collection. Refer to chapter 8, Working with Media Collections, to learn how to create a scrapbook.

To start printing a scrapbook

1. Open the database containing individuals for whom you want to print the scrapbook.

2. In the **File** menu, click **Print Reports**.

   The **Reports and Charts** form will be displayed.

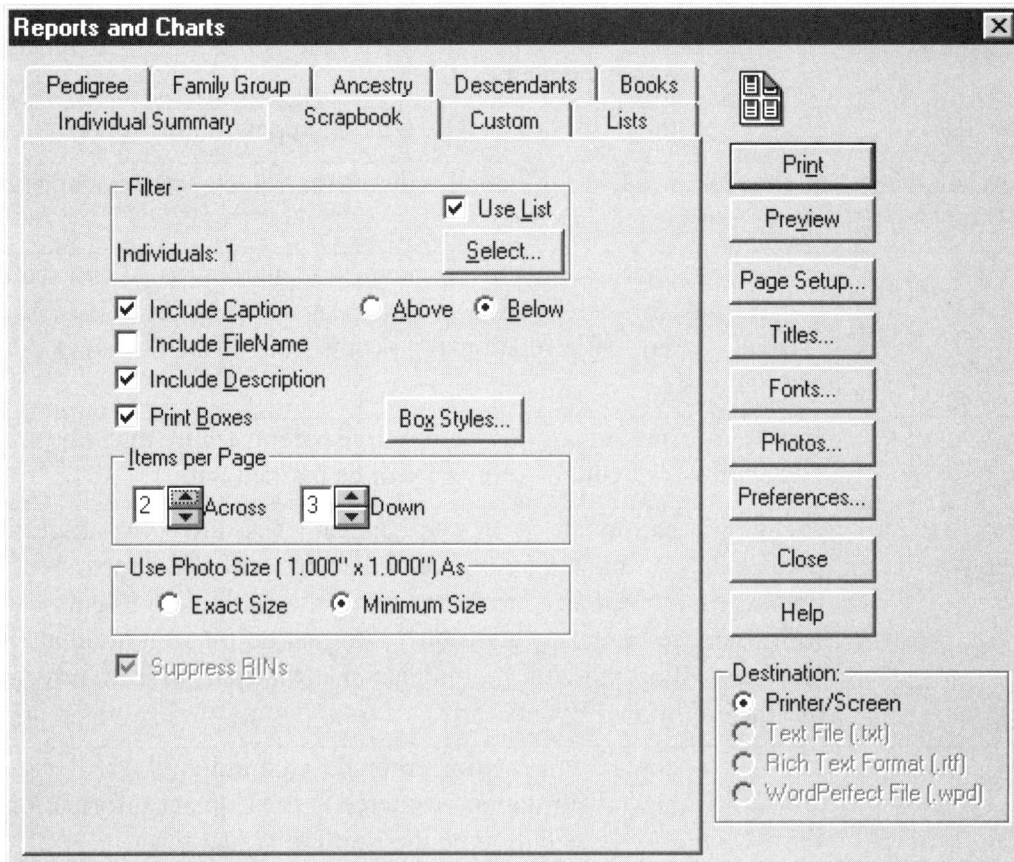

3. Click the **Scrapbook** tab at the top of the form.

To select an individual for the scrapbook

1. By default, the subject of the scrapbook is the individual currently highlighted in the Ancestry Family Tree view. You can select a different person to be the subject of the scrapbook by doing one of the following:

   - To search the database for an individual whose scrapbook will be printed, click the **Search** button and then proceed to step 2, or

   - to view a list of all individuals in the database from which you can select, click the **Use List** box and then proceed to step 3.

2. The **Find Individual** form will be displayed.

   Refer to "Searching the entire database" in chapter 9, Searching the Database, to learn how to use the Find Individual form.

3. The **Select Set of Individuals** form will be displayed.

   An Individual Summary report will be created for each individual you select. Refer to "Searching for an individual using filters" in chapter 9, Searching the Database, to learn how to select individuals using the Select Set of Individuals form.

To define the content of the scrapbook

The Scrapbook page contains a number of controls that affect the content of the scrapbook. Refer to the table below to learn about the purpose of each control and then enter the appropriate information.

Note: As you select various options to define the scrapbook's content, it is very useful to use the **Preview** button to view the scrapbook as it will appear when printed. You will be able to see as you go along how the options you select (or do not select) affect the appearance of the scrapbook.

Field	Description
Include Caption	If checked, the caption defined for the scrapbook image will appear in the scrapbook. Select the adjacent **Above** or **Below** option to determine the placement of the caption.
Include File Name	If checked, the path and file name of the scrapbook image will appear.
Include Description	If checked, the description defined for the scrapbook image will appear.
Print Boxes	If checked, a decorative box will surround each scrapbook image. Refer to "To define a box style," below, to learn how to define options for the box style.
Items per Page	Enter numbers in the **Across** and **Down** boxes to specify how many images will appear on each scrapbook page. The images will be sized to fit on the page. For this reason, the more images per page, the smaller each image will be.
Use Photo Size	"Photo Size" refers to the photo image size currently defined for the scrapbook images. Refer to "Defining options for photo images," below, to learn how to define the photo image size.
	Select the **Exact Size** option if you want each scrapbook image to be printed the requested size; if there isn't enough room on the page, the image will be reduced to fit. Select the **Minimum Size** option if you want the requested size to be regarded as the minimum size allowed for each scrapbook image; the image will be enlarged if space allows.

To define a box style

1. On the Scrapbook page, click the **Box Style** button.

    The **Box Style** form will be displayed.

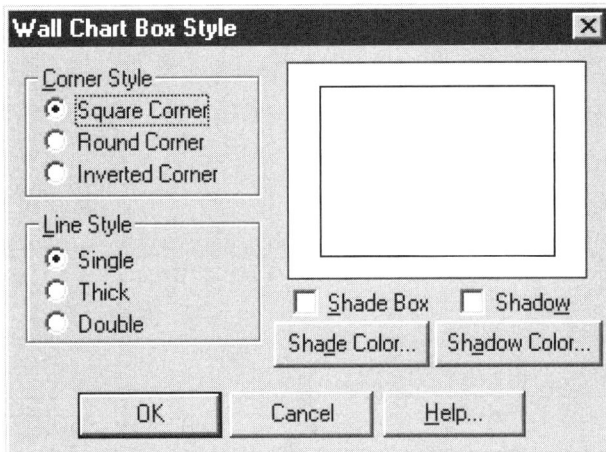

- Under **Corner Style**, select **Square Corner**, **Round Corner**, or **Inverted Corner** to determine the corner style for the box.

   Note: As you select options for the box style, they become visible in the sample image in the upper-right corner of the form.

- Under **Line Style**, select **Single**, **Thick**, or **Double** to determine the line style for the box.

- The **Shade Box** and **Shadow** boxes determine whether the box will contain shading and a "shadow," respectively.

   Check one or both boxes to cause the box to be shaded or "shadowed."

2. If you want to select a color for the box shading or shadow, click the **Shade Color** or **Shadow Color** or button.

   The **Color** form will be displayed.

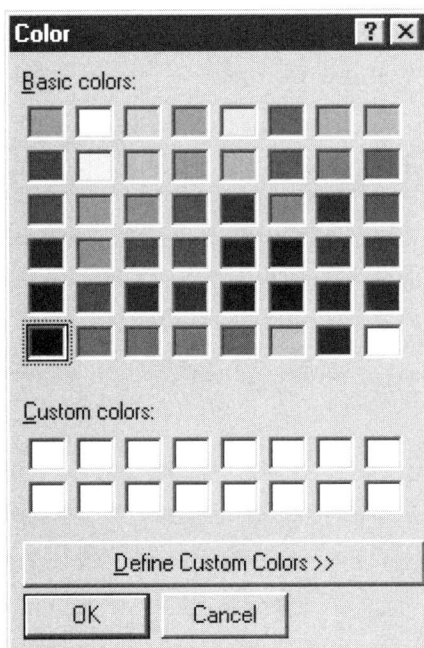

3. Under **Basic colors**, select the color you want to use and then click the **OK** button to close the Color form and return to the Box Style form.

4. If you want to create and assign custom colors for report shading, click the **Define Custom Colors** button.

   The Color form expands to include the custom color design controls. Refer to "To create custom colors for the Ancestry Family Tree views" in chapter 2, Installation and Setup, to learn how to use the form to create and select custom colors.

To print the scrapbook

You can now print the scrapbook as it is by clicking the **Print** button. However, you can define a number of general preferences and print options that will further affect the appearance of the printed scrapbook. Refer to "Defining general report preferences" and "Printing a report," below, to finish preparing the scrapbook for printing.

Defining a custom report

A custom report contains selected information about selected individuals. You select one or more individuals who will be the subjects of the report, and you select specific information (name, parents, birth place, marriage status, etc.) about them that will appear on the report. On the report, each specific type of information is presented in a vertical column. You can place the columns in any order you want and create your own headers (labels) for them. You can also determine the sort order for the information presented in the report. Finally, after creating a custom report, you can name it and save it to use or modify later.

To start a custom report

1. Open the database containing individuals for whom you want to create the custom report.

2. In the **File** menu, click **Print Reports**.

   The **Reports and Charts** form will be displayed.

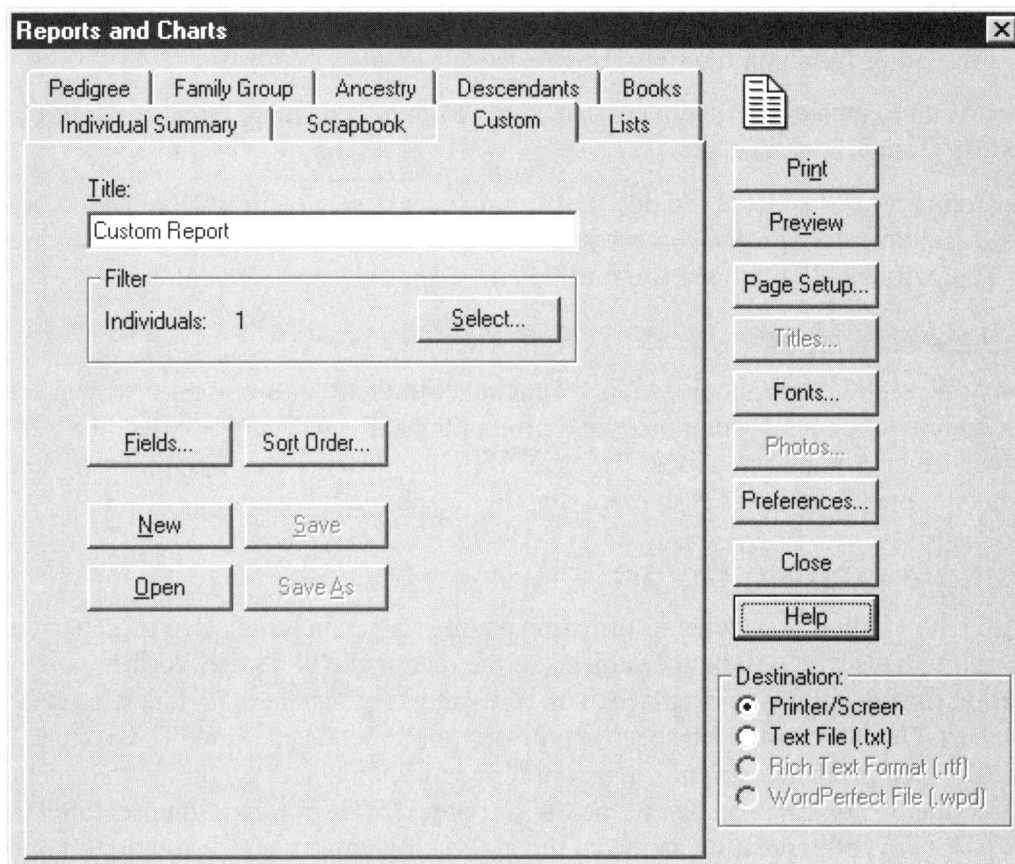

3. Click the **Custom** tab at the top of the form.

Note: As you select various options to define the report's content, it is very useful to use the **Preview** button to view the report as it will appear when printed. You will be able to see as you go along how the options you select (or do not select) affect the appearance of the report.

To select individuals for the custom report

Click the **Select** button.

The **Select Set of Individuals** form will be displayed.

Each individual you select will appear on the custom report. Refer to "Searching for an individual using filters" in chapter 9, Searching the Database, to learn how to select individuals using the Select Set of Individuals form.

To select information that will appear on the custom report

1. On the Custom page, click the **Fields** button.

   The **Report Fields** form will be displayed. It lets you select database fields; the information contained in those fields for each individual will appear on the report.

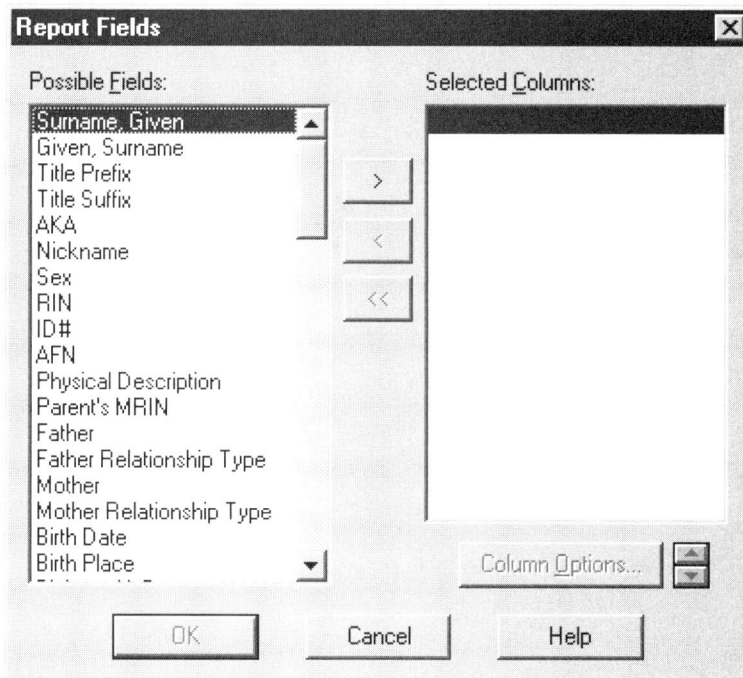

2. In the **Possible Fields** list, highlight a field that you want to appear on the report and then click the > button.

   The field is added to the **Selected Columns** list. (The information for each selected field will appear in a column on the report—for example, a name column, birth date column, birth place column, etc.)

3. Select additional fields that you want to appear on the report and add them to the Selected Columns list.

To arrange the order in which columns will appear on the report

The columns of information on the report will appear in the order in which the fields appear in the **Selected Columns** list.

- Highlight a field in the Selected Columns list and then click the arrow buttons below the list to place the field where you want it in the list. Repeat with additional fields until the list is ordered as you prefer.

To define the column header and width

1. In the **Selected Columns** list, highlight a field and then click the **Column Options** button.

   The **Column Options** form will be displayed.

Column Options: Surname, Given [X]

Header: Surname, Given

Width: 25   Characters

[OK]   [Cancel]

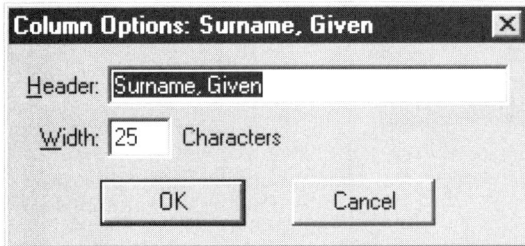

- The **Header** box contains the current header for the column.

    If you want to replace the current header with a different one, enter the new header in the Header box.

- The **Width** box lets you specify how wide (in characters) the column should be.

    If you want to change the width of the column, enter the desired number of characters in the Width box.

2. Click the **OK** button to close the Column Options form and return to the Report Fields form.

3. After you have selected the fields that you want to appear on the report, arranged them in the order you want, and defined any column options, click the **OK** button on the Report Fields form to close it and return to the Reports and Charts form.

To define the sort order

1. On the **Reports and Charts** form, click the **Sort Order** button.

    The **Sort Order** form will be displayed.

Sort Order [X]

Possible Fields:

Surname, Given
Given, Surname
Title Prefix
Title Suffix
AKA
Nickname
Sex
RIN
ID#
AFN
Physical Description
Parent's MRIN

Order List:

Sort Order
⦿ Ascending
○ Descending

[OK]   [Cancel]   [Help...]

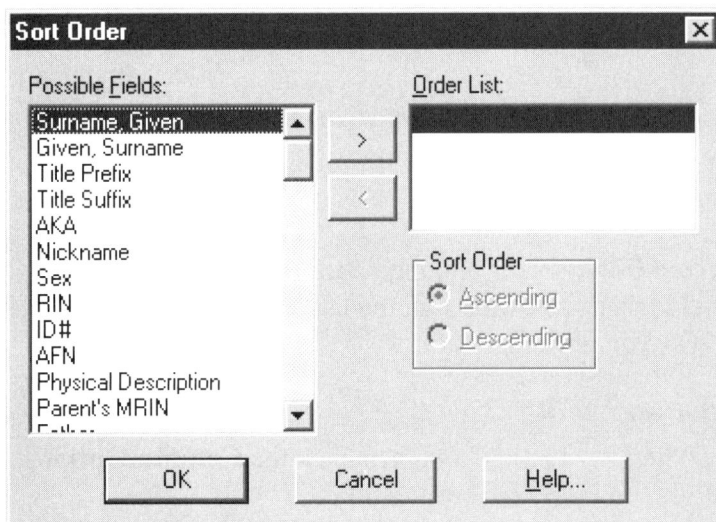

This form lets you determine how the information presented on the report is sorted. For example, suppose you have selected all the descendents of an individual to be included in the report. You could elect to have them sorted first by father and then by birth date. The individuals would be grouped on the report by father and listed chronologically by birth date.

A field does not have to be included in the report to be used as a sort field. For example, you could have individuals sorted by Death Date, even if the death date is not included in the report.

2. In the **Possible Fields** list, highlight a field that you want to sort by and then click the > button.

   The field is added to the **Order List**.

3. Select additional fields that you want to sort by and add them to the Possible Fields list. You can select up to three sort fields.

4. The options under **Sort Order** determine whether the information will be listed in alphabetical or numerical order (ascending) or reverse alphabetical or numerical order (descending) based on the contents of the selected field. For example, if you select the Birth Date field and elect to sort it in descending order, individuals will be grouped by birth date with the most recent date first and the oldest last.

   Highlight a field in the Order List and then click **Ascending** or **Descending** to determine the alphabetical or numerical order.

5. After you have finished selecting fields to sort by, click the **OK** button to close the Sort Fields form and return to the Reports and Charts form.

To print the custom report

You can now print the report as it is by clicking the **Print** button. However, you can define a number of general report preferences and print options that will further affect the appearance of the printed report. Refer to "Defining general report preferences" and "Printing a report," below, to finish preparing the report for printing.

To save a new custom report

On the **Reports and Charts** form, after you have defined your preferences for the custom report, enter a title for the report in the **Title** box and then click the **Save** button.

The custom report will be saved.

To retrieve a saved custom report

1. On the **Custom** page of the **Reports and Charts** form, click the **Open** button.

   The **Open Report Layout** form will be displayed.

Open Report Layout ☒

Custom Report Name:

```
Custom1
FatherBirthDate
```

[Open] [Cancel] [Delete]

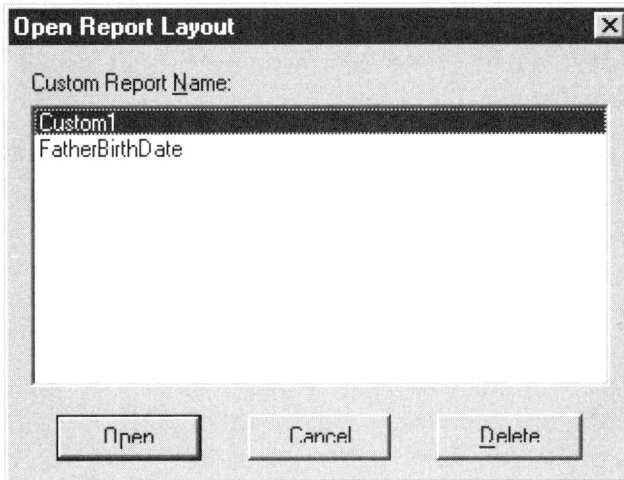

2. Highlight the report you want to retrieve and then click the **Open** button.

The Open Report Layout form is closed and the report is opened in the Reports and Charts form. You can run the report or modify the report properties.

To copy an existing custom report

1. Retrieve a saved custom report and modify the report properties as necessary.

2. On the **Reports and Charts** form, click the **Save As** button.

The **Save Report Layout** form will be displayed.

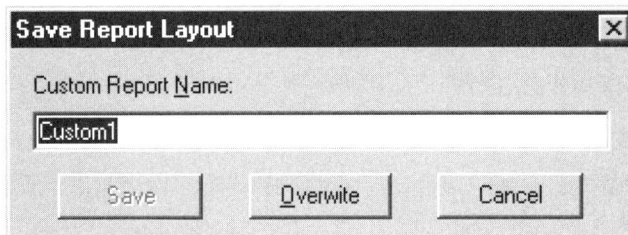

Save Report Layout ☒

Custom Report Name:

```
Custom1
```

[Save] [Overwrite] [Cancel]

3. Enter a unique name for the new custom report in place of the existing name and then click the **Save** button.

The report will be saved as a new custom report and the Save Report Layout form is closed. (The original custom report will still exist.)

Defining a list report

List reports contain lists of individuals, events, places, etc., drawn from a database. There are 11 different types of list reports. For most of them, you can define a number of options that affect the content.

To start a list report

1. Open the database containing individuals for whom you want to create the list report.

2. In the **File** menu, click **Print Reports**.

The **Reports and Charts** form will be displayed.

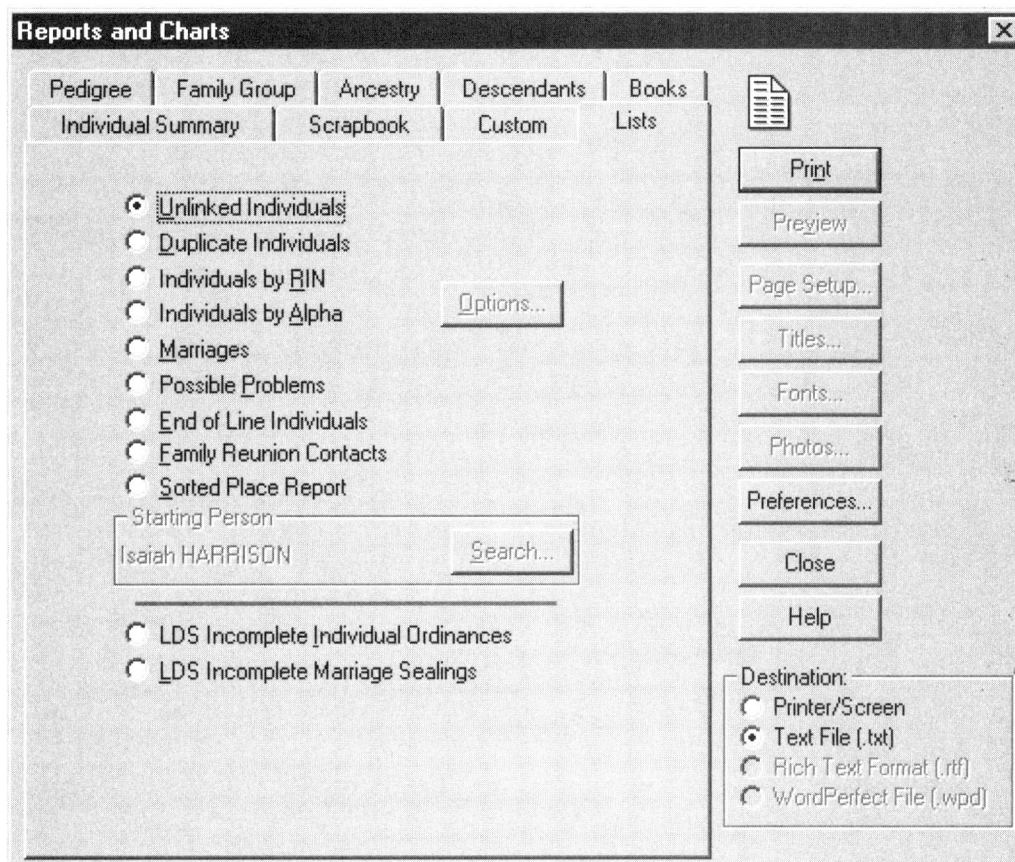

3. Click the **Lists** tab at the top of the form.

Defining an unlinked individuals report

The unlinked individuals report comprises a complete list of individuals in your database who are not linked to a family or spouse.

To define an unlinked individuals report

1. Click the **Unlinked Individuals** option on the **Lists** page of the **Reports and Charts** form.

2. Refer to "Defining print preferences," below, to define print options for the report

Defining a duplicate individuals report

The duplicate individuals report comprises a complete list of individual records that appear to be duplicates.

To define a duplicate individuals report

1. Click the **Duplicate Individuals** option on the **Lists** page of the **Reports and Charts** form.

2. Click the **Options** button.

   The **Duplicate Individuals Report Options** form will be displayed.

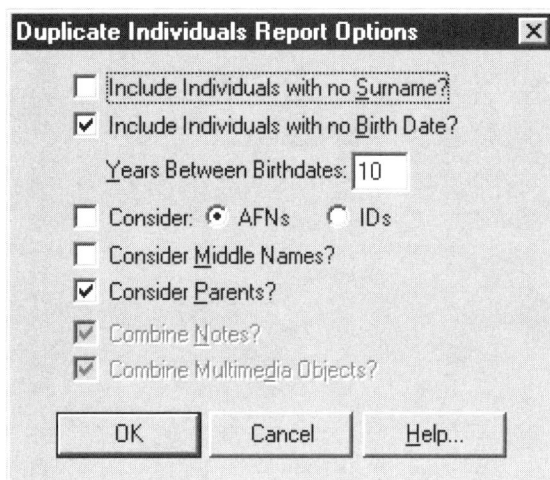

3. This form contains a number of controls that affect the content of the duplicate individuals report. Refer to the table below to learn about the purpose of each and then make the appropriate selections.

Field	Description
Include Individuals with No Surname?	If checked, individuals without surnames will be included.
Include Individuals with No Birth Date?	If checked, individuals without birth dates will be included.
Consider	If checked, you can elect whether to include duplicate Ancestral File numbers or Ancestry Family Tree ID numbers. Check the box and select the **AFNs** or **IDs** option to include duplicate numbers in the report.
Consider Middle Names?	If checked, middle names will be considered. Individuals who have the same first name and surname but different middle names will not be considered duplicates.
Consider Parents?	If checked, parents will be considered. Individuals who have the same name but who have different parents will not be considered duplicates.

4. Click the **OK** button to close the Duplicate Individuals Report Options form.

5. Refer to "Defining print preferences," below, to define print options for the report.

Defining an Individuals by RIN report

The Individuals by RIN report comprises a list of individuals sorted by RIN. For each individual the report will include name, date of birth, date of death, MRIN, and the name of the first spouse, parent (if there is no spouse), or first child (if there is no spouse or parent).

To define an Individuals by RIN report

1. Click the **Individuals by RIN** option on the **Lists** page of the **Reports and Charts** form.

2. Click the **Options** button.

   The **Individuals by RIN** form will be displayed.

3. In the **Start RIN** box, enter the RIN of the individual with whom you want the list to begin; and in the **End RIN** box, enter the RIN of the individual with whom you want the list to end.

4. Click the **OK** button to close the Individuals by RIN form.

5. Refer to "Defining print preferences," below, to define print options for the report.

Defining an Individuals by Alpha report

The Individuals by Alpha report comprises a list of individuals sorted alphabetically by surname. For each individual the report will include name, date of birth, date of death, MRIN, and the name of the first spouse, parent (if there is no spouse), or first child (if there is no spouse or parent).

To define an Individuals by Alpha report

1. Click the **Individuals by Alpha** option on the **Lists** page of the **Reports and Charts** form.

2. Click the **Options** button.

   The **Individuals by Alpha** form will be displayed.

3. In the **Start Name** box, enter a letter, name, or partial name to specify where you want the list to begin; and in the **End Name** box, enter a letter, name, or partial name to specify where you want the list to end. (If you do not specify starting and ending names, all individuals in the database will appear in the report.)

4. Click the **OK** button to close the Individuals by Alpha form.

5. Refer to "Defining print preferences," below, to define print options for the report.

Defining a Marriages report

The Marriages report comprises a list of individuals sorted by MRIN or alphabetically by husband or wife's name. For each individual the report will include MRIN, husband, wife, marriage date, and place of marriage.

To define a Marriages report

1. Click the **Marriages** option on the **Lists** page of the **Reports and Charts** form.

2. Click the **Options** button.

   The **Marriage List Options** form will be displayed.

3. Under **Sort by**, click the **MRIN**, **Husband**, or **Wife** option to determine how the individuals will be sorted.

4. Do one of the following:

   • If sorting by MRIN, enter the MRIN of the marriage with which you want the list to begin in the **Start MRIN** box; and in the **End MRIN** box, enter the MRIN of the marriage with which you want the list to end; or

   • if sorting by husband or wife, enter a letter, name, or partial name to specify where you want the list to begin in the **Start Name** box; and in the **End Name** box, enter a letter, name, or partial name to specify where you want the list to end.

   If you don't specify starting and ending MRINs or names, all marriages will appear in the report.

5. Click the **OK** button to close the Marriage List Options form.

6. Refer to "Defining print preferences," below, to define print options for the report.

Defining a Possible Problems report

The Possible Problems report comprises a list of records that contain discrepancies, such as a death date prior to a birth date or a birth date after a parent's death date. For each individual the list will include RIN, name, and a description of the discrepancy.

To define a Possible Problems report

1. Click the **Possible Problems** option on the **Lists** page of the **Reports and Charts** form.

2. Click the **Options** button.

   The **Possible Problems List** form will be displayed.

3. Under **Sort**, click the **RIN** or **Alphabetic** option to determine how the individuals will be sorted.

4. Do one of the following:

   - If sorting by RIN, enter the RIN of the individual with whom you want the list to begin in the **Start** box; and in the **End** box, enter the RIN of the individual with whom you want the list to end; or

   - if sorting alphabetically, enter a letter, name, or partial name to specify where you want the list to begin in the **Start** box; and in the **End** box, enter a letter, name, or partial name to specify where you want the list to end.

   (If you do not specify starting and ending RINs or names, all individual records in the database will be searched for discrepancies.)

5. Refer to the table below to learn about the purpose of each of the remaining controls and then make the appropriate selections.

Field	Description
Mother's age should be between *n* and *n* Father's age should be between *n* and *n*	Lets you specify what age ranges should be considered normal for a mother or father. A mother or father having an age outside the range specified here will be considered a discrepancy. Enter numbers in the boxes if you want to change the normal ranges.

Field	Description
Age difference of husband and wife	Lets you specify what age difference between a husband and wife should be considered normal. A husband and wife having an age difference greater than the number of years specified here will be considered a discrepancy.
	Enter a number in the box if you want to change the age difference.
Check LDS Data	If checked, LDS ordinance information will be checked for possible discrepancies.
Check Marriage and Children Order	If checked, the order of marriages (for individuals who have multiple marriages) will be compared with the actual dates of the marriages. The order of the children will also be compared with their birth dates. If either the marriages or children are out of order based on their dates, they will be reported.

6. Click the **OK** button to close the Possible Problems List form.

7. Refer to "Defining print preferences," below, to define print options for the report.

Defining an End-of-Line Individuals report

The End-of-Line Individuals report comprises a list of individuals for whom there are no parents. Such an individual represents the end of an ancestral line.

To define an End-of-Line Individuals report

1. Click the **End-of-Line Individuals** option on the **Lists** page of the **Reports and Charts** form.

2. If you want to include every ancestor of a selected individual for whom there are no parents, click the **Search** button. Otherwise, proceed to step 3.

   The **Find Individual** form will be displayed. It lets you find the individual whose end-of-line ancestors will appear on the report. Refer to "Searching the entire database" in chapter 9, Searching the Database, to learn how to use the Find Individual form.

3. Click the **Options** button.

   The **End-of-Line Individuals Options** form will be displayed.

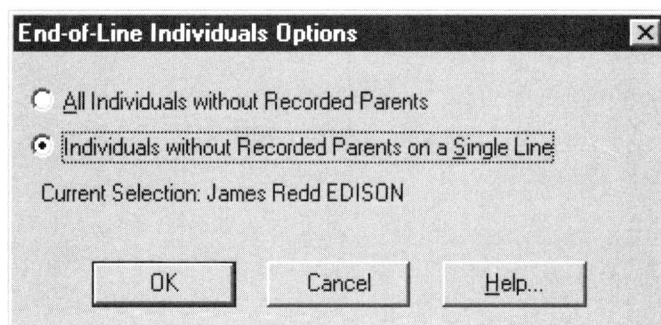

4. Do one of the following:

- Select the **All Individuals without Recorded Parents** option to include every individual in the database for whom there are no parents.

- Select the **Individuals without Recorded Parents on a Single Line** option to include every ancestor of the selected individual for whom there are no parents

5. Click the **OK** button to close the End-of-Line Individuals Options form.

6. Refer to "Defining print preferences," below, to define print options for the report.

Defining a Family Reunion Contacts report

The Family Reunion Contacts report comprises a list of contact information for selected individuals in the database. Refer to "Adding contact information for an individual" in chapter 4, Working with Individuals in a Database, to learn how to enter contact information.

Note: A Family Reunion Contacts report can be printed only to a text file. If you opt to create an address list, you can then open the text file in a word processing application to format it for printing labels.

To define a Family Reunion Contacts report

1. Click the **Family Reunion Contacts** option on the **Lists** page of the **Reports and Charts** form.

2. Click the **Search** button.

   The **Find Individual** form will be displayed. It lets you select a group of individuals in the database whose contact information will be printed. Refer to "Searching the entire database" in chapter 9, Searching the Database, to learn how to use the Find Individual form.

3. Click the **Options** button.

   The **Family Reunion List Options** form will be displayed.

Family Reunion List Options
C Phone List
⊙ Address List
C Email List
☐ Include descendants with no contact information
Born before: 1984
OK Cancel Help...

4. Click the **Phone List** option to print a list of telephone numbers for the selected individuals; click the **Address List** option to print an address list; or click the **Email List** option to print a list of e-mail addresses.

- If you want to include descendants (of the selected individuals) for whom there is no contact information, check the **Include descendants with no contact information** box.

  - The **Born before** box lets you specify a year of birth to omit young descendants from the list. For example, if you don't want descendants who are less than 18 years old to be on the list, you would enter the corresponding year of birth here.

    Enter a year of birth if you want to omit young descendants from the list.

5. Click the **OK** button to close the Family Reunion List Options form.

6. Refer to "Defining print preferences," below, to define print options for the report.

Defining a Sorted Places report

The Sorted Places report comprises a list of places associated with individuals in the database. You can elect to include places for all individuals or for selected individuals.

To define a Sorted Places report

1. Click the **Sorted Places Report** option on the **Lists** page of the **Reports and Charts** form.

2. Click the **Options** button.

   The **Sorted Places List Options** form will be displayed.

3. Do one of the following:

   - Click the **All** option if you want to print a list of places associated with every individual in the database and then proceed to step 5, or

   - click the **Partial** option if you want to print a list of places associated with selected individuals.

4. Click the **Select** button.

   The **Select Set of Individuals** form will be displayed. Refer to "Searching for an individual using filters" in chapter 9, Searching the Database, to learn how to use the form to select one or more individuals for whom places will be printed. (The Select Set of Individuals form is essentially identical to the Search for Individual form described in chapter 9.)

5. Click the **OK** button to close the Sorted Places List Options form.

6. Refer to "Defining print preferences," below, to define print options for the report.

Defining a pedigree chart

A pedigree chart presents the line of descent from a starting individual to the person's earliest known ancestors—similar to the Pedigree view in Ancestry Family Tree. From four to six generations can appear on a page. The chart includes dates and places of birth, marriage, and death, when available, for every person represented. (If there is no birth date but there is an alternate birth event date, the alternate date will appear with *A:* as the event label.) You can also elect to include an index that lists all individuals represented and indicates the position of each on the chart.

To start a pedigree chart

1. Open the database containing individuals for whom you want to create the pedigree chart.

2. In the **File** menu, click **Print Reports**.

    The **Reports and Charts** form will be displayed.

3. Click the **Pedigree** tab at the top of the form.

To select the starting person

By default, the starting person is the individual currently selected in the Ancestry Family Tree view.

To select a different starting person, click the **Search** button under **Starting Person**.

The **Find Individual** form will be displayed. Refer to "Searching the entire database" in chapter 9, Searching the Database, to learn how to use the Find Individual form.

To define the content of the pedigree chart

Refer to the table below to learn about the purpose of each control on the Pedigree page and then select the options you want to use.

Note: As you select various options to define the chart's content, it is very useful to use the **Preview** button to view the chart as it will appear when printed. You will be able to see as you go along how the options you select (or do not select) affect the appearance of the chart.

Field	Description
Chart Type	Select the **Single** option to print a one-page pedigree chart (it can contain up to six generations); **Cascading** to print a multi-page chart containing the number of generations that you specify under Number of Generations to Print; or **Blank Form** to print a one-page, blank pedigree chart that you can fill in by hand.
Index Options	These options define the index preferences. If printed, the index lists all individuals represented on the chart and their dates of birth and death, and it indicates the position of each on the chart. Select the **No Index** option to include no index with the pedigree chart; **Include Index** to include an index on the final page of the chart; or **Index Only** to print only the index for the chart.
Generations per Page	Determines how many generations will appear on a single page (four, five, or six). Note that the more generations are on a page, the less space is available to spell out birth, marriage, and death data. Click the arrow button to the right of the field and select the number of generations to appear on a single page.
Chart Number of 1st Chart	Lets you specify the chart number for the first page of the pedigree chart. (Each page of a pedigree chart is labeled with a "Chart no." The first page is chart no. 1, the second page chart no. 2, etc.) You might want to use this feature if you are printing a replacement page for an existing cascading (multi-page) chart. Enter the chart number for the first page in the box.
Start Person Is Same As: *n* on Chart *n*	Lets you indicate if the starting person on the chart is included on another pedigree chart. This information will be included on the first page of the chart—for example: *No. 1 on this*

Field	Description
	chart is the same as no. 6 on chart no. 5. Enter the number assigned to the person on the other chart you are referring to and then the number of the other chart.
Starting Number of Continuation Charts	Lets you specify the chart number for the second page of a cascading pedigree chart. Enter a chart number here if you don't want the second page of a multi-page chart to be numbered consecutively after the first page.
Number of Generations to Print	Lets you determine on a cascading chart the number of generations that will be included. The default number is 999, which will effectively include all generations. Enter a number if you want to specify the number of generations to be included.
Include Submitter Box	If checked, the submitter's information (name, address, telephone number, etc.) will be included on each page of the chart. (The submitter's information is entered in the Compiler page of the Preferences form. Refer to chapter 2, Installation and Setup, to learn how to define overall Ancestry Family Tree preferences.)
Suppress RINs	RINs are suppressed by default; they cannot be printed on a pedigree chart.
Display Rel. Codes	If checked, relationship codes denoting adopted {A}, guardian {G}, and sealed {S} will appear in brackets after each name on the chart (if such information exists for the individual). (A "sealed" relationship results from an LDS ordinance.)
Allow Last Gen to Split	If checked, Ancestry Family Tree may "split" the last generation to appear on a page, causing the wife to appear to the right of her husband. Depending on the options selected for the chart, splitting may allow more information to appear on the page.
Include Photos	If checked, the default photo image in the media collection for the individual (if there is one) will appear for each individual. Refer to "Defining options for photo images," below, to learn how to customize the photo image size and placement on the report.
Suppress MRINs	If checked, MRINs will not appear on the chart. Uncheck the box if you want MRINs to be printed. The MRIN will appear after the marriage date.
Display Multiple Par. Ind.	If checked, individuals who have multiple sets of parents will be marked with + in brackets after the individual's name. (If

Field	Description
	relationship codes are selected to appear as well, relationship codes and the multiple-parent indicator will appear within the same set of brackets.)

To print the pedigree chart

You can now print the pedigree chart as it is by clicking the **Print** button. However, you can define a number of general report preferences and print options that will further affect the appearance of the printed pedigree chart. Refer to "Defining general report preferences" and "Printing a report," below, to finish preparing the pedigree chart for printing.

Defining a family group record

A family group record contains detailed information (including alternate events, custom events, sources, etc.) about the individuals in single family (husband, wife, and their children). You can elect to print family group records for one family only, for multiple generations beginning with a starting individual, or for any number of selected marriage records.

To start a family group record

1. Open the database containing individuals for whom you want to create the family group record.

2. In the **File** menu, click **Print Reports**.

   The **Reports and Charts** form will be displayed.

3. Click the **Family Group** tab at the top of the form.

Selecting families to appear in family group records

There are two options for selecting the families for which family group records will be created:

- You can create a family group record based on a starting individual. The ancestors or descendants of that individual can then appear in their own family group records as well, if you create *cascading* family group records.

- You can select one or more marriages; a family group record will be created for each marriage you select.

To select a starting individual

1. Under **Selected Family Member**, click the **Parent** or **Child** option to determine whether the starting person will appear as a parent (the family group record will present him or her as a parent and include his or her wife and children) or as a child (the family group record will present him or her as a child and include his or her parents and siblings).

2. By default, the starting person is the individual currently selected in the Ancestry Family Tree view. To select a different starting person, ensure that the **Use List** box is *not* checked and then click the **Search** button.

The **Find Individual** form will be displayed. Refer to "Searching the entire database" in chapter 9, Searching the Database, to learn how to use the Find Individual form.

To select marriages

1. Under **Selected Family Member**, ensure that the **Use List** box is checked and then, if necessary, click the **Edit List** button. (If the Use List box is not checked, the following form will be displayed when you check it.)

The **FGR Marriages List** form will be displayed. It allows you to select one or more marriage records. A family group record will be created for each marriage you select.

2. Do one of the following:

   • To specify one or more marriages by MRIN, enter the MRINs in the **MRIN List** box and then proceed to step 3. (Indicate ranges of numbers with hyphens; separate numbers and ranges of numbers with commas—for example, 6,21,25,235-240,456.)

   • To view a list of marriage records, click the **Browse** button.

   The **Search for Marriage** form will be displayed.

Search for Marriage

1	James Redd EDISON	Emma Valentina EDISON	15 Dec 1886
2	Alma Robert EDISON	Anne Jewett EDISON	3 Aug 1860
3	Jonathan Anton EDISON	Echo EDWARDS	
4	Jeremiah ANDREWS	Amelia MORTON	
5		Henrietta SMITH	
6	Ansel EDISON		
7	Jonathan BRADLEY		
8	Harrison BERGER		
9		Emma EDISON	
10	James Redd EDISON		
11	James Redd EDISON		
12	James Redd EDISON	Emma Valentina LANDERS	15 Dec 1886

OK   Cancel   Help...

Highlight a marriage for which you want to create a family group record and then click the **OK** button to return to the FGR Marriages List form. (You can scroll up or down in the list to find a marriage, or you can enter a number in the text box at the top of the form to go immediately to that position in the list.)

3. On the **FGR Marriages List** form, click the **OK** button to return to the Family Group page of the Reports and Charts form.

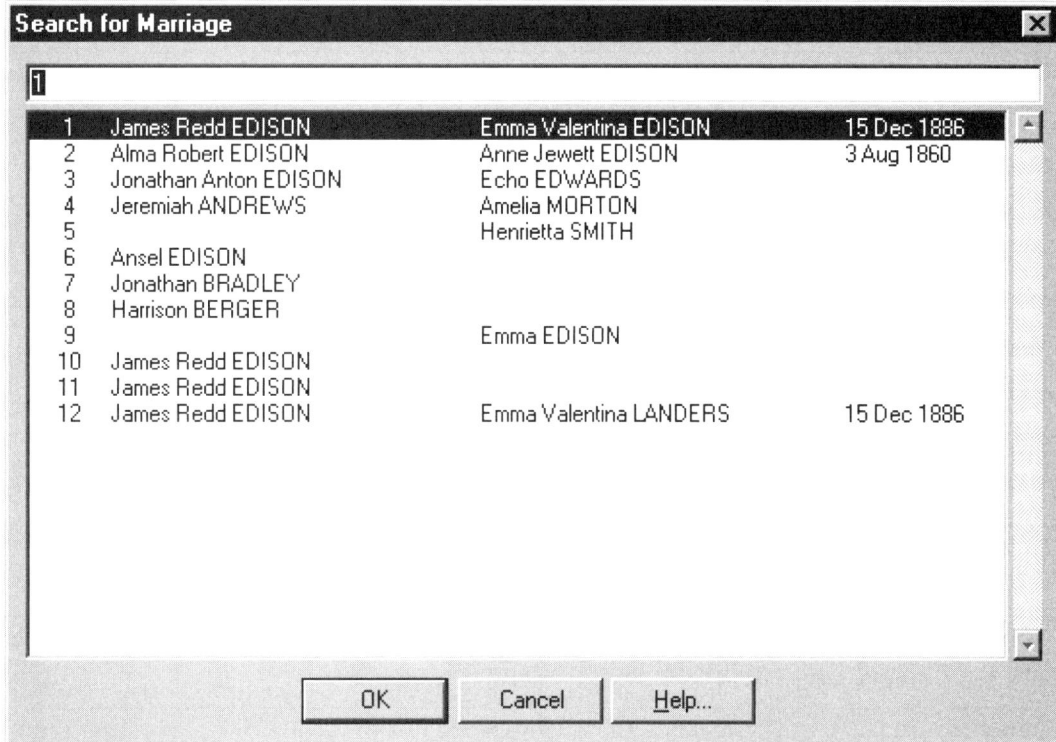

To define the content of the family group record

Refer to the table below to learn about the purpose of each control on the Family Group page and then select the options you want to use.

Note: As you select various options to define the family group record's content, it is very useful to use the **Preview** button to view the record as it will appear when printed. You will be able to see as you go along how the options you select (or do not select) affect the appearance of the record.

Field	Description
Sheet Options	
	Select the **Single** option to create a group record for the immediate family of the starting individual or for each of one or more marriage records that you select; **Cascading** to print group records for the number of generations that you specify under Number of Generations; or **Blank Form** to print a one-page, blank family group record that you can fill in by hand.
	Select the **Expanded** option to include four children on the first

Field	Description
	sheet and six on each additional sheet; **Medium** to include six children on the first sheet and eight on each additional sheet; or **Condensed** to include eight children on the first sheet and ten on each additional sheet. (If you elect to include the submitter's information on the record [see Inc. Submitter Box, below], less space will be available on each sheet; fewer children might therefore appear on each sheet.)
Notes Options	
Sources	If checked, sources cited for each individual will appear.
Titles Only	If checked, only the titles of the cited sources will appear. (Available only if Sources is checked.)
Actual Text	If checked, actual text entered for the source citation will appear. (Available only if Sources is checked.)
Comments	If checked, comments entered for the source citation will appear. (Available only if Sources is checked.)
General Notes	If checked, all notes that are not preceded by an exclamation mark (!) will appear.
Marked Notes (!)	If checked, note paragraphs that are preceded by an exclamation mark will appear (in addition to notes that are not marked).
Parents Only	If checked, notes will appear only for the parents of each family. (If you are creating a cascading family group record, the children's notes will be shown when they appear as parents for their own families. However, the notes for children who are not direct ancestors or descendants of the starting individual will not appear on the family group record.)
Notes on 1st Page	If checked, notes for family members will begin immediately after the last child in each family. If not checked, notes will begin on the first sheet after the family.
Number of Generations	Lets you determine the number of generations that will be included on a cascading family group record. The default number is 999, which will effectively include all generations.

Enter a number if you want to specify the number of generations to be included.

Click the **Up** option or the **Down** option to determine whether the ancestors of the starting person (Up) or the descendants of the starting person (Down) will be included. |
| Other Options | |
| Inc. Submitter Box | If checked, the submitter's information (name, address, telephone |

Field	Description
	number, etc.) will be included on each page of the record. (The submitter's information is entered on the Compiler page of the Preferences form. Refer to chapter 2, Installation and Setup, to learn how to define overall Ancestry Family Tree preferences.)
Include Photos	If checked, the default photo image in the media collection for an individual (if there is one) will appear for each individual. Refer to "Defining options for photo images," below, to learn how to customize the photo image size and placement on the record.
Include "Other" Events	If checked, additional events for individuals and marriages will appear on the family group record. (Refer to "Entering additional information for an individual" in chapter 4, Working with Individuals in a Database, to learn how to create additional events.)
Display Relationship Codes	If checked, relationship codes denoting adopted {A}, guardian {G}, and sealed {S} will appear in brackets after each name on the record (if such information exists for the individual). (A "sealed" relationship results from an LDS ordinance.)
Print Std Event Boxes When Blank	If checked, boxes for all of the standard events (birth, alternate birth event, death, burial, and marriage) will appear for each individual on the family group record even if there is no data for one or more of the events.
	Uncheck the box if you don't want boxes to appear for standard events for which there is no data. (Note that if Use LDS Data is selected on the General page of the Preferences form, standard event boxes for which there is no data can appear if LDS ordinances data appears on the same line.)
Confidential Notes (~) and Events	If checked, confidential notes (note paragraphs that are preceded by a tilde [~]) will appear.
Other Marriages	If checked, marriages for an individual other than the one selected for a family group record will appear in the notes.
Suppress RINs	RINs are suppressed by default; they cannot be printed on a family group record.
Suppress MRINs	If checked, MRINs will not appear on the family group record. If not checked, the MRIN for the parents of the husband and the parents of the wife in the family group record will be printed.
Display Mult. Par. Ind.	If checked, individuals who have multiple sets of parents will be marked with + in brackets after the individual's name. (If relationship codes are selected to appear as well, relationship codes and the multiple-parent indicator will appear within the same set of brackets.)

Field	Description
Mark Direct Line	If checked, each child in cascading family group records who is a direct descendant of the starting individual will be marked with an *X*.

To print the family group record(s)

You can now print the family group records by clicking the **Print** button. However, you can define a number of general report preferences and print options that will further affect the appearance of the printed family group records. Refer to "Defining general report preferences" and "Printing a report," below, to finish preparing the family group records for printing.

Defining an ancestry chart or a descendants chart

An *ancestry chart* presents the ancestors of a starting individual. The arrangement of individuals on an ancestry chart is very similar to that of a pedigree chart; however, the ancestry chart gives you many more choices regarding the amount of data to be included for each individual.

A *descendants chart* presents all descendants of a selected individual. You have many options regarding the amount of information that will be included for each individual.

For both an ancestry chart and a descendants chart, you can create the following:

- a *standard chart,* which occupies the width of an 8 1/2 by 11-inch sheet and extends down to additional sheets as necessary, or

- a *wall chart,* which can be printed on much larger sheets and can contain more information.

To start an ancestry chart or a descendants chart

1. Open the database containing an individual for whom you want to create the chart.

2. In the **File** menu, click **Print Reports**.

    The **Reports and Charts** form will be displayed.

3. Click the **Ancestry** tab or the **Descendants** tab at the top of the form.

   Note that the fields on the Ancestry tab and the Descendants tab are identical.

To select the starting person

By default, the starting person is the individual currently selected in the Ancestry Family Tree view.

To select a different starting person, click the **Search** button under **Starting Person**.

The **Find Individual** form will be displayed. Refer to "Searching the entire database" in chapter 9, Searching the Database, to learn how to use the Find Individual form.

Defining the contents that are common to standard charts and wall charts

There are several fields that affect the contents of both the standard chart and the wall chart.

To define the contents of standard and wall charts

Refer to the table below to learn about the purpose of the controls that affect both the standard chart and the wall chart and then select the options you want to use.

Note: As you select various options to define the chart's content, it is very useful to use the **Preview** button to view the chart as it will appear when printed. You will be able to see as you go along how the options you select (or do not select) affect the appearance of the chart.

Field	Description
Max generations to print	Lets you determine the number of generations that will be included. The default number is 999, which will effectively include all generations. Enter a number if you want to specify the number of generations to be included.
Suppress RINs	RINs are suppressed by default; they cannot be printed on an ancestry chart or a descendants chart.
Display Rel. Codes	If checked, relationship codes denoting adopted {A}, guardian {G}, and sealed {S} will appear in brackets after each name on the chart (if such information exists for the individual). (A "sealed" relationship results from an LDS ordinance.)
Display Multiple Par. Ind.	If checked, individuals who have multiple sets of parents will be marked with + in brackets after the individual's name. (If relationship codes are selected to appear as well, relationship codes and the multiple-parent indicator will appear within the same set of brackets.)

Defining the contents of a standard chart

After you have defined content that is common to both standard and wall charts, you can select options that are unique to standard charts. When selecting the information that you want to include in standard ancestry charts (such as dates and places of events), keep in mind that the more information is included for each individual, the more the chart will have to be condensed to fit the width of an 8 1/2 by 11-inch sheet.

To define the content of a standard chart

1. Under **Chart Options**, click the **Standard Chart** option.

2. Refer to the table below to learn about the controls that affect the content of the standard chart and then select the options you want to use.

Field	Description
Max indent each generation	Lets you specify how much each preceding generation should be indented. The starting individual will not be indented at all; the individuals in each preceding generation will be indented by the amount you enter here. (If there is not enough space to allow the amount of indentation you specify, Ancestry Family Tree will reduce the amount as necessary.) Enter the amount of indentation (in tenths of an inch) for each preceding generation.
Titles printed on each page	If checked, the chart title will appear on each page of the chart. (If not checked, the title will appear on the first page only.)

Field	Description
Print generation numbers	If checked, the generation number will appear before each name on the chart.
Date Format	For each name on the chart, the birth (or alternate birth event) and death (or burial) date can appear (if the information exists). Select the **No Dates** option to cause no date information to appear; select the **Year Only** option to cause only the year of the event to appear; or select the **Full Dates** option to cause the full date to appear.
Birth Place	If checked, the place of birth will appear for each individual (if the information exists).
Death Place	If checked, the place of death will appear for each individual (if the information exists).

Defining the contents of a wall chart

After you have defined content that is common to both standard and wall charts, you can select options that are unique to wall charts. Wall charts offer you many choices regarding the amount and type of data to be included for each individual.

To define the general contents of a wall chart

1. Under **Chart Options**, click the **Wall Chart** option.

   The wall chart controls are displayed under Chart Options.

   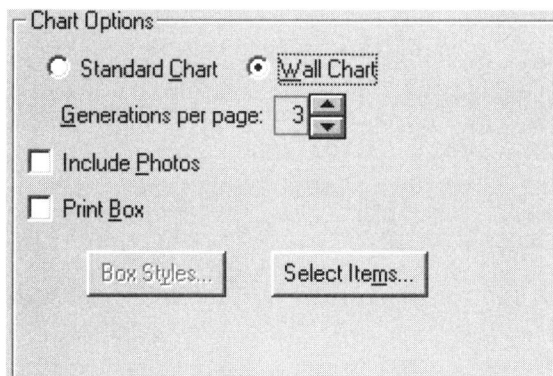

2. Refer to the table below to learn about the controls that affect the general content of the wall chart and then select the options you want to use.

Field	Description
Generations per page	Lets you specify how many generations will appear on each page of the chart. Enter the number of generations that you want to appear on each page.

Field	Description
Include Photos	If checked, the default photo image in the media collection for an individual (if there is one) will appear for each individual. Refer to "Defining options for photo images," below, to learn how to customize the photo image size and placement on the record.
Print Box	If checked, a decorative box will surround each individual on the chart. Refer to "To define a box style" in "Defining a scrapbook," above, to learn how to define options for the box style.

To select information that will appear on the wall chart

1. Under Chart Options, click the **Select Items** button.

   The **Wall Chart Item Selection** form will be displayed.

2. Refer to the table below to learn about the controls that affect the content of the wall chart and then select the options you want to use.

Field	Description
Birth (or Alt. Birth)	If checked, the year of birth (or alternate birth event if there is no birth date) will appear after an individual's name. **Note:** As you check (or uncheck) the Birth, Marriage, and Death boxes, the example under Name Line will show you how a name will appear on the chart with the options you have selected.
Marriage	If checked, the year of marriage will appear after an individual's name.

Field	Description
Death (or Burial)	If checked, the year of death (or burial if there is no death date) will appear after an individual's name.
Tag1, Tag2	Each lets you select a tagged note that will appear below the individual's name. Therefore, you can select up to two tagged notes. (If you have created a custom note tag and it doesn't appear in the list, you can enter the name in the box.) (Refer to "Working with note tags" in chapter 6, Working with Notes, to learn how to create tagged notes.) **Note:** If you select tagged notes to appear on the chart, space will be reserved below every name on the chart even if there are no such tagged notes for an individual. Click the arrow button to the right of the box and select the tagged note that you want to appear.
Tag Name	If checked, the note tag name will appear. Uncheck the box if you don't want the tag name to appear. (This will leave more space for the text of the note.)
Lines/Note	Lets you determine how many lines should be allowed below an individual's name for each tagged note. You can allow up to three lines. **Note:** The number of lines you specify will be added below every name on the chart even if there are no tagged notes of the type you selected for the individual. Click the arrow button to the right of the box and select the number of lines to reserve for each tagged note.
Cause of Death	If checked, a cause of death entered on the Additional Individual Information form for an individual will be included. (Refer to "Entering additional information for an individual" in chapter 4, Working with Individuals in a Database, to learn how to enter the cause of death.)
ID	If checked, the ID number entered for an individual on the Edit Individual form (if there is one) will appear on the chart.
AFN	If checked, the Ancestral File number associated with an individual (if there is one) will appear on the chart.
LDS Ordinance Codes	If checked, LDS ordinance codes will appear on the chart.
Birth	If checked, the date and place of birth will appear below each individual's name (if the information exists).
Alt Birth	If checked, the date and place of an alternate birth event will

Field	Description
	appear below each individual's name (if the information exists).
Birth or Alternate	If checked, the date and place of birth will appear below each individual's name (if the information exists); otherwise, the date and place of an alternate birth event will appear.
Death	If checked, the date and place of death will appear below each individual's name (if the information exists).
Burial	If checked, the date and place of burial will appear below each individual's name (if the information exists).
Death or Burial	If checked, the date and place of death will appear below each individual's name (if the information exists); otherwise, the date and place of burial will appear.
Marriage	If checked, the date and place of marriage will appear below each individual's name (if the information exists).
Other Events	Each box lets you select an alternate event for which the date and place will appear (if the information exists). You can therefore select up to two alternate events.
	Click the arrow button to the right of the box and select an alternate event.
Date on own line	If checked, the date of an event will appear on its own line.
Place on own line	If checked, the place of an event will appear on its own line.
Date and place together	If checked, the date and place of an event will appear on the same line.
Description on own line	If checked and if there are additional events for individuals that have physical descriptions associated with them, the description will appear on its own line. (Refer to "Entering additional information for an individual" in chapter 4, Working with Individuals in a Database, to learn how to enter a physical description.)
	If not checked, the description will appear after the date and place of the alternate event.

3. On the **Wall Chart Item Selection** form, click the **OK** button to save your selections and return to the Reports and Charts form.

To print the ancestry chart or descendants chart

You can now print the chart as it is by clicking the **Print** button. However, you can define a number of general report preferences and print options that will further affect the appearance of the printed chart. Refer to "Defining general report preferences" and "Printing a report," below, to finish preparing the chart for printing.

Defining a book report

Book reports present birth, marriage, death, and burial data in narrative form. There are two types of book reports: the *Ahnentafel* report and the *modified register* report.

- An Ahnentafel report begins with a specified person and presents that person's ancestors. Ahnentafel reports are distinguished by the unique numbering system they use: The starting person is number one. The number of each father is two times the number of his child. The mother's number is two times the child's number plus one. For example, the father of number 16 would be number 32, and the mother of number 16 would be number 33. Number 16 would be the great-great-grandfather of number 1. There is a limit of 32 generations for an Ahnentafel report.

- A modified register report presents the descendants of a starting person. The starting person is number one, and descendants are numbered sequentially as they are encountered.

Each type of book report can include notes and an index.

To start a book report

1. Open the database containing an individual for whom you want to create the book report.

2. In the **File** menu, click **Print Reports**.

   The **Reports and Charts** form will be displayed.

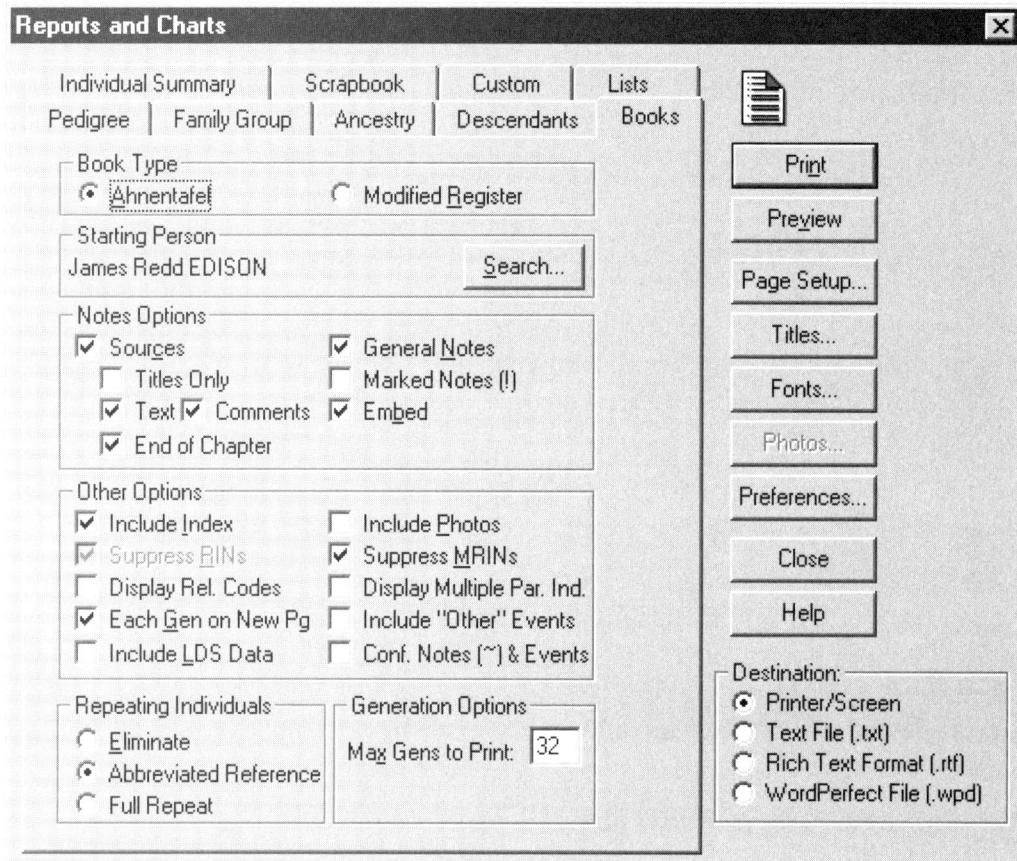

3. Click the **Books** tab at the top of the form.

4. Under **Book Type**, click the **Ahnentafel** option or the **Modified Register** option to determine which type of book report you are creating.

To select the starting person

By default, the starting person is the individual currently selected in the Ancestry Family Tree view.

To select a different starting person, click the **Search** button under **Starting Person**.

The **Find Individual** form will be displayed. Refer to "Searching the entire database" in chapter 9, Searching the Database, to learn how to use the Find Individual form.

To define the content of the book report

Refer to the table below to learn about the purpose of each control on the Books page and then select the options you want to use.

Note: As you select various options to define the report's content, it is very useful to use the **Preview** button to view the report as it will appear when printed. You will be able to see as you go along how the options you select (or do not select) affect the appearance of the report.

Field	Description
Notes Options	
Sources	If checked, sources cited for the individual will appear.
Titles Only	If checked, only the titles of the cited sources will appear. (Available only if Sources is checked.)
Text	If checked, actual text entered for the source citation will appear. (Available only if Sources is checked.)
Comments	If checked, comments entered for the source citation will appear. (Available only if Sources is checked.)
End of Chapter	If checked, sources will appear at the end of each chapter. (A single generation in a book report comprises a chapter.) If not checked, sources will appear in an appendix at the end of the book report.
General Notes	If checked, all notes that are not preceded by an exclamation mark (!) will appear.
Marked Notes (!)	If checked, note paragraphs that are preceded by an exclamation mark will appear (in addition to notes that are not marked).
Embed	If checked, notes will appear directly below the individual to whom they relate. If not checked, notes will appear in an appendix at the end of the book report.
Other Options	
Include Index	If checked, an alphabetical index of names in the book report (but not names included in notes) will be included at the end of the report.
Suppress RINs	RINs are suppressed by default; they cannot be printed on a book report.
Display Rel. Codes	If checked, relationship codes denoting adopted {A}, guardian {G}, and sealed {S} will appear in brackets after each name on the chart (if such information exists for the individual). (A "sealed" relationship results from an LDS ordinance.)
Each Gen on New Pg	If checked, each generation will begin on a new page.
Include LDS Data	If checked, LDS ordinance information will appear for each individual (if it exists). (This option is available only if Use LDS Data is checked on the General page of the Preferences form.)
Include Photos	If checked, the default photo image in the media collection for an individual (if there is one) will appear for each individual. Refer to "Defining options for photo images," below, to learn how to customize the photo image size and placement on the record.

Field	Description
Suppress MRINs	If checked, MRINs will not appear on the family group record.
	Uncheck the box if you want MRINs to be printed. They will be inserted into the narrative where applicable.
Display Multiple Par. Ind.	If checked, individuals who have multiple sets of parents will be marked with + in brackets after the individual's name. (If relationship codes are selected to appear as well, relationship codes and the multiple-parent indicator will appear within the same set of brackets.)
Include "Other" Events	If checked, additional events for individuals and marriages will appear on the family group record. (Refer to "Entering additional information for an individual" in chapter 4, Working with Individuals in a Database, to learn how to create additional events.)
Conf. Notes (~) and Events	If checked, confidential notes (note paragraphs that are preceded by a tilde [~]) will appear.
Repeating Individuals	If your database contains cousins who married, duplicate family lines will result. Select the **Eliminate** option to cause duplicate lines to be omitted from the report (a reference to the single line that has been fully presented will be included); select the **Abbreviated Reference** option to cause all duplicate individuals to be included with a reference to the first occurrence of the individual instead of complete information for the duplicate individual; or select the **Full Repeat** option to allow complete information to be printed for duplicate individuals, regardless of how many times they appear.
Generation Options	
Max. Gens. to Print	For an Ahnentafel book report, lets you determine the number of generations that will be included. The default number is 32, which is the maximum number of generations allowed for an Ahnentafel book report.
	Enter a number if you want to specify the number of generations to be included.
Gens. Traceback	For a modified register book report, lets you determine the number of generations that will be included. The default number is 999, which will effectively include all generations.
	Enter a number if you want to specify the number of generations to be included.

To print the book report

You can now print the book report as it is by clicking the **Print** button. However, you can define a number of general report preferences and print options that will further affect the appearance of the printed report. Refer to "Defining general report preferences" and "Printing a report," below, to finish preparing the report for printing.

Defining general report preferences

In addition to selecting the type of report you want to print and the preferences associated with it, you can select a number of general print preferences that will apply to all or some of the report types. Depending on the type of report you are printing, you will be able to do some or all of the following: preview the report on-screen; define the page setup (margins, etc.); modify the report title; select the fonts for selected portions of the report; define options for photo images; and select some print preferences for the type of report you are printing.

Previewing a report

You can preview most reports on-screen to see what they will look like before you actually print them. This feature is very useful for viewing the effect of various report and print options that you select.

To preview a report

1. On the **Reports and Charts** form, click the **Preview** button to view the report on-screen before you print it.

   The print preview window will be displayed. It contains an image of the first report page as it will appear when printed.

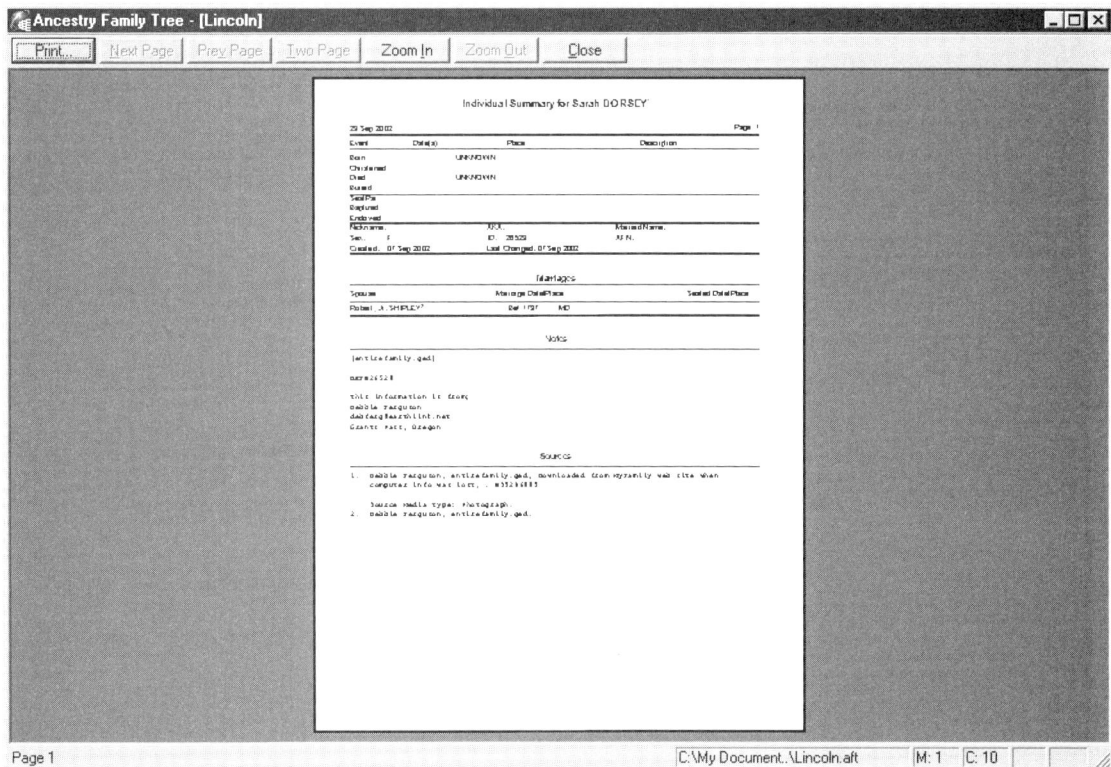

2. Several command buttons in the button bar allow you to manipulate the preview image. Refer to the table below to learn their functions.

Command Button	Description
Print	Print the report. (Refer to "Printing a chart or report," below.)
Next Page, Prev Page	If there is more than one page in the report, click to view previous and subsequent pages.
Two Page	If there is more than one page in the report, click to view two pages at a time. (Click the resulting **One Page** button to revert to a single-page view.)
Zoom In, Zoom Out	Click to enlarge or reduce the size of the preview image.
Close	Close the print preview window.

3. Click the **Close** button to close the preview window and return to the Reports and Charts form.

Defining the page setup

You can specify the page size and orientation and how much space should appear around the margins of the report pages.

To define the page setup

1. Click the **Page Setup** button.

   The **Page Setup** form will be displayed.

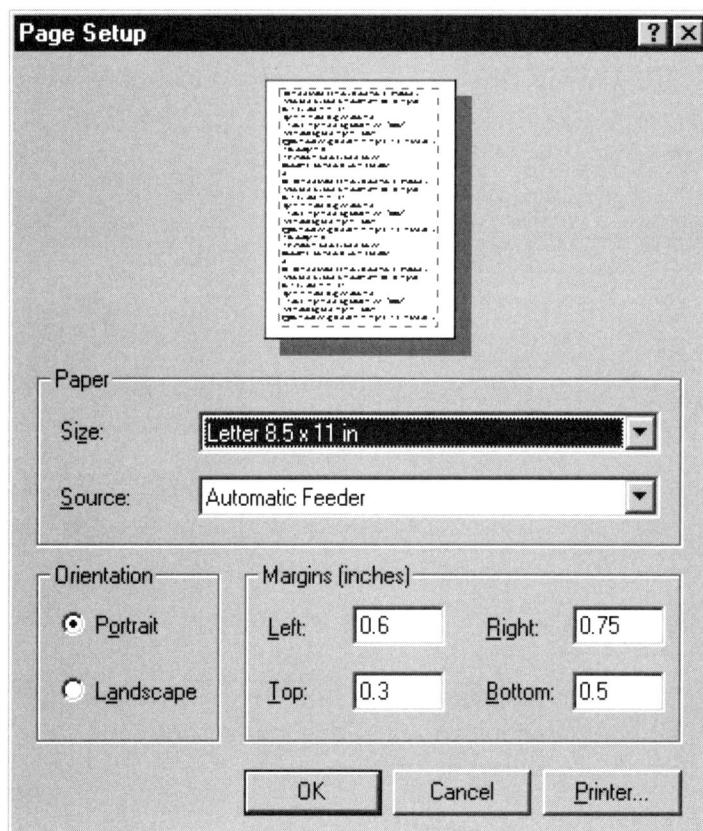

This form contains a number of fields that affect the page setup. Refer to the table below to learn about the purpose of each field and then enter the appropriate information in the fields.

Note: As you make selections on the Page Setup form, the page sample at the top of the form will change to show you how your selections affect the page setup.

Field	Description
Size	Lets you specify what size paper you will use to print the report. Click the arrow button to the right of the box and select a size option.
Source	If your printer has more than one paper source, lets you select the one you want to use. Click the arrow button to the right of the box and select a paper source.
Orientation	Use to specify the orientation of the paper. Click **Portrait** or **Landscape**.
Margins	Lets you specify the margins (in inches) around the report text. Enter amounts in the **Left**, **Right**, **Top**, and **Bottom** boxes to specify the margins around the report text.

2. Click the **OK** button to close the Page Setup form and return to the Reports and Charts form.

Modifying the report title

A number of reports have default titles that you can modify.

To modify the report title

1. On the **Reports and Charts** form, click the **Titles** button.

   A title form similar to the one shown below will be displayed.

2. Refer to the table below to learn about the purpose of each field and then enter the appropriate information in the fields.

Field	Description
Include Name	If checked, the individual's name will be included in the report title.
Prefix, Suffix	The **Prefix** box lets you enter text that will appear before the individual's name, and the **Suffix** box lets you enter text that will follow the individual's name. Enter any text that you want to precede or follow the individual's name in the report title.

3. Click the **OK** button to close the title form and return to the Reports and Charts form.

Defining report font preferences

You can specify the font preferences for one or more text elements in the report. The text elements that you can modify vary depending on the report type you are working with.

To define font preferences

1. Click the **Fonts** button.

    A report font form similar to the one shown below will be displayed.

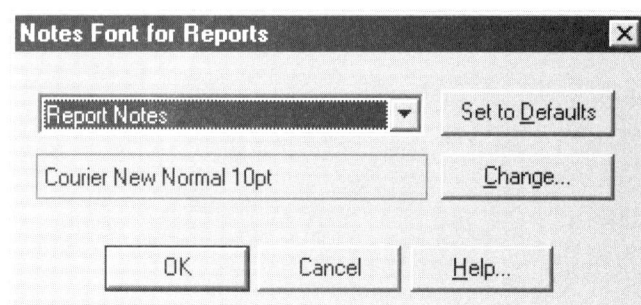

    ```
    ┌─────────────────────────────────────────────┐
    │ Notes Font for Reports                  [X]  │
    │                                              │
    │  ┌──────────────────────┬─┐  ┌────────────┐  │
    │  │ Report Notes         │▼│  │Set to Defaults│ │
    │  └──────────────────────┴─┘  └────────────┘  │
    │  ┌──────────────────────┐    ┌────────────┐  │
    │  │ Courier New Normal 10pt│   │ Change...  │  │
    │  └──────────────────────┘    └────────────┘  │
    │                                              │
    │   ┌────────┐  ┌────────┐  ┌────────┐          │
    │   │   OK   │  │ Cancel │  │ Help...│          │
    │   └────────┘  └────────┘  └────────┘          │
    └─────────────────────────────────────────────┘
    ```

2. Click the arrow button to the right of the text element selection box and select the text element for which you want to modify the font properties.

3. Click the **Change** button.

    The **Font** form will be displayed. Refer to the steps in "To define fonts for the Pedigree and Family views" in chapter 2, Installation and Setup, to learn how to use the Font form.

To restore the default font properties

If you want to restore the default font properties for the selected text element, click the **Set to Defaults** button.

To save the modified font properties

Click the **OK** button to close the report Font form and return to the Reports and Charts form.

Defining options for photo images

The Photo Options form lets you specify the maximum space allowed for a photo image and, for the Individual Summary report, its position relative to associated text.

To define options for photo images

1. Click the **Photos** button.

   The **Photo Options** form will be displayed.

2. Refer to the table below to learn about the purpose of each field and then enter the appropriate information in the fields.

Field	Description
Size	The **Height** and **Width** boxes let you specify the maximum amount of space allowed for photo images on the type of report you are working with. For example, if you are working with an Individual Summary report, the amount of space you specify here will be allowed for all Individual Summary reports that contain photos. Individual photos, however, may be adjusted as necessary by Ancestry Family Tree to fit in that space. Enter the amount of vertical and horizontal space (in inches) to be allowed for photo images in the type of report you are working with.
Reserve space for missing photos	Determines whether all reports of the type you are working with will contain space for a photo (whether there is one or not). Uncheck the box to if you don't want space to be allocated for a photo on every report of the type you are working with.
Photo Placement	Lets you determine where the photo image will be positioned in relation to the associated text. (The text associated with a photo in the Individual Summary report, for example, is the report title.)

Field	Description
	Check one of the available options to specify whether the photo should be positioned to the **Left**, **Right**, **Center**, **Above**, or **Below** the associated text. (Depending on the type of report you are working with, some options may not be available.)

3. Click the **OK** button to close the Photo Options form and return to the Reports and Charts form.

Defining print preferences

Depending on the type of report you are working with, you can select a number of print preferences, such as whether to include LDS ordinance information and color of shading.

To define print preferences

1. Click the **Preferences** button.

    The **Report Preferences** form will be displayed.

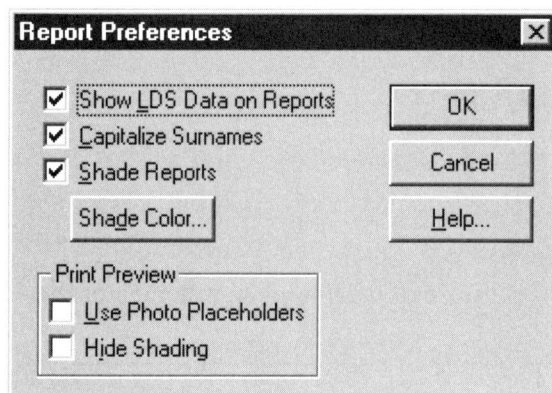

    Report Preferences

    ☑ Show LDS Data on Reports
    ☑ Capitalize Surnames
    ☑ Shade Reports
    [Shade Color...]

    [OK]
    [Cancel]
    [Help...]

    Print Preview
    ☐ Use Photo Placeholders
    ☐ Hide Shading

2. Refer to the table below to learn about the purpose of each field and then enter the appropriate information in the fields.

Field	Description
Show LDS Data on Reports	Determines whether LDS ordinance data for individuals will appear on reports.
	Uncheck the box if you don't want LDS ordinance data to appear on reports.
Capitalize Surnames	Determines whether surnames will appear in all-uppercase letters on reports.
	Uncheck the box if you don't want surnames to appear in all-uppercase letters. (They will appear as you entered them.)
Shade Reports	Indicates whether reports that allow shading will be shaded.
	Uncheck the box if you don't want reports to be shaded.
Use Photo	Determines whether a placeholder will be used instead of the photo

Field	Description
Placeholders	image when you are previewing a report. The placeholder appears as a gray box. Using placeholders can speed up viewing of the report preview.
	Check the box to use placeholders instead of photo images in report previews. (The photo image will appear on the printed report.)
Hide Shading	Determines whether report shading (if enabled) will appear when you are previewing a report.
	Check the box if you don't want report shading to appear in report previews. (Shading will appear on the printed report, if enabled.)

To select a report shading color

1. Click the **Shade Color** button.

   The **Color** form will be displayed. It lets you select and assign one of 48 basic colors for the report shading; it also lets you create custom colors that you can assign.

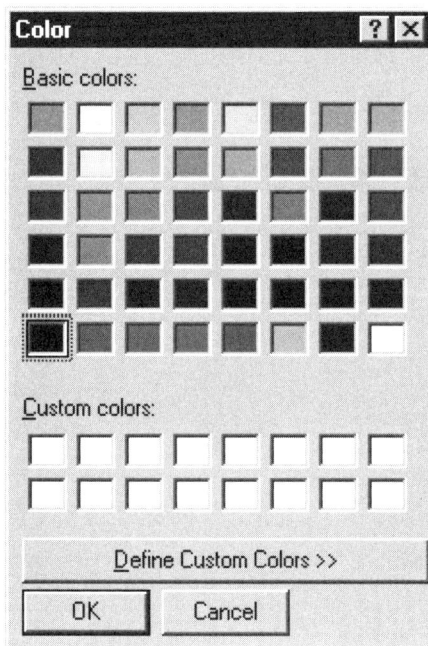

2. Under **Basic colors**, select the color you want to use and then click the **OK** button to close the Color form and return to the Report Preferences form.

3. If you want to create and assign custom colors for report shading, click the **Define Custom Colors** button.

   The Color form expands to include the custom color design controls. Refer to "To create custom colors for the Ancestry Family Tree views" in chapter 2, Installation and Setup, to learn how to use the form to create and select custom colors.

To save the print properties

Click the **OK** button to close the Report Preferences form and return to the Reports and Charts form.

Printing a chart or report

After you have defined the properties for the specific report type and the general report properties, you are ready to print the report. You can print hard (paper) copies of a report, or you can "print" it by saving it as a text (.txt) file. Saving a report as a text file allows you to store it indefinitely on a hard or floppy disk and then open and view or print it any time you want.

To print a hard copy of a report

1. On the **Reports and Charts** form, ensure that the **Printer/Screen** option is selected.

   Destination:
   - Printer/Screen
   - Text File (.txt)
   - Rich Text Format (.rtf)
   - WordPerfect File (.wpd)

2. Click the **Print** button.

   The **Print** form will be displayed.

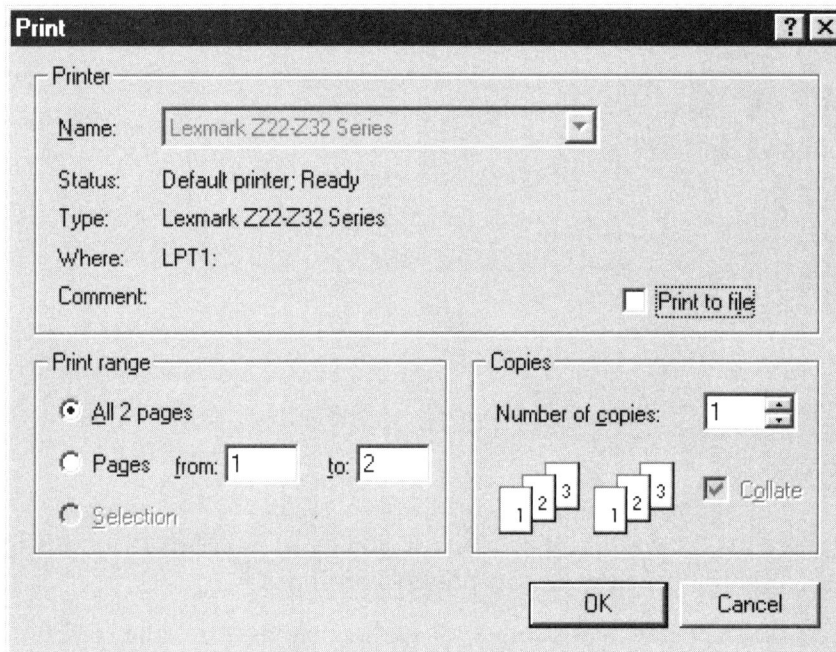

   Print

   Printer
   Name: Lexmark Z22-Z32 Series
   Status: Default printer; Ready
   Type: Lexmark Z22-Z32 Series
   Where: LPT1:
   Comment: ☐ Print to file

   Print range
   - All 2 pages
   - Pages from: 1 to: 2
   - Selection

   Copies
   Number of copies: 1
   ☑ Collate

   OK   Cancel

   - If you have more than one printer connected to your computer, click the arrow button to the right of the **Name** box and select the printer you want to use.

   - Under **Print range**, specify which pages of the report you want to print. Do one of the following:

     - Click **All *n* Pages** to print the entire report, or

- to print selected pages, click **Pages** and then enter a range of page numbers in the **from** and **to** boxes.

- In the **Number of copies** box, enter the number of copies of the report you want to print.

3. Click the **OK** button to send the report to the printer.

To save a report as a text file

1. On the **Reports and Charts** form, ensure that the **Text File (.txt)** option is selected.

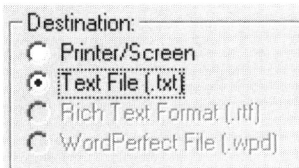

   Note: You cannot print a Scrapbook report to a text file.

2. Click the **Print** button.

   The **Save As** form will be displayed.

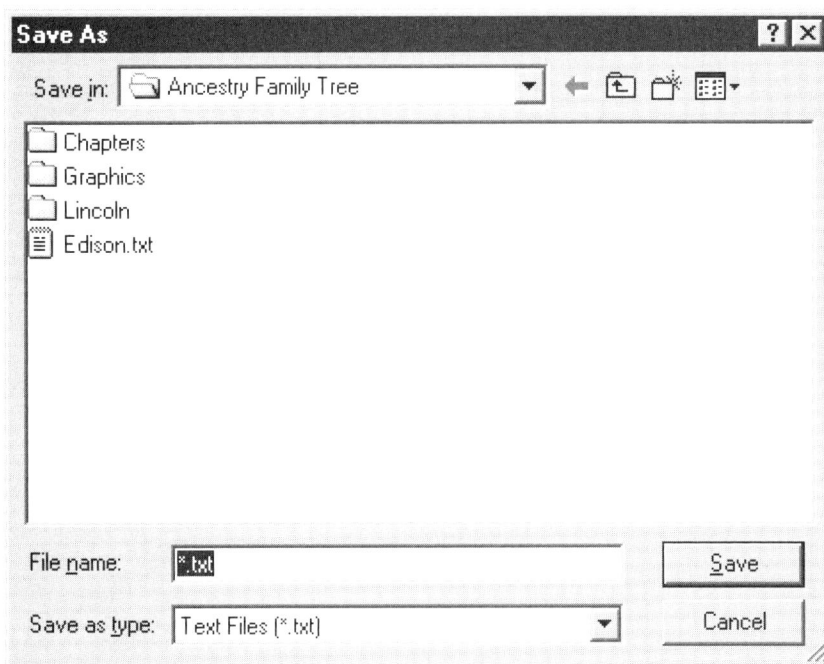

3. Use the controls described below to locate the directory in which you want to save the text file.

   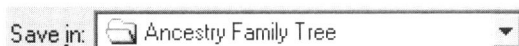 Click the drop-down button to the right of the **Save In** box to view the contents of the disk drives and folders on your computer.

    Click the Up One Level button to view the contents of the folder one level above the folder you are currently viewing.

    Click the New Folder button to create a new folder in the current directory.

4. In the **File name** box, enter the name of the text file. It must have a suffix of *.txt*.

5. Click the **Save** button to save the report as a text file and close the Save As form.

CHAPTER 12

Searching for Information on the World Wide Web

This chapter describes how you can use Ancestry Family Tree to search the fantastic genealogical resource that is the World Wide Web. A vast amount of genealogical information is available on the World Wide Web, ranging from the data contained in the websites of individual researchers to the holdings of large enterprises such as Ancestry.com and public and private institutions. Ancestry Family Tree lets you maintain a list of your favorite websites and search them for information quickly and conveniently.

In this chapter

• Maintaining a list of favorite websites
• Searching for information on the Web

Maintaining a list of favorite websites

Ancestry Family Tree allows you to maintain a list of favorite websites. Using the list, you can connect to those sites directly from Ancestry Family Tree. If a site is one that can be searched for data about individuals, you can also add *search text* to the URL that will let you search automatically for the individual currently highlighted in your database.

To add a website to the list of favorites

1. On the Internet menu, click Favorite Sites.

    The **My Favorite Web Sites** form will be displayed. Note that the list already contains an entry for Ancestry.com.

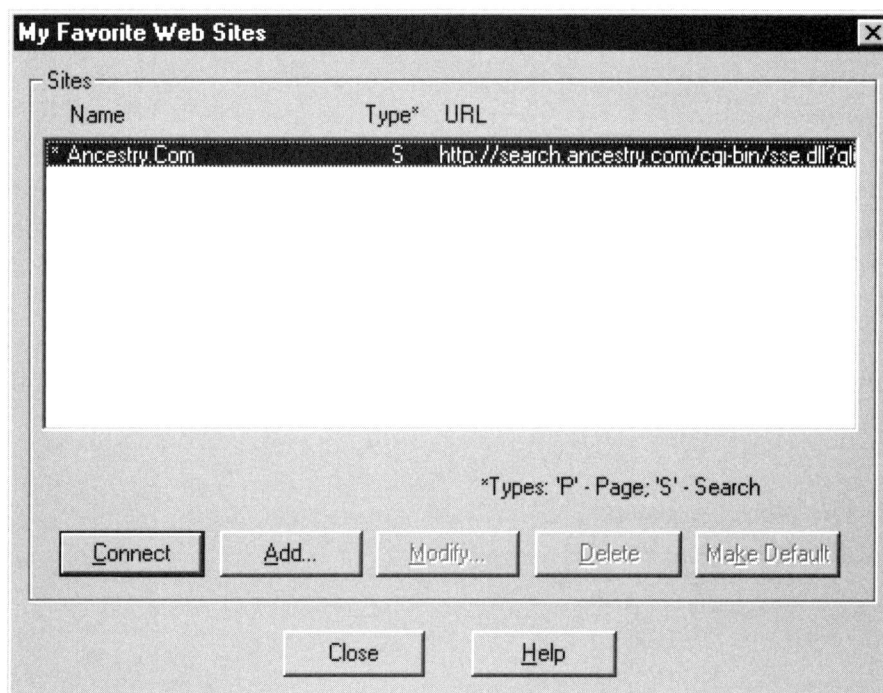

2. Click the **Add** button.

    The **Add/Edit Favorite Site** form will be displayed.

```
Add/Edit Favorite Site                                    [X]

    Title: [                                              ]

     URL: [                                               ]

          [ ] Search this site    Represent space with: [    ]

    For sites that you will not search, enter the full URL, for example,
    "http://www.ancestry.com".

    For sites that you will search, enter the full URL, including the search text. You can tell AFT
    to insert first and last name by placing "%%FN%%" and "%%LN%%" in the text. For example,

    http://www.mysearch.com/cgi-bin/searchfor?first_name=%%FN%%last_name=%%LN%%

              [   OK   ]      [  Cancel  ]      [  Help  ]
```

3. In the **Title** box, enter a title to represent the website (for example, Ancestry.com).

4. In the **URL** box, enter the full address of the website, beginning with *http://* (for example, *http://www.ancestry.com)*.

5. Click the **OK** button to add the site to the list of favorites.

To add a searchable website to the list of favorites

1. Click the **Add** button on the **My Favorite Web Sites** form.

   The **Add/Edit Favorite Site** form will be displayed.

2. In the **Title** box, enter a title to represent the website (for example, FamilySearch.org).

3. Check the **Search this site** box.

4. Add the search text to the address in the **URL** box.

   Hint: To determine what search text you should enter, go to the website and perform a search for any individual. Copy the full address from your Web browser's address line and paste it into the URL box. Then, in place of the first and last names in the search text, enter *%%FN%%* and *%%LN%%,* respectively. For example, if you search for John Jones on the FamilySearch.org site, you will see the following address:

   http://www.familysearch.org/Search/ancestorsearchresults.asp?first_name=John&last_name=Jones

   You would replace the first name, *John,* with *%%FN%%;* and the last name, *Jones,* with *%%LN%%.* The full address in the URL box would look like this:

   http://www.familysearch.org/Search/ancestorsearchresults.asp?first_name=%%FN%%&last_name=%%LN%%

   When requesting the website to perform a search, Ancestry Family Tree will automatically insert the first and last names of the individual highlighted in the Ancestry Family Tree view.

5. The **Represent space with** box lets you specify characters that should be substituted for spaces within names when searching websites automatically.

   For example, if the last name of an ancestor is Mc Pherson, the space will cause problems in Internet URLs. Most searchable websites get around this by substituting one or more characters for a space. To determine what code to use, enter a name with spaces into a name field for the search and then watch the address line of your browser. For example, if you do this in an Ancestry.com search, you will find that Mc Pherson gets replaced with Mc+Pherson. In this case you would enter a + in the **Represent space with** box. On the FamilySearch.org site, you will find that Mc%20Pherson is used; you would enter %20 in **Represent space with** box to represent all spaces as %20.

   Enter the appropriate character(s) in the box.

6. Click the **OK** button to add the site to the list of favorites.

To modify a site in the list of favorites

1. On the **My Favorite Web Sites** form, highlight the site you want to modify and then click the **Modify** button.

   The **Add/Edit Favorite Site** form will be displayed.

2. Modify the existing information for the website as necessary (refer to the steps in "To add a website to the list of favorites" and "To add a searchable website to the list of favorites," above) and then click the **OK** button to close the Add/Edit Favorite Site form and return to the My Favorite Web Sites form.

To remove a site from the list of favorites

1. On the **My Favorite Web Sites** form, highlight the site you want to remove and then click the **Delete** button.

   A warning form similar to the one shown below will be displayed.

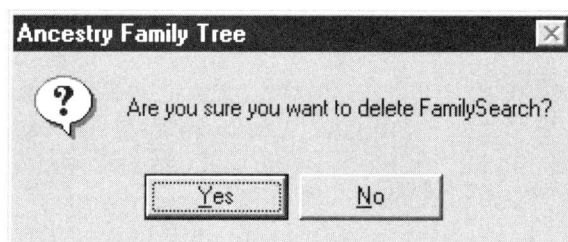

2. Click the **Yes** button to remove the website from the list (or click the **No** button to cancel the deletion).

Searching for information on the Web

You can access the Ancestry.com website and the vast amount of genealogical information it contains very easily through Ancestry Family Tree. Ancestry Family Tree also lets you maintain a list of all of your other favorite websites and search them for information quickly and conveniently.

Searching your favorite sites

After you have added your favorite sites to the My Favorite Web Sites form, it is very easy to connect to and search those that you have designated as searchable. Searchable sites are those that allow you to search for individuals and for which you have included search text using the My Favorite Web Sites form. The individual who is currently highlighted in Ancestry Family Tree will be the subject of the search.

To search a favorite site

1. Sign on to the World Wide Web through your Web provider.

2. In the Ancestry Family Tree view, highlight the individual for whom you want to find information.

3. On the **Internet** menu, click **Search Favorite Sites**.

   The **Search a Web Site** form will be displayed.

4. In the **Site to Search** list, highlight the site you want to search. (Only the sites that you designated as searchable using the My Favorite Web Sites form will appear on the list.)

5. The individual currently highlighted in Ancestry Family Tree appears under **Person to Search for**. If you want a different individual in your database to be the subject of the website search, click the **Change** button.

   The **Find Individual** form will be displayed. Refer to "Searching the entire database" in chapter 9, Searching the Database, to learn how to use the Find Individual form.

6. Click the **Perform Internet Search** button to connect to the highlighted site and perform the search.

Searching on Ancestry.com

Ancestry Family Tree's Internet menu lets you instantly connect to and search several of the most popular resources at Ancestry.com for genealogical information. The individual who is currently highlighted in Ancestry Family Tree will be the subject of the search.

To search on Ancestry.com

1. Sign on to the World Wide Web through your Web provider.

2. In Ancestry Family Tree, highlight the individual for whom you want to find information.

3. On the **Internet** menu,

   - click **Search Ancestry.com** to perform a general search of the databases at Ancestry.com,

   - click **Search Ancestry World Tree** to search the Ancestry World Tree, which contains genealogical data submitted by researchers for millions of individuals, or

   - click **Search Ancestry Message Boards** to search the message boards at Ancestry.com for information about the selected individual.

After you log in to Ancestry.com, the search will be performed and you will see a list of records that contain the highlighted name (or similar names). You will then be able to view the found records and perform additional searches if you want to.

CHAPTER 13

Publishing Your Data on the World Wide Web

This chapter describes how you can use Ancestry Family Tree to publish your family history data on the World Wide Web, where other researchers can see it and use it to enhance their own research.

- You can use Ancestry Family Tree to publish your own family database as a webpage that anyone can access via the World Wide Web.
- You can create an Online Family Tree hosted by Ancestry.com. Using this free service, you can quickly place your family history data online, where you and anyone else whom you allow can continue contributing to it.

Both of these publishing options require Web browser software on your computer and access to the Web through a Web provider.

In this chapter

- Creating your own webpage
- Creating an Online Family Tree

Creating your own webpage

Using Ancestry Family Tree, you can create a webpage containing all of the information, including multimedia files, for any number of individuals in a family database. You select the individuals whom you want to appear on the webpage, specify what information should be included for each individual, and define other preferences that determine the content and appearance of the webpage. You can then upload the webpage to a Web host, where it will be accessible to anyone on the Web. And, if you so choose, visitors to your site can download your data in GEDCOM format.

To start creating a webpage

1. In Ancestry Family Tree, open the database for which you want to create a webpage.

2. Do one of the following:

   • In the **Internet** menu, click **Create Web Page**, or

   • click the Create Web Page button ✳ on the button bar.

   The **Web Page Wizard** form will be displayed.

3. Under **Page Type**, select one of the following options:

    - **Ancestry** if you want to create a webpage showing the ancestry of a selected individual in your database,

    - **Descendents** if you want to create a webpage showing the descendants of a selected individual in your database, or

    - **Selected** if you want to create a webpage showing one or more selected individuals from your database.

Selecting the individuals who will appear on the webpage

If you are creating an Ancestry or Descendants type of webpage, you need to select an individual with whom the webpage will begin; that person and all of his or her ancestors or descendants will be shown. If you are creating a Selected-type webpage, you need to select one or more individuals from your database who will be shown.

To select the starting person for an Ancestry or Descendants webpage

By default, the starting person is the individual currently selected in the Ancestry Family Tree view.

To select a different starting person, click the **Search** button under **Starting Person**. (The Search button is available only if you clicked Ancestry or Descendants under Page Type.)

The **Find Individual** form will be displayed. Refer to "Searching the entire database" in chapter 9, Searching the Database, to learn how to use the Find Individual form.

To select individuals for a selected webpage

Under **Filter**, click the **Select** button. (The Select button is available only if you clicked Selected under Page Type.)

The **Select Set of Individuals** form will be displayed. Refer to "Searching for an individual using filters" in chapter 9, Searching the Database, to learn how to use the form to select one or more individuals who will be shown on the webpage. (The Select Set of Individuals form is essentially identical to the Search for Individual form described in chapter 9.)

Defining the content of the webpage

The Web Page Wizard form contains a number of controls that affect the content of the webpage.

To define the content of the webpage

Refer to the table below to learn about the purpose of each control on the Web Page Wizard and then use them to define the content of your webpage.

Field	Description
Notes	
Source	If checked, sources cited for each individual will appear.
Actual Text	If checked, actual text entered for the source citation will appear. (Available only if Source is checked.)
Comments	If checked, comments entered for the source citation will appear. (Available only if Source is checked.)
General	If checked, all notes that are not preceded by an exclamation mark (!) will appear.
Marked (!)	If checked, note paragraphs that are preceded by an exclamation mark will appear (in addition to notes that are not marked).
Embed	If selected, the notes will be included with the standard information for the individual.
Link	If selected, the notes will be included in a separate HTML file; there will be a link from the individual to the HTML file.
Other Options	
Include GEDCOM File	If checked, a GEDCOM file containing the individuals on your webpage will be included. Visitors to your page will be able to download the GEDCOM file. If you use this option, specify whether you want the GEDCOM file to be created as a GEDCOM version 4 or version 5.5 file by clicking **Version 4** or **Version 5**.
Include Your Name/Address	If checked, the submitter's name and address will be included on the webpage. (This information is entered on the Compiler page of the Preferences form. Refer to chapter 2, Installation and Setup, to learn how to define preferences in Ancestry Family Tree.)
Include Your Email Address	If checked, the submitter's e-mail address will be included on the webpage. (The submitter's e-mail address is also entered on the Compiler page of the Preferences form.)
Display Rel. Indicators	If checked, relationship codes denoting adopted {A}, guardian {G}, and sealed {S} will appear in brackets after each name on the record (if such information exists for the individual). (A "sealed" relationship results from an LDS ordinance.)
Display Multiple Parent Ind.	If checked, individuals who have multiple sets of parents will be marked with + in brackets after the individual's name. (If relationship codes are selected to appear as well, relationship codes and the multiple-parent indicator will appear within the same set of brackets.)
Include "Other" Events	If checked, additional events for individuals and marriages will appear on the webpage. (Refer to "Entering additional information for

Field	Description
Events	an individual" in chapter 4, Working with Individuals in a Database, to learn how to create additional events.)
Max Generations to Trace Back	For a Descendants-type webpage, lets you determine the number of generations that will be included. The default number is 999, which will effectively include all generations. Enter a number if you want to specify the number of generations to be included.
Max Generations to Prepare	For an Ancestry-type webpage, lets you determine the number of generations that will be included. The default number is 32, which is the maximum number of generations allowed. Enter a number if you want to specify the number of generations to be included.
Continue Duplicate Lines	If selected, duplicate family lines on an Ancestry-type webpage will be continued. (Using this option will preserve the integrity of the Ahnentafel numbering used on Ancestry-type webpages).
Hide Details for the Living	If checked, each living individual will be indicated by the notation "Living." No other information will be included.
Show Names	If checked, only the names of living persons will be included.
Include Places in Name Index	If checked, places associated with events will be included in the webpage's name index.
Include LDS Info	If checked, LDS ordinance information will appear for each individual (if it exists). (This option is available only if Use LDS Data is checked on the General page of the Preferences form.)
Scrapbook Options	Select one of the following options: • **None** – includes no multimedia items with your webpage, • **Primary Image Only** – includes the default photo image in the media collection for an individual (if there is one), or • **Full Scrapbook** - includes scrapbooks you have created for individuals.
Embed Primary Image	If checked, the default photo image for an individual will appear on the main webpage with the individual's information. If not checked, the image will be included separately; there will be a link from the individual to the image.
Include Video Clips	If checked, video clips in an individual's multimedia collection will be included on the webpage.
Include Audio Clips	If checked, audio clips in an individual's multimedia collection will be included on the webpage.

To define additional preferences for the default photo images and scrapbook images

1. Ensure that the **Primary Image Only** or **Full Scrapbook** option is selected.

2. Click the **Embedded Image** button or **Scrapbook Image** button.

   The **Web Page Image Size** form will be displayed.

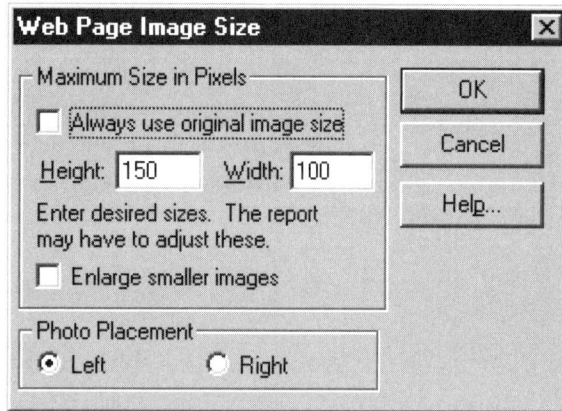

3. Refer to the table below to learn about the purpose of the controls on the form and then use them to define options for the individuals' default photo images.

Field	Description
Always use original image size	If checked, each image will appear in its original size. If not checked, each image will be sized to the dimensions (in pixels) entered in the **Height** and **Width** boxes. Enter the number of pixels in the boxes if you want to change the size. (If an image does not fit the width/height ratio you specify, these dimensions will be altered to retain the image's original proportions.)
Enlarge smaller images	If checked, images that are smaller than the size specified in the Height and Width boxes will be enlarged to those dimensions. (This will likely result in reduced image quality.)
Photo Placement	Select the **Left** or **Right** option to specify whether the image should appear to the left or right of the text associated with an individual.

To continue defining the webpage

1. On the **Web Page Wizard** form, click the **Next >** button.

   The second Web Page Wizard form will be displayed.

2. In the **Web Page Description** box, enter a brief description of the page's contents.

3. In the **Local Web Page Directory** box, enter a name for the folder that will be created to contain the webpage files.

   Ancestry Family Tree will save your webpage files in the folder, which will be stored on your hard disk in the location shown under **Local Web Page Path**.

To change the webpage title

1. Under **Title** you will see the default title for the webpage. (The title appears at the top of the initial page of your webpage. If you want to change it, click the **Change** button.

   The **Web Page Ancestors Title** form will be displayed.

- If checked, the **Include Name** box causes the name of the starting person to be included in the title.

  If you don't want the name to be included, uncheck the box.

- In the **Prefix** and **Suffix** boxes, enter or modify the text that you want to precede and follow the name of the starting person.

2. Click the **OK** button to close the form and return to the Web Page Wizard.

To select a background image for the webpage

1. On the second **Web Page Wizard** form, click the **Select** button under **Background Image**.

   The **Open Photo File** form will be displayed.

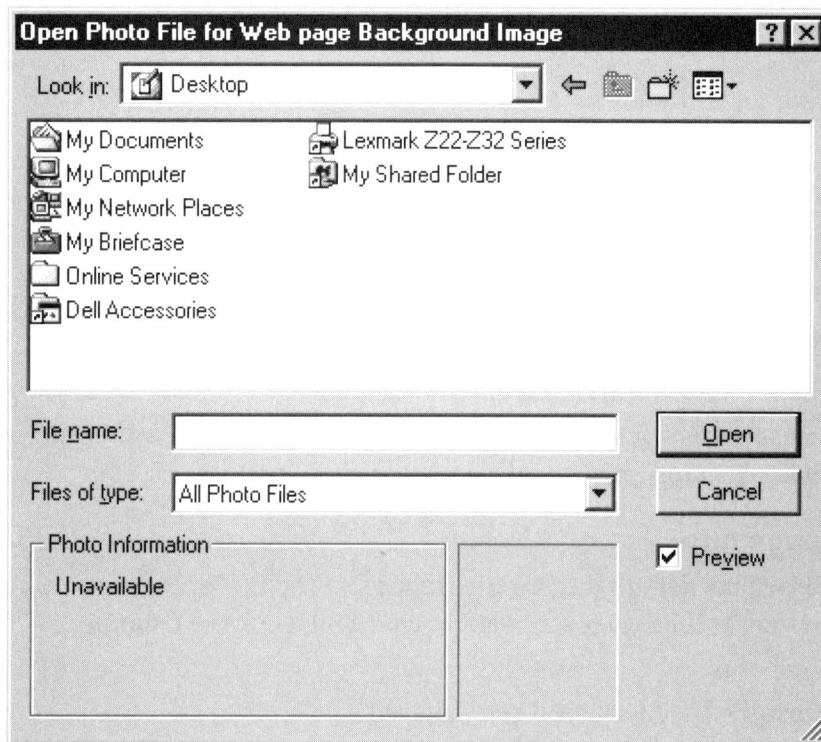

2. Use the controls described below to locate the image file you want to use.

   - Click the drop-down button to the right of the **Look In** box to view the contents of the disk drives and folders on your computer.

   - Click the ⬆ button to view the contents of the folder one level above the folder you are currently viewing.

3. After you have located and highlighted the image file you want to use, click the **Open** button to close the form and return to the Web Page Wizard.

   The image file is selected and the full path to its location is shown on the Web Page Wizard.

To create an introduction for your webpage

In the **Introduction** box on the second **Web Page Wizard** form, you can enter text for an introduction to your webpage. This introduction will appear below the title on the initial page of your webpage.

Enter the introduction text in the box.

Defining advanced webpage options

Advanced Web page options let you enter a webpage file prefix and select some other settings that determine how your webpage is saved on the Web host. Defining these options is not required.

To define advanced webpage preferences

1. On the second **Web Page Wizard** form, click the **Advanced Options** button.

   The **Web Page Advanced Options** form will be displayed.

   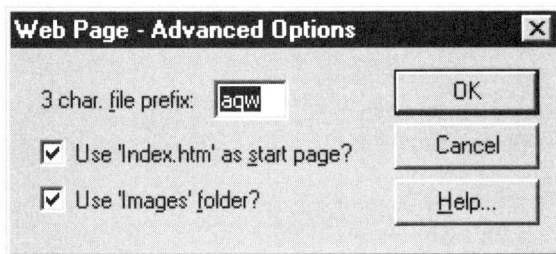

   - The **3 char. file prefix** box lets you enter a file prefix for the webpage you are creating.

     If you intend to create only one webpage using Ancestry Family Tree, you can use the default prefix. You can also use the default prefix if you can create separate folders on your Web host for each genealogy page. However, if you are limited to a single folder on your Web host, you will need to specify a unique three-character prefix for each webpage.

     Enter a file prefix if necessary.

   - If checked, the **Use 'Index.htm' as start page?** box causes index.htm to be used as the name of the main file of your webpage. However, some Web hosts require this name for other uses.

     Uncheck the box if necessary. Ancestry Family Tree will use the three-character prefix as part of a start name.

   - If checked, the **Use 'Images' folder?** box causes an image sub-folder to be created for image files. However, some Web hosts will not allow you to use sub-folders.

     Uncheck the box if necessary. Ancestry Family Tree will not create an images sub-folder but will instead place all .htm and image files in the same folder.

2. Click the **OK** button to close the form and return to the Web Page Wizard.

Defining advanced HTML options

Advanced HTML options let you add a link from the webpage you are creating to a parent webpage. You can also add HTML code that will define the contents of the webpage header and footer—for example, a family logo for the header or a copyright notice for the footer. Defining these options is not required.

To define advanced HTML options

On the second **Web Page Wizard** form, click the **Advanced Options** button.

The **Web Page Advanced HTML** form will be displayed.

```
Web Page - Advanced HTML                              [X]

    URL of page to link back to: [                    ]

         Text of link back: [                         ]

    HTML Code to appear on top of each page:   [✓] HTML From a File

    File Name [                          ]    [ Browse ]

    HTML Code to appear on bottom of each page: [✓] HTML From a File

    File Name [                          ]    [ Browse ]


         [ OK ]      [ Cancel ]      [ Help... ]
```

To add a link to a parent webpage

- The **URL of page to link back to** box lets you specify the URL of a parent webpage that the page you are creating will be linked back to.

  If there is a parent webpage that you want the page you are creating to link back to, enter the URL.

- The **Text of link back** box lets you enter the text for the link back to a parent webpage.

  If there is a parent webpage that you want the page you are creating to link back to, enter the text for the link here.

To select an .htm file for a webpage header or footer

By default, Ancestry Family tree lets you select an .htm file containing the HTML code that will define the contents of the webpage header or footer.

To select an .htm file, do one of the following:

- In the **File Name** box under **HTML code to appear on top of each page** or **HTML code to appear on bottom of each page**, enter the path and file name of the .htm file you want to use, or

- click the **Browse** button to the right of one of the boxes to navigate to and select the .htm file you want to use.

To enter HTML code for a webpage header or footer

1. If you want to enter an HTML code that will define the contents of the header or footer, uncheck the **HTML From a File** box adjacent to **HTML code to appear on top of each page** or **HTML code to appear on bottom of each page**.

   The **Web Page Advanced HTML** form is modified as shown below:

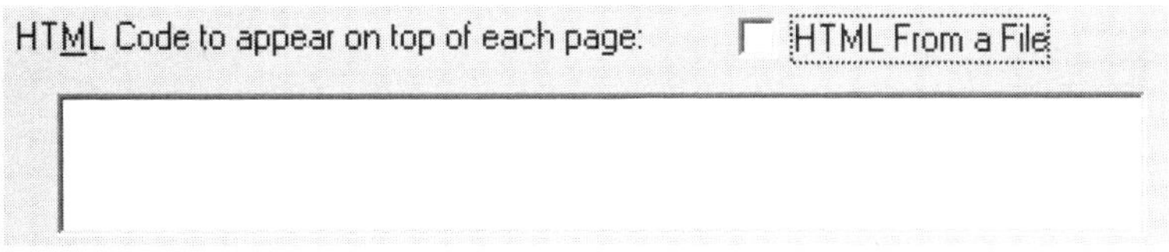

   HT_ML Code to appear on top of each page: ☐ HTML From a File

2. Enter the HTML code in the text box.

To save the advanced HTML options

Click the **OK** button to close the Web Page Advanced HTML form and return to the Web Page Wizard.

Finishing your webpage

Ancestry Family Tree will save your webpage files on your computer's hard disk. The final step in the process is to upload the files to your Web host. (A Web host is required for you to publish a webpage accessible via the World Wide Web.)

To finish creating your webpage

1. On the second **Web Page Wizard** form, click the **Finish** button.

   The **GEDCOM Export** form will be displayed while the webpage files are created.

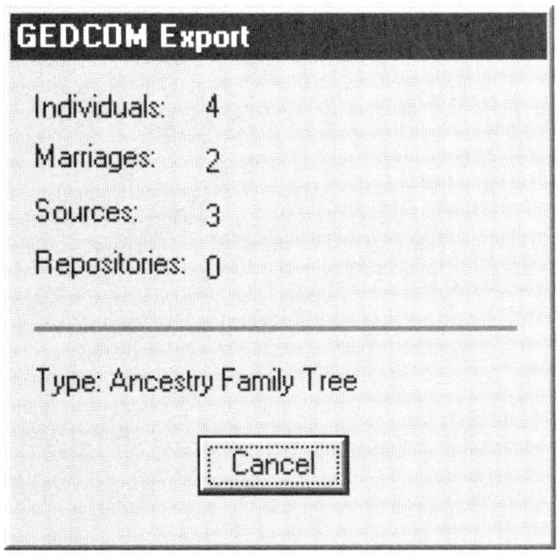

   GEDCOM Export

   Individuals: 4
   Marriages: 2
   Sources: 3
   Repositories: 0

   Type: Ancestry Family Tree

   [Cancel]

   You can click the **Cancel** button to cancel the creation of your webpage.

   When the webpage files are complete, the following **GEDCOM Export** form will be displayed.

GEDCOM Export

4 Individuals Exported
2 Marriages Exported

OK

2. Click the **OK** button to finish creating the webpage files.

   A form similar to the one shown below will be displayed.

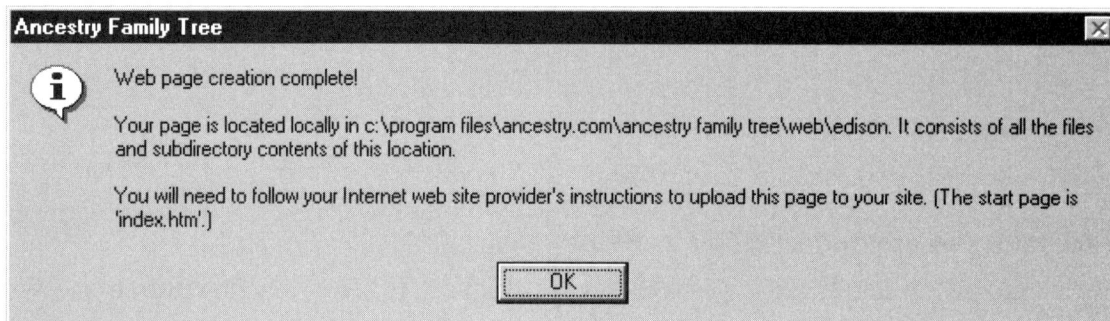

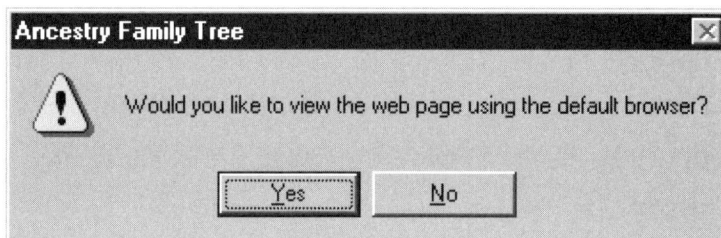

Ancestry Family Tree

Web page creation complete!

Your page is located locally in c:\program files\ancestry.com\ancestry family tree\web\edison. It consists of all the files and subdirectory contents of this location.

You will need to follow your Internet web site provider's instructions to upload this page to your site. (The start page is 'index.htm'.)

OK

Ancestry Family Tree will have placed your webpage files in the path and folder identified here.

3. Click the **OK** button.

   A form similar to the one shown below will be displayed.

Ancestry Family Tree

Would you like to view the web page using the default browser?

Yes   No

4. Click the **Yes** button to view your completed webpage (or click the **No** button to close the form and return to the Ancestry Family Tree view).

   You can view your webpage any time you want to by going to the folder where the Web files were saved and double-clicking index.htm to open the page.

Transferring your webpage to your Web host

To make your webpage available on the Internet, you will need to upload the files to your Web host. Follow your Web host's directions for uploading the files. You will need to upload all files, folders, and sub-folders created for your webpage.

Creating an Online Family Tree

You can export Ancestry Family Tree data to create an Online Family Tree hosted by Ancestry.com. Using this free service, you and others to whom you grant access can all contribute to your Online Family Tree. As with a webpage, you select the individuals whom you want to appear in the Online Family Tree, specify what information should be included for each individual, and define other preferences that determine the content and appearance of the Online Family Tree. However, there are several differences between creating an Online Family Tree and creating a webpage of your own:

- An Online Family Tree is hosted by Ancestry.com at no charge. (Creating your own webpage requires that you have a Web host where you can post your webpage.)

- You can create your Online Family Tree and have it online in a very short time.

- You and others to whom you grant access can all add, edit, or delete information in your Online Family Tree at the same time.

Also, users who are granted access can download the data from your Online Family Tree. (Refer to chapter 10, Importing and Exporting Files and Merging Records, to learn how to download Online Family Tree data.)

To create an Online Family Tree

1. Sign on to the World Wide Web through your Web provider.

2. In Ancestry Family Tree, open the database that contains data you want to export.

3. In the **File** menu, click **Export to Web**.

   The **GEDCOM Export** form will be displayed.

4. Under **Include** you can select from a number of options that determine what type of information will be exported from each individual record. Refer to the table below to learn about each option, then check or uncheck the boxes to set the options you want.

Option	Description
Notes	This box determines whether all notes in all note fields (including those beginning with *!*) will be included in the exported data. (An exclamation point [!] can be used to mark note paragraphs, allowing them to be excluded from some charts and reports at your discretion. Refer to chapter 6, Working with Notes, for details.)
	Uncheck the box if you don't want notes to be included.
Sources	This box determines whether sources, source citations, and repositories will be included in the exported data.
	Uncheck the box if you don't want this information to be included.
Contact Info	This box determines whether the contact information entered for an individual will be included in the exported data.
	Check the box if you want contact information to be included.
Confidential Data	This box determines whether confidential notes will be included in the exported data. (Confidential *notes* are denoted by a tilde [~] at the beginning of the first line of confidential text and a blank line before and after; refer to chapter 6, Working with Notes, for details. *Events* can be marked confidential using the Additional Event form; refer to chapter 4, Working with Individuals in a Database, to learn how to use the Additional Event form.)
	Uncheck the box if you do not want confidential notes to be included.
Full Info on Living	This box determines whether all information will be included in the exported data for individuals in the database who are still living. (Ancestry Family Tree defines any individual with no entry in the death date field and less than 110 years old as living.)
	If you choose not to include all information for living individuals, only relationship information will be included for them.
	Uncheck the box if you do not want to include all information for living individuals.
Names on Living	If you choose not to include all information for living individuals by unchecking the Full Info on Living box, the **Names on Living** box becomes available. This box determines whether the names of living individuals will be included in the exported data.
	If you choose not to include the names of living individuals, their names will be replaced by the word *Living*.
	Uncheck the box if you do not want to include the names of living individuals.

Option	Description
Submitter	This box determines whether the information entered for the compiler of the database will be included in the exported data. (This information is entered on the Compiler page of the Preferences form. Refer to chapter 2, Installation and Setup, to learn how to define preferences.) Uncheck the box if you don't want to include information for the compiler.
MultiMedia Links	Not applicable when creating an Online Family Tree.
Encode Media	Not applicable when creating an Online Family Tree.
LDS Data	This box determines whether LDS data (such as date and place of baptism, endowment, etc.) will be included in the exported data. This box is available only if Use LDS Data is selected on the General page of the Preferences form. Uncheck the box if you do not want LDS data to be included.

5. Do one of the following:

   - To export all individuals in the database, ensure that **All** is selected under **Selected Individuals** and then proceed to the following step, or

   - to export one or more selected individuals, click the **Partial** option under **Selected Individuals** and then click the **Select** button.

     The **Select Set of Individuals** form will be displayed. This form lets you select individuals from a list and lets you search for individuals in the database using various search filters. Refer to chapter 9, Searching the Database, to learn how to use the Select Set of Individuals form to search for and select individuals.

     After you have selected the individual(s) whom you want to include in the exported data, proceed to the following step.

6. When you have finished selecting individuals and specifying what type of information will be exported, click the **Export** button on the **GEDCOM Export** form.

   If you are not currently logged in to Ancestry.com, the **Login** form will be displayed.

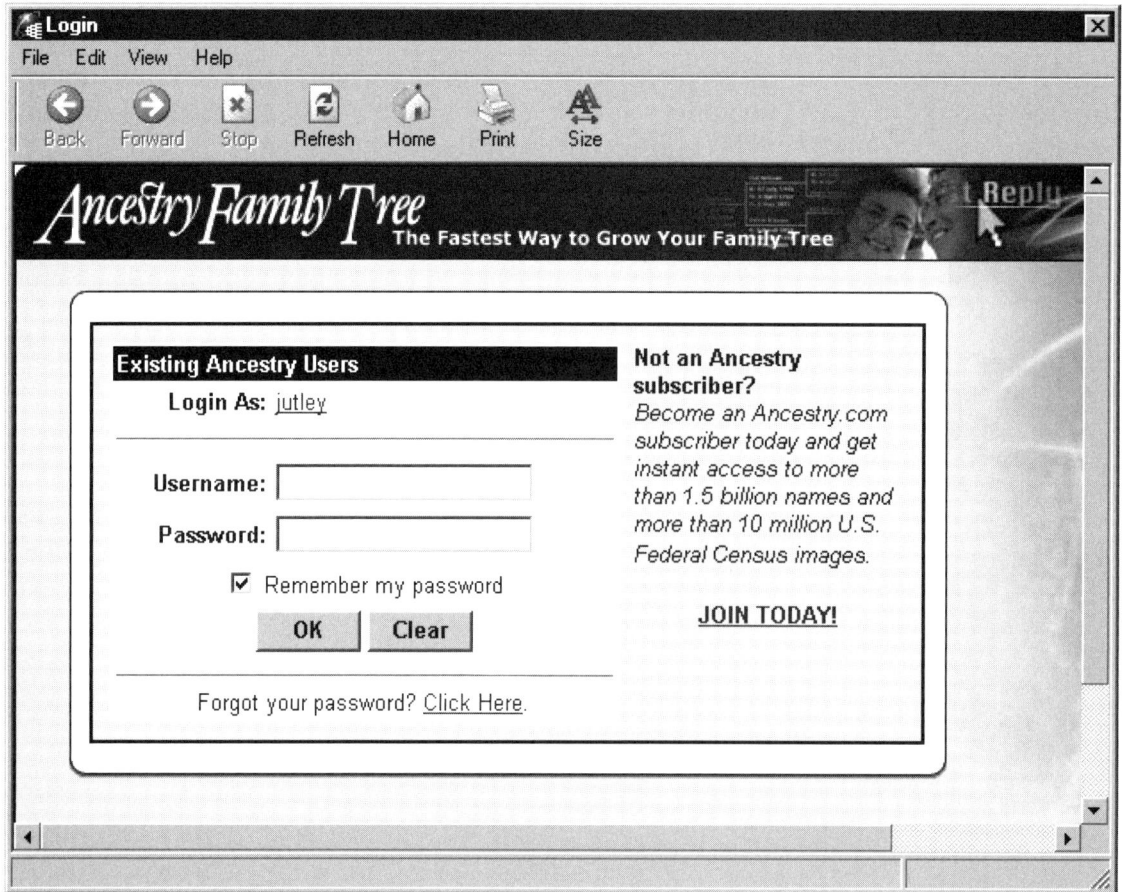

7. Do one of the following:

   - If you are a registered user of Ancestry.com, log in.

   - If you are not a registered user, you can register to use the free services at
     Ancestry.com or you can subscribe to access additional resources on
     Ancestry.com.

8. After you have logged in or registered, the **Online Family Trees** form will be
   displayed.

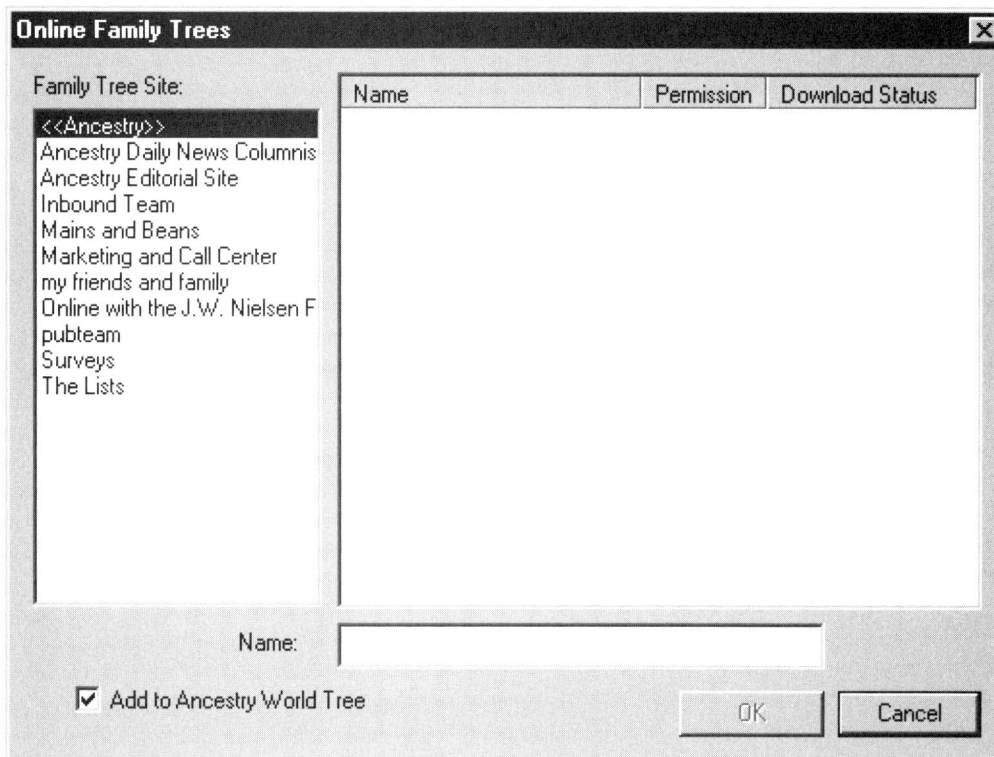

If you have previously created one or more Online Family Trees, they will be listed in the Name/Permission/Download Status list.

9. Do one of the following:

    - If you are creating a new Online Family Tree, enter a name for it in the **Name** box.

    - If you want to update an existing Online Family Tree, highlight it in the Name/Permission/Download Status list.

    Note: If the **Add to Ancestry World Tree** box is checked, the data will also be added to the Ancestry World Tree at Ancestry.com. This is a collection of data on millions of individuals submitted by researchers from all over the world.

10. Click the **OK** button.

    - If the Add to Ancestry World Tree box is checked, the **World Tree Submission Agreement** form will be displayed.

      Read the form and click **Yes** to proceed (or click **No** to end the export).

    - If you are updating an existing Online Family Tree database, a warning form similar to the one shown below will be displayed.

Ancestry Family Tree

⚠ Grove already exists.
Do you want to replace it?

Yes   No

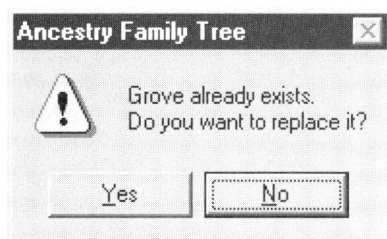

11. Click the **Yes** button to replace the existing Online Family Tree database (or click the **No** button to return to the Online Family Trees form).

    The **Uploading** form will be displayed while the database is exported as a GEDCOM file.

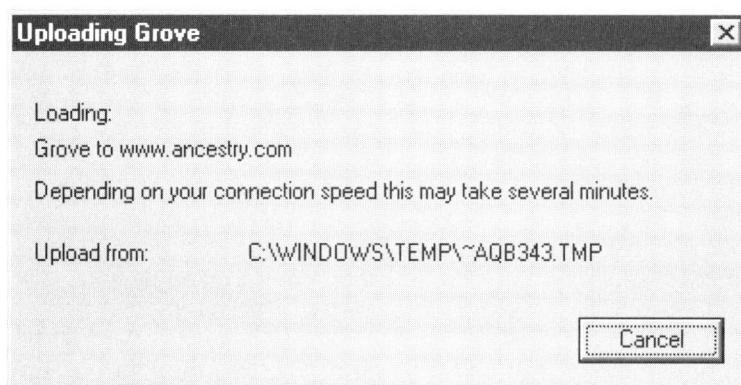

Uploading Grove ✕

Loading:

Grove to www.ancestry.com

Depending on your connection speed this may take several minutes.

Upload from: C:\WINDOWS\TEMP\~AQB343.TMP

Cancel

When the export is complete, the **GEDCOM Export** form will be displayed.

GEDCOM Export ✕

189 Individuals Exported
112 Marriages Exported

OK

12. Click the **OK** button to close the form and return to the Ancestry Family Tree view.

    Your online family tree is now available for viewing and modification (by you and those to whom you grant access) on the Ancestry.com home page.

Index

G